Muay Thai
Peace, At Last

by

Michael Goodison

Copyright © 2015 Michael Goodison

All rights reserved.

ISBN: 9781523807871
ISBN-13: 978-1523807873

If you are reading this book,
it's dedicated to you.

Climb aboard, be entertained;
                         we nameless souls, together,
Burn the candles, light It up.
               The wheels may turn Forever.
                       Swim with mermaids, fly with birds
                                 and sing a freedom song,
In winter hides the summer joy... and drummers!
                           beat them Strong.
Seek it out, that timeless love,
                 run blind at unknown plans,
The worldly light will keep me safe,
                 lest God hath me on His hands.

PROLOGUE
FIGHT NIGHT

> *"How much can you know about yourself
> if you've never been in a fight?"*
> - Chuck Palahniuk, *Fight Club*

There's living, and then there's thriving… But what's the distinction?
If we contend that living consists of nothing more than breathing, eating and sleeping, then mustn't thriving be everything that is above and beyond the barest act of survival?
Coffee shops and music, candles and hot water, road trips and laughter, card games with strangers. When the world moves to the beat of a tune, like a poem brought to life – more magic than science – and when you can really *feel* the rhythms of the universe as it not only surrounds, but encapsulates you…
Thriving is drinking tea.
Thriving is smiling.
Thriving is that which isn't utterly necessary.
There are moments in life when even the sturdiest man of logic is given no choice but to ponder the question: Is it at all possible that someone, or some*thing,* may have composed the music of life?
There are moments in life that are too rare and too beautiful to not *mean* something…
It can be challenging for those of us born into the developed world to fully appreciate the act of thriving, because we were born into it, and we know of nothing else – no other means of existence. Yet, fully appreciate it, we must.
In winter hides the summer joy…
It is only within the deepest throes of suffering that joy is understood, and thus there resides a desire at the heart of the human condition – a compulsion, no less – to seek out and explore the darkness, so as to fully appreciate the light.
Which is all largely how I came to be in Chiang Mai, northern Thailand, getting my hands strapped up in preparation to enter a Muay Thai ring. I was once a stranger to the darkness, but I've become something of a regular

customer. *"I'll just have the usual, thanks,"* is now met with a stoic nod by the universal score-keeper.

You can play a game of cards, or a game of football, but there's no playing Muay Thai. It is the most brutal, most effective martial art in the world.

The fights prior to mine had all ended by way of knockout, and there were dark-skinned bodies writhing on thin, woven mats nearby. They were the Thai fighters – the conquerors and the conquered – recovering from their devastating bouts. They didn't look particularly comfortable.

Mine was the headline fight of the evening. Most of the Thais in the crowd probably didn't like me, which was fair enough. After all, I am a foreigner – a "farang," as the Thais say – stepping into the ring to compete against one of their own, in a sport that is entirely theirs.

There were tourists amongst the crowd as well. Most of them were unknown to me, but some of them were fellow backpackers that I had met along the way, come to watch and support me in my fight.

Also amongst the onlookers was a member of the Thai Mafia. A training partner pointed him out to me and I looked at him – all tattoos and a bikini-clad female escort and prominent facial scars – eyeing me impassively as I got ready to walk down to the ring. There had been a Mafia-connected shooting in Chiang Mai earlier in the week. A local man was found a few blocks away from my hostel with fifteen bullets in his body. He had been shot in the ankles, the knees, the chest, and then a line of bullet holes had been drawn across his forehead. As the Mafia man continued to stare at me, I found myself wondering if he'd had anything to do with the shooting murder.

I returned his dead-eyed stare.

I'd been training and waiting for the better part of a month for the chance to fight, and the moment had finally arrived.

The fight immediately prior to mine came to an abrupt end. I waited as one of the Thai fighters was helped past me, dripping blood onto the concrete floor from a nasty gash above his eyes – the telltale sign of elbow strikes. At least I knew that I wouldn't get lost on the way down to the ring. All I had to do was follow the blood trail.

I am a peaceful person. Fun loving. Easy going. Content. I have a habit of humming to myself. It might be considered strange then, that I felt so nonchalant about the violent spectacle I was about to submit myself to.

I could easily justify my desire to fight by declaring that I love the science, the beauty and the art of fighting, which is true, but that's not really why I was there to fight.

Mine isn't the typical fighter's story, but we'll get to that.

"Time to go, Mike!" my friend and training partner, Stuart, called to me. He had my mouth guard tucked securely behind his ear, and he was holding my little go-pro camera in front of his face.

"Do you realize that it's pointing at your face?" I asked him.

"Sorry?"

"That little lens thing there," I said, nodding at the camera. "It's looking right at your face."

"Oh, shit."

Stuart turned the camera around the right way and I shook my head wearily. *Old people.*

The way ahead was clear and the hands that had been holding me in place were gone.

It was time to fight.

"Showtime," I said quietly.

All of the decisions that I had made in my life up to that moment – the tiny, seemingly innocuous decisions that we all make on a daily basis – had led me to that final stroll.

I was finally headed down to the ring – towards whatever awaited – and *you,* dear reader – well, I'm taking you with me.

CHAPTER ONE
DESTINATION: THAILAND

> *"The one who walks alone is likely to end up in places no one has ever been."*
> \- Albert Einstein

It was almost midnight of July 20th, 2015, and it was a perfect night for flying. Cold and clear – the stars were out on display, and the open sky appeared to be beckoning to me. Somewhere to the north-west I knew that the people of Thailand would be finishing their working day and heading out into the warmth and humidity of the night in search of cheap alcohol, good company and loose environments. Thailand had been calling my name, and I was finally answering the call.

Loitering about, I looked out the window from the departures lounge and checked to make sure the plane I would be boarding had two wings with big whirry-things hanging underneath them, which encompassed the full extent of my aviation knowledge. With those boxes securely ticked, I presented my ticket and got directed down the ramp and onto the plane.

The first flutterings of freedom were beginning to stir in my chest.

Travelling is as much a journey of the soul as it is a journey for the body. Not everyone is called upon to travel. Some people feel quite content in the security of their own home, amongst familiar faces and surrounds, and I can understand that. However, the idea of *not* travelling has never taken hold for me. Wherever we go in our lives, the places that we visit and the people that we meet and the experiences that we live through all inevitably become a part of us. They become a part of our story. They enrich the lines that crease our faces, and they dance behind our eyes when we smile. Choosing not to travel is like only reading the first page in a book.

We landed in Bangkok and I transferred to a domestic flight that was bound for Chiang Mai. We'd flown all through the night, and then, finally, I was in Thailand and the sun was coming up. It was a beautiful morning.

The warmth and humidity hit me the moment I stepped off the plane and onto the hot tarmac.

25 days until the fight.

It had been a long and cold winter back home in Melbourne, and it was a delight to be able to shrug off my woolen jumper and feel the sun and a warm breeze on my skin once again.

Ah, adventure, the arrogant temptress. And, much like any temptress, the potent addiction of adventure is in the suspense and the imaginings and the fantasy and the *possibility* of what could be awaiting.

It's a big world out there.

You won't meet a temptress who lives naked and barefoot. A real temptress understands the power of mystery. Curiosity has killed many a cat, no doubt, but I am sure it has killed many more humans. Just go and spend a minute staring at one of the many corpses that litter the most inhospitable regions of the Himalayan mountain range and ask them what they were pursuing, exactly, to have died in such a way, and in such a place.

They probably won't answer you – owing to being frozen – but you can make a few educated guesses as to what they might say.

I wanted to see what nobody else has seen. I wanted to go where nobody else has gone. I wanted to know the nature of the summit that lay hidden beneath the veil of clouds. I wanted to know if it was possible. I couldn't help myself. I was curious.

Indeed, sometimes the only way to know if the metal is hot is to go right ahead and put your hand on it.

You'll notice as well, upon the trail of adventure, the desire for a *pure* adventure. A virgin adventure. Lands unseen and unspoiled by anybody else. Stories that have never been told before.

Glorious adventure.

And I had arrived.

I exited the airport through a discreet side door, avoiding the sales barrage from premium taxi services. I flagged down a battered old three-wheeler tuk-tuk and asked him if he could take me to a place called KC Muay Thai. I didn't know where it was and I didn't have any bookings or contact names or numbers. I'd simply done a quick Google search for Muay Thai gyms in Chiang Mai before I had flown out of Melbourne and I'd found a website for KC Muay Thai.

The tuk-tuk driver had never heard of it.

I shrugged and made myself comfortable whilst the driver made calls to various people – presumably looking for anybody who knew where KC Muay Thai was.

I had just a small backpack with me, which would carry everything that I needed for the duration of my stay. Into it, I had packed a pair of running shorts, a camera, a book, an iPad, a mouth-guard, a spare pair of socks, and a toothbrush. I was carrying my passport, phone and wallet on my person, and I was wearing clothes, which is optional in Thailand. I had everything I needed, and several things I didn't.

"Did you find it?" I asked the tuk-tuk driver. "KC Muay Thai?"

The Thai man nodded and leapt into the driver's seat. We shot off into the bustling maze of Chiang Mai's streets and I got my first real taste of Thai air in my lungs. There were little fireworks going off in my chest.

And then we arrived in the wrong place.

"What's this?" I asked the tuk-tuk driver.

We were halfway along a dank, narrow, potholed city side-alley, and there were stray dogs approaching to sniff at the wheels of the tuk-tuk. There was a line of closed up shop fronts, with tropical plants growing out of hanging pots. Amidst the mess and the clutter, there was a small walkway, and it was into this that the driver led me.

Amazing, I thought to myself as we emerged from the walkway into a cavernous space. There was a Muay Thai ring in the centre, with a sturdy steel structure above it that was sporting spotlights and music speakers.

It was a Muay Thai stadium, and we had apparently just entered through a discrete side entrance. Which was close to what I wanted, but it definitely wasn't the KC Muay Thai gym that I had asked for. Nonetheless, the stadium felt very authentic and I was enjoying the spectacle.

The driver gestured at me to wait and then he wandered off around the seating area in search of someone... presumably.

With nothing else to do, I climbed into the ring.

I'd been on the ground in Thailand for less than half an hour and I was already standing in a Muay Thai ring. I didn't quite know it at the time, but in less than a month I would be fighting for real in that very same ring. There would be blood and elbows, and a screaming, delirious crowd, all assembled around that little piece of roped-in real estate. It felt good. It felt comforting. A Muay Thai ring is the most honest and fair place I have ever known. That might seem scary to some people. To me, it feels like a breath of the freshest air imaginable. An invigorating change from the monotony and the paperwork and the bullshit of the 21st century way of living.

"Hello? Australia?"

I turned around to see my tuk-tuk driver waving me over.

I climbed out of the ring and followed the driver into a room that turned out to be an office of some kind. There was Thai writing on the front door that I couldn't interpret. An accounting office, perhaps?

Inside, I was introduced to another Thai man. His wife and daughter were also present. The daughter had apparently studied law in Sydney, and so her English was the best. She told me that her dad was the preeminent lawyer in Chiang Mai, and that he also organized Muay Thai fights on the side and represented fighters.

"We train you here," she said, pointing. "In the ring."

I turned around to look at the stadium again. There was nobody else around. I had been expecting a fight camp. I had been expecting a community of fighters. People to talk to, etcetera.

"Who will train me?" I asked, looking doubtfully at her frail old father.

"We have the best trainer in Chiang Mai," the girl assured me. "Lumpinee champion. He will train you in the ring."

I frowned. Why wouldn't the best trainer in Chiang Mai work out of a fight camp with lots of foreigners? It didn't make much sense to me.

The girl sensed my doubts and she smiled. "He used to train tourists in Pai," she said.

I'd heard of Pai. Apparently it was a sleepy, hippie town in the mountains to the west of Chiang Mai, close to the border with Burma. *Maybe I'll visit Pai whilst I'm here…*

"He worked at Charn Chai Muay Thai gym," the girl explained. "But he was caught taking drugs, so now he cannot find work. My dad is the only person who will give him work. But still, he is the best trainer in Chiang Mai. And cheap, too."

That got my attention.

"How cheap?"

"How long you want?"

"A month," I said.

"And you will fight for us?" she asked. "Against a Thai fighter?"

"Yes."

"6,000 Baht," she said. "And you get to keep your prize money. Training is individual – one on one – 2 hours every morning at 10 o'clock in the ring. It's up to you how often you come, but the trainer will be here every morning at 10."

I considered the offer. 6,000 Baht was extremely cheap for private training. Around 200 Australian dollars, maybe a touch more. I'd been expecting to pay nearly double that for group classes at KC Muay Thai, and group classes were nowhere near as effective for someone training to fight as private lessons would be.

I nodded to her. "I want to do one training session first," I said. "If he is as good as you say, I'll pay for a month upfront. 6,000 Baht."

The girl turned and spoke to her dad in Thai and then nodded. "Ok," she said. "You come back tomorrow at 10 o'clock in the morning for training."

"What about a place to stay?" I asked, glancing around. I had absolutely no idea where I was in the city of Chiang Mai. I hadn't had a chance to get my bearings yet. The tuk-tuk driver had left me there with my backpack, but that wasn't of any concern to me. Travel is cheap and easily acquired in Chiang Mai. So long as you can stick your thumb out, you can get around. If you don't have any thumbs, you can wave your arms around. If you don't have any arms, getting around might be more difficult.

The Thai girl smiled again. Thai people are a friendly, hospitable people, as a general rule. "You came in the side entrance," she explained. "The main entrance is on Loi Kroh road, which is a major tourist road. You go out that way," she pointed, "and you will find many places to stay."

"And markets?" I asked.

She nodded. "Yes."

"Ok then," I said, grabbing my backpack. "Cool… I'll be back in the morning."

The old man saw that I was leaving and grabbed his daughters arm and spoke to her hurriedly.

I waited.

The Thai man handed me a business card, which was printed in Thai on one side and English on the other. It gave his name – and it began with Doctor – and his business address and mobile number.

"My father says to say that he is the best lawyer in Chiang Mai," the girl relayed to me. "He says that if you have any trouble in Chiang Mai with police, you call him straight away. His English is fine, he just doesn't like using it unless he has to. No problems if you call him."

I looked again at the card, stunned. Was I holding a get out of jail free card? I fished out my wallet and placed the card carefully inside. That could be very useful.

I felt as if the stars were aligning. I hadn't been in Thailand long at all and I was already well on the way to getting myself organized. So what if I wasn't at KC Muay Thai? I didn't even know anything about the place other than the fact that it had a website and catered to tourists. Maybe that little law office that doubled as a Muay Thai promotions team would be even better… More authentic. Less tailored, perhaps…

I hitched my backpack across my shoulders and strolled out towards the main street, feeling Thailand underfoot good and properly. It was a long walk along a line of closed up shop fronts before I reached the street. The signs suggested that I was in a classic Thai bar alley, which would come alive at night with strippers, ladyboys, dance poles, cheap alcohol, music, and liberal-minded old expats. Lining the walls were action photos of old Muay Thai fights that had evidently taken place in the ring I had just left behind.

It had a sepia feel to it – the whole place. Like there was history in the air. Stories to be told, if only the walls could speak. Tethered as they were to the moorings of history, the walls simply watched silently as I strolled along, maintaining their impassive vigil.

I finally emerged onto the street and stopped for a moment to take in the noise and bustle of the scene. There were scooters and tuk-tuks driving past, honking their horns at each other and prospective clients respectively. I was briefly distracted by the flash of bare skin as a cute foreign girl cruised past on a bright yellow scooter, her tiny singlet billowing out behind her. I could smell stale water and petrol fumes and the other usual confluence of hot-climate, old-city smells.

A shirtless, tattooed dwarf walked past.

I turned and watched him walk into the alley that I had just exited, pushing a small cart in front of himself. He looked angry about something.

Welcome to Thailand, I thought to myself with a wry grin.

I was eager to find a place where I could put my backpack down so that I could throw myself into the city. I was full of energy and I was excited, despite having not slept on the plane overnight.

In such a situation going left felt just as a good as right, and so I turned left and walked along the narrow street. I stopped at the first backpacker hostel I encountered and booked myself in for a night, so that I could drop off my bag. I was put into a twelve-bed dormitory room. The three female, German occupants of the room appeared to have just recently roused themselves to meet the day.

The hostel was full to bursting with young travelers. It was clean and the whole place felt energetic. There were voices filtering through from various sources, talking in different languages and with different accents.

And it was relatively cheap.

I talked the nightly fee down to 200 Baht, which is around $7.00 AUD.

"How you going, mate?" I said to a guy in the elevator. His name was Carter and he was American. Sporting curly dark hair and chubby in the way that only Americans can reliably be, Carter, it turned out, would be staying in that same backpacker hostel for the better part of the forthcoming two weeks. I was pleased by the news and I decided then that I too would stay put, given that my training ring was within easy walking distance. I had myself a companion. It's somewhat unusual for backpackers to stay in the same place for a period of time longer than a few days, but Carter was an entrepreneurial online gamer, and so he moved around at a slower pace than most, independent as he was of financial pressures. It was a charmed existence and it was reflective of Carter himself – carefree and whimsical, with a throwaway speaking style that suggested there was nothing that might resemble a filter occupying the space between his brain, his imagination, and his voice box. He was the sort of guy that could talk his way out of anything, as if nothing ever stuck to him, and he had the timeless American confidence to match – the sort of confidence only garnered by those organically aware that they've the might of history's greatest military power standing resolutely in their corner. They're a breed of a different sort; Americans.

"You just arrived here, did you?" Carter asked. "Come and meet my friend. He spent the night downstairs in the common room. You wanna get some food?"

"Yeah, food would be nice."

Carter's friend was handsome and dapper – or at least he would've been, were he not lying passed out on a couch with a small pile of dead insects balanced precariously on his face and gathering in his crotch.

"Ah, see, he always does this," Carter explained, gesturing at the couch situation with an air of apparent exasperation. "I thought he would've been awake by now." He clapped his hands in front of the guy's face. "Hey… Antony!" he called, clapping again. "Wake up, dude!"

Antony came awake slowly. Some of the insects slid off his face and he groaned. "Not again, Carter," he said, slumping back and brushing himself off. The insects scattered everywhere and I picked one up to inspect it.

"What?" Carter was laughing. "I thought you might be hungry when you woke up."

Sure enough, I saw that the insects had actually been deep-fried.

"This guy's an Aussie," Carter said, introducing me. "And *this* is Antony. He's from Canada."

I shook Antony's hand. "Good sleep?" I asked.

Antony nodded. "Yes, it was quite nice, thank you," he said seriously, sitting up and looking around at his couch fondly. Then he looked around the common room and frowned. "This place is a lot cleaner than I remember it," he said.

"The cleaners were in this morning," Carter said. "I caught them trying to put the insects in your mouth."

"Oh yeah, I remember something like that," Antony said thoughtfully. "Are we getting food? I'm starving."

"Yeah, let's do that," I said. I was running on Melbourne time and I hadn't eaten breakfast yet, and it was lunchtime in Thailand.

The two travelers led the way and we meandered down the street, into a typical Thai establishment, complete with half-naked girls and stripper poles. And it was only noon. It was at roughly that moment, as the girls came and led us to our table, that I realized our backpacker hostel and my Muay Thai stadium were right in the beating heart of Chiang Mai's red light district. I shrugged it off, feeling somewhat bemused by the development.

Indeed, I am forever battling a lack of stimulation. Australia is far too safe and regulated for any real fun to ever legally transpire. Thailand felt much more appropriate for someone with an inclination for life, intrigue and adventure.

Too often we apologize for being alive, as if we must justify our very existence to the society that we inherit. Surely, there is nothing for us to feel guilty for. This is my world and it is your world as much as it is anybody else's. Nobody else has done any more or less to deserve being alive. What awaits us on the paths we avoid? Nothing. There's nothing to be gained by indecision or second guessing. There's nothing awaiting us on the paths we don't walk. Conviction, decisiveness and a refusal to be wrong have proven themselves to be useful catalysts for life, in my experience. Open minds – like open doors – are easily invaded, and the contents soiled, vandalized, stolen or corrupted.

Never apologize for being alive.

Such was the mood for me on that first day of travel. Emboldened are those with disregard for the intellectual trends and fashions. The world belongs to all of us and we don't have to get along or share if we don't feel like it. Just ask the capitalists. Do whatever you want.

After lunch our eclectic little trio was joined by a Swiss girl, and together, we delved into the "Old City" part of Chiang Mai and went exploring.

Commonly referred to as the Old City, central Chiang Mai is shaped like a perfect square, and is walled off by a partially destroyed brick wall, which would have been gargantuan in the 13th century, when it was built to defend the city against attacks by the ever-warring Burmese and Cambodians. The wall is surrounded by a moat, with bridges spanning the tepid water to allow traffic and pedestrians to cross. "Old City" would imply ancient building materials and techniques and an overall feeling of being behind the times. This is all partly true, but gentrification is taking place within the city walls, by degrees – as is the case all over Thailand. There is electricity now, for starters. There are satellite dishes and power cables criss-crossing and tangled. A lot of the roads aren't wide enough to accommodate cars, which is fine because most of the Thai populace commute on two wheels anyway.

This is a fast-developing part of the world, and it's exciting to see the contrast between the very old and the very new.

Tourists run rampant throughout Chiang Mai, the vast majority of whom appear to be Chinese.

I was still hungry after lunch, and so I perused the street vendors as we explored the city. I bought freshly fried and salted fish, and delicious mango and various other fruits. It cost mere cents.

Together with Carter, Antony and Daniela – the girl from Switzerland – I spent the afternoon exploring temples and intricate alleyways, better acquainting myself with the city of Chiang Mai. I would be calling this place home for the next month.

And indeed, describing Thailand is a practice fraught with hyperbole. Think of serious men doing serious things with serious expressions on their faces. Think of people in suits and ties, hurrying to places unknown with a frantic, determined stride, desperate to look important, whilst simultaneously choking off the oxygen to their brain in the name of fashionable neck-pieces. Think of efficiency and paperwork and regulation and law enforcement. Think of stern looking women with permanent, easy disdain etched into their very soul. Think all of those things and then laugh foolishly, for Thailand is nothing like that. No, this is a place that operates at a slower pace, with time allowed for conversation and leisurely indulgence. This is a place where you can say and do as you please, to whomever you wish, and to feel free from watching eyes. This is a place where, truly, you can dance when people are looking, and you can sing when people are listening, and you can live fearlessly, and however you wish to do so. It's a place of overt sexuality of all sorts, with liberal attitudes and a relaxed, all-on-the-same-page atmosphere. It is a place of vibrant colour, with nothing bland or ordinary to be seen, with people unafraid to connect with one another. And it's hot. Hot and humid. Combine hot weather and humidity with religious freedom and democratic values, and you have for yourself a recipe for sex. Throw that recipe into a cauldron of liberal-mindedness, and coupled with a melting pot of heritage, violence, culture and visitors, and what you'll soon come to discover is that Thailand is the greatest, most bizarre experiment in human life that has ever existed or been attempted in the modern age.

And it was into this experiment that I plunged, wholeheartedly and eager, with my head on a swivel.

Courtesy of my swiveling head, I spotted a cat sitting on top of a tabletop nearby, licking itself. It would be considered impolite for you or I to lick ourselves like that in public, but there are different rules for cats. It is a profound lesson, indeed, to consider the ease with which that cat approached the task of licking itself. In fact, I can think of no better way to sum up Thailand than to present to you the image of a cat, carelessly lifting its leg and licking itself on a public bench. Truly profound.

"Should we have a drink tonight?" Daniela suggested. She had a pretty accent.

"Of course," Antony said.

I liked the sound of that. I felt like celebrating my arrival in Thailand, and the freedom that I was feeling, and the company of my new friends. I was feeling a little bit lost, if I was completely honest. I'd arrived in Thailand feeling utterly bent in a certain direction. I was there to train and to fight in a professional Muay Thai bout. On that first afternoon, however, there was little I could do to take myself further in that direction. I would have my first training session the following morning, and I could take it from there. In the meantime, I figured I might as well relax and enjoy myself.

We whiled away the afternoon avoiding the stifling heat and humidity by sipping coke out of glass bottles and playing pool and exchanging travel stories in a friendly bar. As the sun set in the west and the lights started flicking on across Chiang Mai, we ordered up beers and clinked our glasses together.

The night moved along with good conversation, competitive games of pool against unruly Dutch lads, and plenty more beer.

Despite my earlier misgivings, I was soon feeling like I had found my place in the world. Beer has a way of helping with that, of course, but it was the warmth and homely nature of Thailand itself that was the real star of the show. Throw away your doubts, was the message, received loud and clear. You're allowed to live.

The tropical rains started hammering against the tin roof just as the bar was winding down for the evening.

Daniela bundled me up for a quick kiss in the warm rain before the four of us all stumbled back to the hostel and fell into bed. I walked alongside Daniela and we spent the walk deliberately rubbing shoulders with each other and talking about life.

There's a period of time in a young man's life where he is utterly invincible. Tell him otherwise and he'll think you mad. Invincible, infallible – a shepherd for the luckiest of sheep – destined to live and reign forever as the king of the universe. Mortality is a hilarious notion to that young man. You can tell him that it's impossible to lift the Earth. He won't believe you. You can tell him that not every woman on the planet is going to want him. He won't believe you. You can tell him that there are other men out there who are even more invincible and infallible than he. He won't believe you.

Such is the tragedy of being a young man.

You're infallible right up until you're not.

Michael Goodison

Enlightened are senses that learn to ignore;
    To look without seeing is to Open a door,
And let it blow through, come, the Winds of the World;
    More wisdom's in Breathing than all scrolls left unfurled.
So, breathe and keep breathing; there's More yet to learn,
A drop in the Ocean might be all for tides turn.

CHAPTER 2
AND SO IT STARTS

*"So we beat on, boats against the current,
born back ceaselessly into the past."*
- F. Scott Fitzgerald, *The Great Gatsby*

There are few places left for wild souls to roam. No Wild West frontier. No new world. No anarchical battlefields. For those who do not wish to be ruled or governed, there is no place for them. Banishment is no longer an option. Either fight for your freedom and end up imprisoned, or imprison yourself within a society that you cannot stand, with people who make no sense to you, and be bombarded by a lifestyle that bears no interest or similarity to that which you envision in dreams. Either way, the choice is imprisonment. I'm sure it would've once been claimed that the free spirit of men and women could never be chained, but the governments of the world have proven otherwise.

If there is one place in the world where there remains a *taste* of freedom, it probably exists in South-East Asia somewhere. It certainly won't be found in the developed world. It won't be found in a place where everybody is forced to run at the slowest person's pace. Thailand feels right to me. It feels alive and dynamic. There are no robots disguised in business clothes trying to live a life as financially efficient as possible. Instead, there are people, talking and laughing and fighting and crying with one another. There are people falling in and out of love. There are people living and dying. There is passion. Life is the only currency that matters to me, and Thailand is full to positively bursting with it.

I've never subscribed to the apparently unspoken theory that safer equals better. To me, that is in no way a self-evident truth. I am comfortable in my central philosophy of life – I am here to be entertained – and for me, I ask only to be surrounded by the madness of life as it transpires in its natural state. Give me the bold and the outrageous – those raging against the chains, ready and willing to fling themselves at the world. In a world in which no two moments are ever the same, and an entirely new universe is created with each passing millisecond, it is an abhorrent, disturbing, utterly repugnant spectacle to experience that most devilish thing: boredom.

And so, there I was, having flung myself out of the nest to see if those wings are for show or for function, on the ground in Thailand and itching to live…

Adjusting to time zones is relatively easy when you're travelling west around the world, chasing the sun. The difference between Chiang Mai and Melbourne is three hours. In Melbourne, I had been in the habit of sleeping in until 9am, and so, after my first night in Thailand, I awoke naturally at 6am, feeling fully rested, energized and re-charged.

The dorm room had filled up overnight without my noticing, and now eleven of the twelve beds were filled with sweaty, snoring bodies. I was loving the warmth and humidity of the environment – so different from the cold, frosty winter mornings I had left behind.

Daniela was awake on the bed beneath mine and she smiled in greeting as I climbed down the ladder. I nodded towards the door and we went down onto the street in search of breakfast together.

The streets were almost silent at that hour of morning. Shop fronts were closed up, and we had to walk for half an hour before we found a street vendor. Daniela was travelling onwards to Chiang Rai that same day, bound for a slow-boat journey down the Mekong River into bordering Laos and eventually arriving in Vietnam.

Travelling can all too easily become a bit of an emotional roller-coaster ride. You meet new, unique, vibrant people in exotic places and you get to know them and you laugh with them and you fall in love with them and you trust them completely, and you go and do things together that you will remember fondly for the rest of your lives, and then a few moments later you go your separate ways and it feels like you've broken up. And then you get to the next location, or the next person or group of persons arrive at your location, and you do it all again. By the time you return home, you've met the love of your life a hundred times over and been through a hundred different break-ups.

There's a knack to it, as there is most things.

Daniela and I ate breakfast together and strolled back to the hostel. I was checking my watch as we went. I needed to be ready for my first Muay Thai training session by 10am.

I was feeling good as Daniela and I parted ways. The air felt fresh and the warmth and humidity was invigorating in the early hours of the day. The rain from the night before had long since evaporated or drained away, leaving everything feeling clear and clean. Renewed. As if the cleaners had been in overnight to sweep away the accumulation of clutter and dust from the day before.

There was very little on my mind that morning, which was unusual, to say the least. I'd had a full night's sleep, which was also unusual.

I've come to notice that the world becomes a far nicer place when you are on the road. There are fewer bombs dropped. There are fewer murders and robberies. There are fewer arguments. Fewer politicians caught in lies. There's less suffering and anguish. There's less complaining. There are fewer celebrities being regurgitated into the public consciousness for lack of anything worthwhile to talk about. For no readily apparent reason – other than the fact that there are fewer opportunities to watch the news – being on the road makes the world seem like a nicer place. Perhaps there's a lesson in that.

It was time for Muay Thai training.

24 days until the fight.

The shirtless, tattooed Thai dwarf was there again, sweeping the floor in the alleyway.

I nodded to him and continued down to the ring.

There was an old guy waiting for me.

I groaned inwardly.

This guy was too old for me to spar with. There was no way he was the champion trainer that I had been promised.

"Sawasdeekap," I said, bowing conservatively to him, as per the Muay Thai custom. *Hello.*

We introduced ourselves quickly.

"Your trainer come three days," the old man said in broken English, holding up three fingers. "He come Bangkok. Fight Bangkok. Come back Chiang Mai three days for training."

"Ok, sure," I said, nodding. "My trainer will be here in three days."

"Today, me train," the old man said, gesturing to himself.

I shrugged. "Sure."

I was ok to train with the old guy for a few days, just so long as I wasn't expected to pay the agreed 6,000 Baht until I had met with my promised champion trainer. I wasn't going to be ripped off.

In fact, I was secretly relieved to get the chance to ease into the training with an older trainer, given that I knew my fitness wasn't quite where it ought to be for Muay Thai training in Thailand. I'd been a little slack leading up to the trip, but not to worry. The old guy would be a nice buffer before the real training began in three days.

As it turned out, I was wrong.

The old man was borderline psychotic in his training approach.

Forget about technique. This guy was all about *conditioning.*

The session began easily enough, with a slow, fifteen minute jog around the extremities of the stadium, followed by another fifteen minutes of skipping and then another fifteen minutes of hitting a heavy bag however I liked.

I was drenched in sweat after hitting the bag. The humidity in Thailand is tough to get used to. I was losing water faster than I could replace it.

"In the ring," the old man said.

The warm-up was over. Now it was time to get down to business.

"Business" consisted of seemingly relentless rounds of kicking the thick Thai pads, with no comment or attention paid to technique. In between rounds, the old guy would have me lay in the centre of the ring and tense my muscles whilst he slammed the Thai boxing pads into every inch of my body he could find. Then he had me doing push-ups and sit-ups. Then it was more kicking.

"Muay Thai, you get hit, you get kick," the old man said, slamming a kick into my left thigh as he spoke. I sat all my weight down on the leg to take the heavy impact. That seemed only to embolden the old man, who threw more furious kicks and knees at my legs and ribcage as I tried to focus on hitting the pads.

Two hours felt like forever.

At the end of the session, the old man produced a bottle containing a clear Thai boxing ointment, which he rubbed into my leg muscles. The ointment burned hot on my legs, like deep-heat on steroids.

"Kapkunkap," I said to the old man, which means *thank you* in Thai.

"See you tomorrow," the old man said gruffly. "10 o'clock."

"10 o'clock," I called back over my shoulder.

The shirtless, angry-looking dwarf smirked as I tried not to limp along the alley and back out to the main street.

I returned the smirk, as if agreeing with him. There was something curious about that dwarf – some quirk, trait or otherwise which is difficult to describe – that made me want to bundle him into a garbage bin full of enraged monkeys and then nudge the whole thing down a flight of stairs.

Back at the hostel, I stepped into the shower fully clothed and found an old soap canister which I used to help wash my clothes. I didn't want to admit it, but I was close to collapse at that point. My legs were badly swollen and shaking.

"Fuck's sake," I groaned as I stripped off and inspected my thighs and torso, which were covered in angry welts.

It's just day one, I told myself. *I'll get used to it.*

I wondered what Daniela was doing and briefly fantasized about what might've been had I gone with her to take the slow boat along the Mekong down to Vietnam. She had been a really nice girl. I rubbed a hand over the welts on my side and grimaced, suddenly wishing I'd gone with Daniela.

I must've been in the shower for over half an hour, with my head pressed up against the cool tiles, trying to recover both mentally and physically from the battering I had taken in my first training session.

I was trying not to think about the month that I had in front of me.

I was doing it a little tough after that first day, but such is life. I'd fought previously in seven victorious professional Muay Thai fights and I knew intimately the commitment and sacrifice that was required of me if I was to be victorious in my eighth.

The showers were communal and the doors were broken, leaving them wide open to anybody walking past along the hallway.

"You alright, Mick?" I heard somebody say.

I pushed myself off from the tiles and saw that Carter was standing there in the hall, looking concerned.

I stood up straight. "Yeah, mate," I said coolly. "What are you up to?"

Carter leaned against the wall and frowned. "Antony wants to go up to the temple," he said. "The one on the mountain. You know it?"

I nodded. "Yeah, what's it called again?"

"Doi Suthep."

I nodded thoughtfully. "Yeah. Let me get something to eat and then I'll come along with you guys."

Carter nodded. "You have injuries," he said, pointing at my body.

I checked out my body again. "Yep, tough day at the office," I admitted. My left side was quickly turning purple and black, and my legs were swollen. I realized the skin had split on the side of my knee where I had been kicked repeatedly, and blood was mixing with the water from the shower and running down my shin.

"Looks painful," Carter observed.

I nodded. "Not too bad," I said, shrugging. "What do you wanna do for food?"

"Anything."

"Cool. I'll be out in a minute," I said.

Carter nodded. "Shame you're such a pussy," he said offhandedly, and then he left.

"Ok then," I said to the suddenly vacant bathroom.

I sighed and pressed my head against the tiles again for a moment before turning the water off. Despite his flaws – his conspicuous American-ness and his silly, curly hair – Carter had broken the spell. I could easily have been in the cold shower all day long if he hadn't come and spoken to me. Just having someone to talk to had lightened the load on my mind and I was feeling a lot better. That was why I had been reluctant to do individual training, as opposed to joining a fight camp with other fighters. Fight training can be a very difficult undertaking, and having people to share the load is invaluable. I didn't have other fighters to talk to, but at least I had other travelers and English speakers around me there at the hostel.

If Carter was the best I had, well then so be it. Even misshapen, unripe lemons can produce a lemonade of sorts.

I gathered up my soaking wet clothes off the floor and tiptoed back to the dorm room. "Sorry, sorry," I said hurriedly as I entered the dorm room and saw many pairs of bleary eyes looking at me. It was after noon and most of the room's occupants were still in bed.

"What happened to you?" one of the German girls asked.

"Hm?" I said. I didn't want to keep talking about my injuries. I wanted to ignore them and hope that they would go away. I was a little embarrassed by my bruised appearance. It was a blow to my ego. I'd forgotten how much Muay Thai can hurt.

"Oh, *ouch*," another of the girls said, propping herself up in bed to look anxiously at me.

I blew off the questions and invited the German girls to come along to find something to eat with Antony and Carter.

They joined us in the hostel foyer and we set off into the maze of streets and alleyways once again, in search of decent food.

After lunch, the five of us bartered for a red taxi to take us up to the temple on the mountain overlooking Chiang Mai. It was a beautiful day and the twisting road up the mountainside, coupled with the warm breeze, had me dosing off with my arm draped outside the taxi.

We arrived at the foot of the temple in the middle of the afternoon and I dragged my weary limbs out of the taxi and gazed up at the vast array of steps I'd have to climb to reach the temple at the top. I'm loathe to look soft in front of pretty girls. It's one of those universal, unwritten laws of the distinctly male brain.

"Well, come on then," one of the German girls said, and thus we climbed.

Dogs and monkeys shared the steps with a myriad of Thai locals, monks, and tourists, all clambering up towards the temple in the afternoon heat.

We got our first look at the temple when we finally crested the steps and beheld the old structure. It was strikingly beautiful. The German girls were told to cover their bare legs with sarongs, which were being handed out to the skin-baring tourist girls by Thai volunteers. There were intricate patterns everywhere and bells and steeple ceilings and shadowy nooks underneath trees and gentle flowing water ponds and burning candles and bald monks in orange robes and battered sandals.

The view over Chiang Mai was even better than that of the temple, in my opinion. I could see the airport and the distinct, square-shaped, moat-encircled brick walls that made up the "old city" part of Chiang Mai. Another mountain range rose up on the far side of the ancient city, as if it were a brother sentinel standing up out of the Earth to protect the 2nd

largest dwelling in Thailand, with a population of just over two hundred thousand.

As the sun began to set, we clambered back down the steep temple steps and rode the red taxi back down to Chiang Mai.

"Hey, Mick. Have you met the English guys yet?" Carter asked as we traipsed back into the hostel.

I shook my head. "I don't think so."

"They're fun guys. Come meet them."

I was feeling an awfully long way from being ready to fight. In fact, during those early days of the trip, I was quick to the suspicion that I wouldn't be fighting at all, despite my best intentions. I can be stubborn, however, and in about three weeks' time, I would indeed be stepping into the ring.

There were four guys hanging out in the common room when Carter, Antony and I arrived. Three Englishmen and one guy from Ireland. We all introduced ourselves quickly and our respective stories were exchanged.

"Beer, mate?" someone pressed a Thai beer into my hand. It was a *Chang*. I opened it and sipped at it gratefully, cautiously aware that I was probably still dehydrated after my Muay Thai workout earlier in the day.

The guy from Ireland was Toddy. The guys from England were Liam, Jack and James. Together with Antony, Carter and I, we made for quite a rowdy group. They were fun guys, and I was quickly caught up in the mood as more beer was proffered and the card games started really heating up.

I was getting swept along in the tide of energy, despite it pulling me conspicuously further and further away from my desired goal of being fit for training the next day. Fight preparation is not something that can be simply switched on and off as applicable. It is a full-time occupation – something which occupies both the mind and the body at all hours of the night and day. I resigned myself to the prospect of suffering through training the following morning, granted the inevitable fact of my being thoroughly hung-over.

The hostel common room had filled up as travelers entered in ones, twos and threes, and a small, friendly crowd had soon gathered around our central table. I got drunk much too quickly, owing partly to the humidity and my dehydration, and partly to my not having drunk anything stronger than tea in almost six months prior to travelling to Thailand.

Occupying centre stage, as seemed so natural and appropriate for him, Carter soon suggested that our little congregation of travelers migrate out onto the streets of Thailand in search of adventure and new experiences.

There were confirmatory grumbles and our rowdy little gang headed out into the darkness and onto the streets of Chiang Mai, singing and dancing with one another.

If there was anyone asleep in that town, we were on something of a mission to wake them up. Not out of malice, no, but only so that they could all join us in the revelry and bask in the magnificence that is northern Thailand at night.

My familiar traveler's sense of elation and freedom returned as we strolled across the moat and the warm, humid air filled my lungs. To hell with training in the morning. I felt alive. I wanted to enjoy myself.

"There's a place up here," James the Englishman pointed. "They've got pool tables and dart boards."

Pool tables appeared to be a staple of the Chiang Mai nightlife entertainment, which suited me just fine.

"And food?" I asked.

"I'm pretty sure they had food," Jack said, frowning thoughtfully. "We were just there last night," he said, slapping Liam on the shoulder.

"Yeah, they had food," Liam said, nodding eagerly.

"Fine then," I agreed. It would do.

We found the bar and made ourselves right at home, ordering up pizzas and more beer and encircling the pool table. It wasn't a very Thai experience, but I didn't mind just then. I was having a good time.

There was more and more beer. I didn't even know who was buying them, but the thick glass mugs seemed to be continually appearing in front of me, and I wasn't about to question their being there.

The conversation moved around from international politics to sports to competing travel stories, with the criteria being general craziness. Strange, I believe, that human-beings require social lubricants such as drugs and alcohol to feel comfortable and at ease with one another. It is surely just one of many symptoms of a more existential problem.

"Ladyboy," announced Carter, suddenly and sharply, standing up and pointing across the bar at a womanly-looking Thai individual who had just entered.

I ran through the checklist for identifying a ladyboy. Tall, prominent Adam's apple, muscle tone, strong looking hands. *Check, check, check and check.*

Thailand nightlife is rife with weirdness, for want of a better word. Ladyboys are unusually common and prominent. Sexuality runs the full gamut on whatever spectrum you care to mention, and it's all on display for anybody to see. It's the oldest business in the world, and even today, prostitution is thriving on the streets of Thailand. Girls young and old dot the streets in huge numbers, looking for potential customers. The sad part is how invisible they become after a few days in Thailand. Indeed, as you come to learn, there are certain currencies in life far more potent than money – those being the likes of fear, violence and sex. Those seeking a family-friendly holiday to a picturesque tropical destination would be best suited to the confines of a South Thailand beach resort – the sort that comes with a certain number of stars in the description. Those more willing can venture out onto the streets with the locals and the backpackers, and it's there that you will encounter the rawness of a culture so far-reaching as to be done justice in naught but the world of exaggeration. Monkey stole your hat and a monk punched your friend? That's just another Tuesday night down at the karaoke bar on Tha Phae Road in Chiang Mai.

"I'm not proud of what I've done," Carter said sheepishly, and we all stood back and watched as he hoisted his respective purchases for his companions to inspect. After moving on from the first bar, the young American had been curtailed into a variety store by a very persuasive old Thai salesman standing out the front and hollering at potential customers. Some moments later, and there we were, all staring at what he had bought. First, there was a t-shirt with a picture of a dog and bold writing printed on the front that said: The Dogfather. Second, there was a pair of reading glasses that came with eyebrows, a nose and an enormous, snowy-white beard attached.

"Nice purchases," Liam observed.

"Love your work," James agreed.

"Be rude not to wear them," I suggested.

Carter looked at me blandly for a moment before taking his shirt off and replacing it with his new one, and then on went the glasses.

We could barely control ourselves, so intently were we laughing.

"Well at least that beard covers up some of the t-shirt," Liam said, pointing.

Carter shrugged miserably and held up his old t-shirt. "And what am I supposed to do with this?" he wondered aloud.

"Just hold onto it."

"Stick it in your pocket."

A stray cat went berserk as Carter approached, and so we dived headlong into an indifferent-looking bar, for fear of being eaten alive.

The bar was dank and smelled funny, but we didn't care. We found a table and continued drinking. Before too long, it was just Carter and myself, though I wasn't sure why.

"Hey, Carter?" I said, turning to my friend.

"Mm?"

"Can you make sure I'm not hung-over tomorrow? I have training and I can't be hung-over. Can you do that for me?"

Carter shrugged nonchalantly. "Of course," he said, and he started brushing my hair with his hands.

"What are you doing?"

"You've got chips in your hair."

"I see... Where did the other guys go?"

"Liam stole a lizard," Carter explained to me, lifting his beard to sip at his beer.

"He stole a lizard?"

"Yeah. I dunno where they went but we should probably leave soon. It's getting light outside."

"Ok then," I agreed.

I hadn't realized how quickly the time had gone.

As we strolled back out onto the streets, the sky was showing the first signs of light in the east.

A new day was dawning, and I was furious with myself.

I had travelled to Thailand for a multitude of reasons, it was true, but my priority was to compete in a Muay Thai fight. I would need to be a lot more careful in the future, to ensure that I didn't compromise the journey to the ring with too much drinking and frequent late nights. As it were, I wasn't feeling good. It was after 5am and I was drunk and dehydrated on the streets of Chiang Mai, with stiff and swollen legs and pain flaring in my ribs whenever I moved too sharply. I wasn't going to be in good shape for another session of conditioning with the Thai elder.

Nevertheless, the night had been an adventure.

The most contested space in the world is that which the future holds. People all have different ideas about what future they want, be it for themselves, their children, their friends. Politicians each represent slightly different futures that we can vote for, and they paint detailed pictures for us as to what those respective futures might hold. Unfortunately, most of the time, those paintings more closely resemble self-portraits, and so the political future almost always appears bleak. I am a part of a generation that wants what we have never had – what the world hasn't had for centuries – a blank canvas, to do with as we please.

Life's a blank canvas – or at least, it should be – and I was filling in the blanks with as many varied and vibrant colours as possible.

Muay Thai: Peace, At Last

Mightn't She, who sees it all, know more than what is seen?
It's possible, I'd like to think, that all what's meant has been.
Consider now, if time weren't told, and Now is all that were.,
Tomorrow's gone, She had us fooled, young men are calling Her.
Contested space, the future realm, if only it'd arrive,
Some distant time that never comes, yet Now we are alive...

CHAPTER 3
LIFE KICKS THE HARDEST

"Sleep late, have fun, get wild, drink whiskey and drive fast on empty streets with nothing in mind but falling in love and not getting arrested."
— Hunter S. Thompson

I am a man with a code. A creed for life. I have life rules, which I have stowed safely away upstairs. Over the course of time, words tentatively written as a child have become etched into a young man's very soul. They provide a direction – a bearing on a compass. Without a code, it's easy to get lost. Indeed, I've come to discover that an increasing number of my generation are simply meandering about, bumping invariably into things as they stare at the socks of the people in front of them.

It's a big world out there, and there's a place for everyone, should only we raise our eyes and walk our own paths. Courage is the forebear of everything else in life, and so it is in this man's creed. Courage to think independently, to speak independently, to question everything, and the courage to love. Like many men, my code revolves around being a gentleman, and what that means, exactly. There are many differing definitions on being a gentleman, of course, but I have found that it often results in a coupling of two broad, distinctly masculine virtues. Aggression and tenderness. Some men believe that it is best to appear outwardly aggressive, whilst harbouring a softer, tender side, which they reveal to their loved ones. I believe it is better to be the opposite. To be outwardly soft and tender, whilst harbouring a fiercely aggressive side, which is revealed only to those who would threaten harm against loved ones. Either way, the recipe for being a gentleman consists of those two key ingredients. It is for every man to decide for himself how he wishes to stir them together.

I found myself pondering the robust virtues of my code as Carter and I walked back to the hostel as the sun rose and the mercury began its swift morning climb. We bought toasted sandwiches from a 7/11 store along the way, and I started drinking water as if it was going out of fashion. I badly needed to hydrate again if I was to be in any kind of state to attend training.

I'd be furious with myself if I missed training because I'd gotten too drunk and succumbed to partying. The first couple of days and nights had been fun, but it was time to get serious. I was there to compete in a Muay Thai fight, and that meant I needed to take the training seriously. Chiang Mai and I had been quick to dispense with the introductions and formalities, and we were each feeling somewhat wary of the other in light of proceedings, which suited us both fine. From that time onwards, training needed to be my first priority.

23 days until the fight.
"Sawasdeekap," I grumbled at the front desk attendant as James and I ambled back into the hostel, both of us looking disheveled and molested.
Hello, sir.

I was wondering whether or not it would be a good idea at that stage to try to get some sleep. What was the best way to get myself ready before training in just a few hours' time?

I decided that sleeping then would be a bad idea. Instead, I went out and purchased water and Gatorade and I sipped at it whilst standing under the shower and trying to motivate myself. My head felt awful, and my body wasn't far behind, but I still believed that I could survive the training session that was yet to come. I had survived worse.

I frowned and watched as a new girl that I didn't recognize came into the bathroom and stumbled into one of the stalls. I considered pointing out that this was the male bathroom, but the girl didn't seem to be in any state to listen, and whether or not the bathroom was gender exclusive seemed to be a matter of opinion, anyway.

"Jesus," I muttered to myself as I listened to her throwing up. What a mess. I didn't feel so bad now, by comparison.

I suddenly found myself wondering whether it was wise to be preparing for a fight whilst living in a backpacker hostel. A fight camp most certainly would have been more suitable. Significantly more conducive to health and fitness. Fewer distractions.

"Alright?" I asked the girl as she emerged from the toilet stall and sat slumped on the dirty tiled floor in front of me.

She nodded and then seemed to realize for the first time that I was there, showering and holding a Gatorade bottle in my hand.

"Want a drink?" I offered her the flavoured drink and she accepted it with a look of relief on her face.

"Long night," the girl groaned, rubbing her eyes. She had a European accent. Dutch, probably.

I nodded my understanding and then stopped the shower and left to get dressed.

There was a bookshelf in the hostel common room that had been setup for travelers to share and trade books with one another whilst on the move, and I spent some time perusing the various titles.

Reading is a tremendous thing. Not only do books contain all of the collective knowledge from thousands of years of human intellect, but books also teach us how to be alone. In my opinion, learning how to spend time on your own and to enjoy your own company is one of the most critical life skills for parents to instill in their children. My parents left me alone with my toys when I was a kid, and I believe that it's one of the best things that they ever did for me – amongst many other extraordinary things, of course. Leaving me alone with my toys taught me how to use my imagination and how to be contented and soothed by my own company. In that regard, I never developed a reliance on anybody else, and my happiness and my thinking were entirely my own responsibility. From playing alone in my room with my toy soldiers and castles and dragons, a love of reading and independent thinking followed only naturally, in the same way that night follows day.

"Hard to choose one, isn't it?" a lovely, mischievous voice entered my consciousness, and I turned to look. There was a girl sitting at a table nearby, already reading a magazine of some kind. I'd walked past her without noticing.

"Oh, hey," I said, waving. "Yeah, I brought a book from home anyway, so I'm just having a look."

"Only one book?" she asked. She had a British accent.

"Yeah. I'll just read it over and over if I have to," I said, shrugging. "I'm hoping to be so busy that I won't have too much time left over for reading."

"Are you from New Zealand?" the girl asked.

I grinned. "Australia," I said. "Are you from China?"

"England."

I gestured to myself. "Michael."

She gestured to herself. "Philly."

"As in… the place… or the cheese?" I asked.

"The horse," she said with a laugh. "My parents love horses."

"I hope you love horses, too, then."

"I do."

"That's lucky… Do you like cats as well?"

"Who doesn't like cats?" she asked, frowning suspiciously around the room.

"Someone told me last night that there's a cat café somewhere here in Chiang Mai," I said.

"A *cat* café?"

I nodded. "Yeah. Apparently it's exactly what you think it is – just a café where you can buy tea or whatever and there are also cats there that will come and sit on your lap."

"That's amazing."

"Do you want to go with me after lunch?" I asked. "I've got things I gotta do this morning…"

"That sounds lovely," Philly said. "I'll wait for you here at, say, one?"

We sat and talked for a while. She was a friendly, amicable person. Her first time travelling and she was doing it entirely on her own.

Then, it was time for training.

I was still feeling awful, and I felt even worse after the usual warm-up of jogging, skipping and hitting the heavy bag.

Carter's promise that I would be hangover free had proven itself empty.

"In the ring," the old man said gruffly.

I nodded and climbed in, breathing deeply as I prepared for the assault on my body to begin.

I noticed that the old man had welts and bruises up his forearms and I couldn't help grinning to myself, satisfied. I'd made sure to kick the pads as hard as I could the day before. No matter how thick they make those pads, you can still damage the arms of the person holding them, and that was exactly what I had been trying to do to that old bastard. I wanted to break his arms, and it looked like I might've gotten closer than I had at first suspected.

I'll be surprised if we do pad work again today.

And so it was. Instead of pad work, the old man had us doing clinch work.

The Muay Thai clinch is a big part of what sets the sport apart from straight up kickboxing. In Muay Thai, when two fighters lock up and get close to each other, the referee doesn't step in and separate them. Instead, they are allowed to continue wrestling with each other, and it is from within the clinch that knees and elbows and throws can be utilized. Clinching is a very dangerous aspect of the sport.

The idea is to get your hands behind your opponent's head, and your elbows dug into their collarbones. From that position, you can wrench your opponent around by his head and force him into positions from which you can drive knees into his body and face. You can also throw them to the ground to score points and stamp your authority on the contest. Thais have no respect for a fighter who cannot handle himself in the clinch – something that foreigners traditionally struggle with.

My trainer and I came to grips in the middle of the ring, grunting and gasping as we wrestled for control.

Strength is only a small aspect in the clinch game. Technique is important, of course, but the main thing is mental agility – the ability to think coolly and swiftly under pressure and in an ever-changing situation – and the ability to *feel* where the weight and inertia of yourself and your opponent is situated, respectively. Clinching is a little bit like playing a game of human, combat chess whilst standing up.

After a minute or so of tangling our arms and then separating, the clinching started to heat up and I got into the positions that I wanted. I wrenched on the old guys neck in such a way that is hard to see from an observers point of view, but which is excruciatingly painful to the person on the receiving end. It's also terrifying. It feels like your neck is about to break if you resist, and that's because it *is*.

I increased the pressure on the hold until the old guy finally relented and went to the canvas. He rolled straight back to his feet and came back at me, leading with a knee strike to my injured ribs.

It's polite in clinch training to throw knees with the inside of your thigh, rather than using the point of the knee, but my trainer didn't seem too fussed about that right now.

It was a good shot and I grimaced soundlessly.

Clinching is a very intimate business. You use your head to press against the other person as a powerful tool to steer them around, and quite often you'll find that the side of your face is pressed up against theirs. From this positioning, you can hear their every pained gasp and desperate breath. Clinching can be a good barometer for how your opponent is feeling, because they can't hide those little things from you when you get that close, and having a poker face is obviously a critical element of combat sports.

I returned the knee to the old guy and felt the air escaping his lungs. He responded by trying to use the momentum of the knee strike to swing me to the ground, but I was ready for it and muscled out of it, and countered *his* momentum to get my arms up under his armpits to lift him into the air and slam him down against the canvas once again.

The trainer was back on his feet in an instant, looking impassive and unbothered.

Inwardly, I was pleased with myself. It had been a while since I had trained or clinched with anyone, and I was holding my own up to that point. I wondered who I needed to talk to in order to book myself in for a proper fight on a professional fight card.

The old guy had stepped out of the ring, and now he returned holding a medicine ball. I knew exactly what that meant. I looked at the ball and nodded my understanding. I lay on my back with my hands behind my head. I took a deep breath and tensed up.

My trainer slammed the medicine ball down onto my stomach, which wasn't a very pleasant feeling. If he were a masseuse, I'd be asking for my money back. I lay there with my hands behind my head and squeezed my eyes shut and did my best to tense up every muscle in my body as hard as I could to protect my organs whilst he stomped on my chest, kicked my legs, pounded the medicine ball into my stomach and then dropped his knees down onto my stomach just to be sure. This went on for some time. He used the Thai pads as clubs and swung them at me. The onslaught finally relented and I curled up in a ball on the floor and gave myself a few minutes to recover. I was lightheaded from holding my breath. I wouldn't have been surprised if I had a hernia after that. I hadn't wanted to breathe for fear that my stomach muscles might relax and then my organs would be exposed. A ruptured spleen would've been a good way to put a stop to my trip. Stomach muscles play a critical body-armour role, in conjunction with the ribs and collar bones. I'd stolen a few tiny little breaths in between blows like I was sipping from a straw, but that was all I had managed. My body was red and raw. My entire torso looked like it was badly sunburnt and my legs felt like they were swelling.

All in the name of fight conditioning.

After a while, I shrugged inwardly and returned to my feet.

I'm just here to be entertained.

It's an attitude towards life that has proven itself time and time again to be of great assistance during difficult times. A wry kind of nonchalance. An acceptance of the way things are, and of who you are. Michael is all I've ever had, Michael is all I've ever needed, and Michael is all I'll ever need.

The rest of the session was much more calm and respectful between the two of us. We focused on some low speed fight strategy and techniques to set up elbow strikes.

"Kapkunkap," I said at last, bowing.

The session was over.

The dwarf watched me as I walked back past his little bar in the alleyway. There was something about that angry little guy that made me want to roll him up in a musty old rug. He didn't seem to own a shirt. Perhaps he couldn't find an appropriate size. All of the other bars were closed up at that hour of the day.

Philly was in the common room when I got back. "Hey," she grinned.

"Hey," I said. "I'm just gonna take a quick shower and then I'll meet you back down here?"

"Sure."

I went back upstairs and found Carter on his bed in the dorm room, deeply ensconced in his world of online gaming, with his headphones in his ears and the whites of his eyes showing around his pupils. I was exhausted and wanted nothing more than to collapse in a heap and fall asleep, but I'd promised Philly we'd find the cat café, and I would be loathe to let her down.

I usually prefer to spend time on my own, but it was still early days in Thailand, and so I felt it wasn't a bad idea to spend some time with other people before I went my own way and did my own thing.

It was difficult at that point to really come to terms with the fact that I would be fighting in just a few weeks' time. It felt as if it wasn't really going to happen. It *was* going to happen, however, and I needed to get myself as settled into a training routine as I could manage.

Wearing dry clothes, I returned to the common room and, together, Philly and I strolled out onto the streets and begun our search for this mysterious feline café.

It was a humid, overcast day, and the walk seemed to sap the last of my energy reserves. When we finally found the cat café on the far side of the city, I collapsed into air-conditioned, cushion-lined, soft and purring comfort. Philly and I sat on cushions and ordered milkshakes and tea and relaxed as a seemingly endless mess of cats strutted around the room and occasionally stopped to examine the new curiosities in their midst.

"They're so *cute!*" Philly gushed, picking up cat after cat and plonking them on her lap, until they were piled so high I could hardly see her for all the meowing and paw-licking that was transpiring.

They *were* quite adorable. I took Philly's phone and snapped off a few photos. We ordered lunch and stayed longer, waiting for the novelty to wear off and then finally accepting that it probably wasn't going to.

I insisted that we catch a three-wheeler tuk-tuk for the journey back across the city. It was starting to rain lightly. Warm, tropical rain.

Arriving back at the hostel, Philly and I went up to the dorm room and discovered that our beds were next to each other.

"Oh, that's *your* bed?" Philly said as I lay down with a stifled groan. "Where were you last night?"

"I was out all night," I replied, not really in the mood for talking.

Philly pulled out a tablet computer from her bag and propped it up so that we could both see it, and, as the afternoon rain intensified on the ceiling, I relaxed into the soft pillows and drifted along with the movie, feeling somewhat serene in my exhaustion.

I awoke to find that the rain had stopped and the sky outside had darkened. Philly was asleep. There were people bustling around in the dorm room, rustling bags and talking to each other in Spanish.

"Hey," I murmured, shaking Philly awake. "Are you hungry?"

She nodded wearily.

We got ourselves ready and then walked down onto the street. Instead of turning left this time, we turned right, away from the old city. We walked over a couple of small bridges and then found ourselves in an extremely crowded precinct. We had found the nightly street-market, and it was jam packed full of tourists and locals like. There were vendors selling everything you could imagine, from knives, tasers and batons to clothes, ice-creams and wooden key rings shaped like penises.

As it so happened, my sparse clothing was already gross with sweat, despite my daily shower-washings, and so I stopped along the way and bartered for a few more white, tropical looking shirts and pairs of billowy shorts with elephant patterns on them. I also found a Thai power adaptor.

Then we went to dinner. Philly and I found a quaint little restaurant that was open to the night air at the very rear of the night market, where it backed onto quiet, leafy streets. There were fans to ward off the oppressive, post-rain humidity and there was a young Thai man on a small stage playing an acoustic guitar and singing softly into a microphone. The entire establishment was illuminated by sporadic candlelight. It was all very romantic.

Philly and I ate together and we talked and laughed quietly – just two more human beings enjoying each other's company in the place – being serenaded by live music and seduced by candlelight.

Just as we were leaving, two Thai men brushed past us and thrust leaflets into our hands. They were advertising Muay Thai fights that were starting in half an hour at Loi Kroh stadium. I recognized the name. That was the same stadium within which I had been training. "Wanna go?" I asked, waving the leaflet at Philly. "I think I might be able to get us in for free."

Philly looked at the leaflet and then smiled and shrugged. "Sure," she said. "Looks interesting."

We meandered back towards the hostel and stopped in along the way at the stadium entrance. The alleyway that I had only seen closed up was now in full swing, with the bars having thrown open their doors to the masses of tourists and locals alike. There were half naked Thai girls everywhere you looked, flirting with tourists and encouraging them to buy more drinks and play another game of pool and stay a little longer. The daughter of the lawyer was there at the gate, with a tin full of Thai Baht currency and a stamp.

She smiled when she saw me. "Come to watch?" she asked, gesturing for my hand. She stamped mine and then Philly's wrists without hesitation or request of payment. "Go. Learn of Thai fighting."

Philly and I thanked her and then proceeded along the alleyway, fighting off hordes of Thai women as they tried to steer us into their respective establishments. Music was thumping from the respective bars, with a new song emanating from each entrance we passed by.

"Wow," Philly said, staring around, wide-eyed.

It's places like that in which people can experience culture shock in Thailand. And in just a few weeks, I would be right at the beating heart of the scene, fighting in the ring. The ring itself was in its own court at the end of the alley, where it held centre stage amongst a stadium of plastic seating.

There were ladyboys parading about in one particular bar, which was aptly named *Ladyboy Bar*.

One Thai woman marched up the alleyway when she saw us coming and pulled her bikini aside to reveal her *very* augmented breasts before grabbing at my arm.

"Imagine if you were my girlfriend," I grinned at Philly as I yanked my arm back and steered the fake-boob-toting Thai woman back in the direction she had come from.

"They just don't seem to care that I'm standing *right* here," Philly said, leaning in closer so that I could hear her over the music. "It's so weird… Normally it's girls that get all the attention. I feel completely invisible."

It's little wonder western men return to Thailand time and time again. Where before they may have had to fight and scratch to try to get a girl to speak to them and received little but disdainful looks in return for their efforts, in Thailand they are idolized and fought over and treated like kings. It's a simple formula, but effective, and it revolves entirely around attention and the feeling of empowerment. Men like to feel and behave like men – something that the politically correct western world increasingly frowns upon.

Philly and I settled ourselves into the ringside chairs and ordered beers from a bikini-clad waitress as she meandered past.

"There are *kids* here!" Philly exclaimed incredulously, pointing into the audience where there were tourist families present to see the spectacular Thai fights that they had all heard about. Perhaps nobody had told them to expect overt sexuality in the same place. Mothers looked suitably horrified, fathers looked uncomfortably sheepish, and children just looked.

And then the fights got underway.

Two teenagers – I guessed their ages to be fourteen – were helped over the ropes and into the ring. They were oiled up, barefoot, and ready to go. The haunting Muay Thai klaxon music started up over the speakers.

Anybody who has ever flicked through the television channels will recognize that primal, pit-of-the-stomach feeling when a boxing or fighting match flicks briefly across the screen. As a spectacle, Muay Thai is possibly the most beautiful fighting art to observe. Lithe and powerful, the athletes move and dance with each other, carefully maintaining and closing and opening up distances, like two positively charged magnets being forced towards one another. Bare skin, raw violence and cheering crowds. Complete with food and sex, and a human being can suddenly be transported back to their most primitive selves, where all other things become irrelevant and infantile by comparison. On those hot, humid nights in Thailand, there are hundreds and possibly even thousands of fights transpiring all around the country, each and every single night, from the isolated Thai islands in the south to the poor, undeveloped eastern fringes in Isaan, to the charged atmospheres in Chiang Mai. It is a martial art that has been tested in competition more thoroughly than any other, and thus the practitioners know precisely what works and what doesn't. Danger is sexy, and there's no competitive martial art in the world more dangerous than genuine Muay Thai in Thailand.

The first round was a little tentative as the two young warriors tried to feel each other out, flirting with distances and throwing glancing jabs and kicks.

The second round was intense. They came out and met in the middle of the ring, with neither boy taking a backwards step. They leaned back and threw kick after kick at each other's legs and torso, and one boy got close enough to land a scything elbow across the side of his opponent's head.

Blood gushed down the young boy's face and onto the canvas, and I noticed Philly clutching her beer so hard that I thought it might break.

The referee stepped in to start an eight-count, but the boy was back on his feet after the referee had reached three. There was fire in his eyes now and the crowd roared their approval and stamped their feet.

The two boys went at each other again, neither one holding anything back, though it was clear that the boy with the cut was losing steam. Then, out of seemingly nowhere, he threw a feinting punch and then came right behind it with a whipping, savage roundhouse kick, aimed directly at his opponent's ear.

Michael Goodison

Show me not a mirrored glass –
    there's nothing there to Learn,
Instead show me a windowed pane –
    the World awaits its turn.
And be it said, that poets all, know nought of ratings, no;
    But write, dear friends,
    of Stars and Moons,
    and show them that it's So.

CHAPTER 4
WITHIN REACH

"We'll never be as young as we are tonight."
— Chuck Palahniuk

"Oh my God!" the woman behind us shrieked.
Philly clutched at her face as one of the young boys crumpled to the ground and fell utterly still. There was no getting up from a kick like that.
"Ouch," I murmured to myself, grimacing sympathetically.
"This is just *awful!*" Philly exclaimed, looking apoplectic with fury. "It's completely *disgusting!*" She rounded on me. "How can you sit here and *watch* this?"
I was thoughtful. "This is normal to them," I said, gesturing to the Thais in the audience. "They grow up doing it. They have a different perspective, I guess."
"They're just kids!" Philly exclaimed. "It would be different if it was adults doing this, but *kids* is *not* ok."
"Well, actually," I said, feeling a little sheepish. "These guys are quite old now. They're teenagers. They would've both started fighting when they were six or seven."
Philly looked suitably horrified.
"But you have to understand," I continued. "That's the best time for people to learn how to fight – when they're young. It's much more dangerous if we create rules that say you can't start fighting until you're eighteen, because by then those boys have developed real strength and power. When they're fighting at aged six or seven, they can fight as much as four or five times per week, because they don't hit hard enough to hurt one another. They can gain experience and learn how to think and slow things down in a fight, which are all absolutely critical things that are extremely hard to learn when you get older." I wanted dearly to impress upon her the beauty of what she was witnessing. The courage and heart that was being displayed by the young warriors in the ring. The boldness required to step over the ropes and look an opponent in the eye. The coming of age that

transpires in the heat of battle. There is so very much more to fighting than simply fighting.

Philly just stared at me disbelievingly.

I shrugged and smiled. "Believe it or not, these Thais know a little more about fighting than you or I do, and they know exactly what they're doing when they put their kids in a ring."

The next pair of fighters were brought out, and, sure enough, these guys looked to be around six or seven years of age.

Philly groaned audibly and I laughed.

"Just watch," I said.

The fight ended with one of the boys getting backed into a corner under a barrage of wild punches in the first round. The referee stepped in and stopped the fight, smiling and chatting to the two young boys in Thai as they were separated and the victor had his tiny, gloved hand raised to the cheering crowd.

Next up was a Muay Boran exhibition show. Muay Boran translates to "Ancient Boxing," from which the modern manifestation of Muay Thai – "Thai Boxing" – traces its roots. Instead of leather gloves, the fighters wrap their knuckles and forearms with toughened ropes or hides. It wasn't unusual in older times for fighters to imbue their bindings with crushed glass or sand. Head-butting was also allowed. It was an extremely dangerous martial art, developed for use on the battlefields against the ever-warring Cambodians and Burmese.

This particular display of Muay Boran was just an exhibition fight, and the crowd clapped politely as the rope-bound warriors pretended to strike one another.

Then it was the turn of two twenty-something women to enter the ring. That fight ended in the third round by way of a spectacular spinning back kick to the liver. Philly was suitably impressed and seemed eager to talk about the prospect of trying Muay Thai for herself now that she had seen other girls do it. She felt empowered by what she had just witnessed. I nodded along receptively as she replayed the action for me in a blow by blow commentary.

Gender is something of an interesting study against a fighting backdrop. I maintain that strength is of only mild importance in a ring, and the main thing that separates men from women in the world of fighting is the durability of the male frame. Simply put, men are capable of enduring greater punishment to their bodies than women are. I often find myself wondering why women weren't granted the same fighting attributes that men were... I maintain that women must possess a certain attribute that is lacking in men so as to even the scales in physical combat, though what that might be, I remain unsure... Surely, *surely,* women have not evolved over the eons to be at the mercy of men. There must be something that we are missing. Granted, that virtue remains something that is yet unseen and unproven, but surely…

Then it was time for the first of two main event fights. This was the first time all night that a foreigner would enter the ring, and the crowd was suddenly deafening as it booed and cheered a Spanish man as he climbed over the top rope and bowed to the audience. He was tall and appeared to be built entirely out of ropy, powerful muscle.

His opponent was a Thai, who was neither tall nor muscular. He was short and fat, and I noticed some westerners in the crowd laughing when they saw who the Spanish guy would be facing. I assumed that most of the westerners in the crowd were with the Spanish camp and were all there to support their fighter.

"Looks a little unfair," Philly observed, eyeing the two fighters as they began performing the Wai Kru – a traditional warrior dance performed before the fight, to give respect to their coaches and to bless the ring, and to rid the ring of bad spirits. The Wai Kru also provides an invaluable insight for gamblers wanting to bet on the fights. It was during this dance that a trained eye could observe the movements of the two warriors and detect any possible injuries or fears or tension that may sway the outcome one way or another.

I watched the two fighters closely, and I also eyed the Thai corner as they chatted with the fight promoter. "I'll bet you a drink that the fight goes all five rounds, but the Thai fighter will win easily," I challenged.

"Really?" Philly stared at me like I was an idiot. *That little fat guy against that athletic guy?* "You're on!" she declared. She was really getting into the fights by that point. The crowd was in full voice, the alcohol was flowing, and there was primitive entertainment on display from all sides. It would be difficult for any red-blooded human being *not* to develop a certain lust in such an environment.

The Spaniard may have been tall and powerfully muscled, but he had looked stiff and calculated during the Wai Kru, as if he needed to really concentrate on where his body was in space. The short, fat Thai on the other hand, had looked relaxed and moved with practiced, languid ease that belied his apparent athletic deficiencies. He moved with a fluidity and grace that the Spaniard lacked, and he appeared so confident as to be bored by proceedings.

I knew it instantly.

This was one extremely talented Thai fighter who had been brought in by the promoter to entertain the crowd whilst also putting the arrogant westerners back in their place. I'd seen it before. They wanted to embarrass the "farang." Who better to send against a tall athlete than a short, fat guy?

Additionally, I've always felt that the most dangerous fighters are short, stocky guys, and this Thai fit the bill almost perfectly. The natural angle created by the height difference will help to protect the chin of the short guy whilst exposing the chin of the taller guy – and the chin is the bull's-eye in a fight. Add all of that to the natural balance advantage that shorter guys have – which makes them harder to unbalance whilst also giving them greater ability to transfer their weight between defensive and offensive power – and I firmly believed that this Spaniard and his fans were in for a rude shock.

The bell rang and the music started, and I leant forward in my chair, utterly fascinated by the match-up. I am a student of fighting.

These Thailand fights in little-known stadiums are different to the fights you might see on television. They're different because the two fighters are strangers to one another. They have never seen the other person fight, and therefore they're stepping into the complete unknown. Fights you see on television are usually between two fighters who have spent months training and studying specifically for their opponent. In this way, they come to understand and know their opponent – what their strongest positions are, what their weak points are, what they do when they're in trouble, how they behave when they're winning, what their favoured strategies and tactics are.

In these Thailand fights however, two fighters come face to face with one another knowing absolutely *nothing* about their opponent, making the experience far more intimidating and scary for the participants than the fights you'll see on television.

In such a context, the first few moments will often set the tone for how the rest of the fight will proceed.

Sure enough, when the bell rang, the Thai was much quicker and more confident in his movements towards the centre of the ring. The Spaniard was slower, less sure of himself, more wary. He stutter-stepped half a step backward when he realized how close the Thai had gotten to him so quickly, and the fat Thai punished the error in footwork by slamming his left shin bone into the meaty, unprotected inside of the Spaniard's lead thigh.

I sat up straighter.

That had gotten my attention.

Not only had the promoters put the hapless Spaniard in against a seasoned fighter, but they had also put him in against a southpaw! The Thai was left-handed, which changes everything in a fight. Fighting a lefty is an entirely different kettle of fish to fighting a right-handed fighter, and if you don't know how to fight against a southpaw, then the fight's already over. Only one out of ten people in the world are left-handed, and so you can readily assume that only one out of ten fighters in the world are left-handed. And you can bet every cent you own that that a trained southpaw will know exactly how to fight a right-handed fighter.

This was going to be a massacre.

The Spaniard was out of his depth, and he was in for a hellish experience.

Not very much else happened for the remainder of the first round. The Thai stalked the Spaniard around the ring, occasionally throwing inside leg kicks, but otherwise keeping his distance from the nervous jabs thrown by the tall Spaniard.

The crowd, which had been silenced by the stunning leg kick in the opening seconds, was beginning to shout encouragement to the westerner. Perhaps they felt that he still had a chance. Perhaps the lack of action for the rest of the round meant that the two fighters were on an even level of fighting skill.

Nothing could've been further from the truth.

The Thai had spent the first round studying the movements of his opponent, proactively moving him around in certain directions to see how the Spaniard responded. Which foot did he move first, which foot did he rest his weight on when he moved, did he cross his feet, etc… The Spaniard on the other hand, hadn't been studying the Thai. Instead, he had been simply reacting and responding.

In the same way that dance partners have leaders, it was plain to see that the Thai was steering the Spaniard around the ring in whichever direction he wanted him to go.

During the break between rounds, the Thai chatted casually with his trainers whilst they rubbed his legs and showered him with ice. They were relaxed and at ease. In the Spanish corner, there was a coach grabbing his fighter's face and screaming at him. Neither relaxed, nor at ease. Intensity in a fight isn't a good thing, though apparently nobody had told the Spaniards. Being tense has the exact same effect as carrying too much muscle. It slows you down. Combat sports are all about power, and it's important to note that there's a distinct difference between strength and power. The equation for power is mass x speed squared. The important thing to note, of course, is the fact that the *speed* part of the equation gets multiplied by itself. Experienced, knowledgeable fighters train for speed, and being fast means being loose. It also means not carrying excess weight, though if you must carry excess weight, it's actually better to carry fat than muscle, because fat doesn't tighten and subsequently resist concentric movements, whereas excess muscle mass will do exactly that. A perfect example of a fighter who got too muscled is George St. Pierre – former welterweight champion of the UFC. Early on his career, he was incredibly lean and explosive, and he garnered a reputation as someone who knocked out the best fighters in the world in the most competitive weight division in the world. GSP's latter fights, however, showed us a different fighter. He was significantly more muscled, and as a consequence, he was significantly slower. His trademark explosiveness was gone and he failed to end those fights, instead grinding out narrow, controversial points victories.

Speed is everything.

Sure enough, the fight went the full five rounds, and the short, fat Thai utterly embarrassed the Spaniard, who collapsed into the arms of his trainers at the final bell and had to be rolled out of the ring.

I glanced at Philly. "You owe me a drink," I said.

The Thai looked as if he had barely broken a sweat, whilst the Spaniard appeared to be on the brink of unconsciousness due to sheer exhaustion. This was in stark contrast to their respective physical appearances. Short and fat versus tall, lean and muscled.

The difference was in energy *efficiency*. It was how the two fighters had spent their energy. Whilst the Spaniard had been tense and jerky in his movement during the fight, the Thai had basically just stood there and occasionally strolled around and thrown easy, highly effective kicks.

There were valuable lessons in this fight for any aspiring fighter, and I was eagerly reviewing the fight in my head.

There was still one more fight left in the evening, but Philly had seen enough.

We returned to the hostel and I climbed into bed, still playing the fights on replay in my head, studying them. Learning. Sleep was a long time coming.

I arrived at the ring the next day to find a young Thai man waiting for me. He smiled politely and introduced himself. He was wearing Muay Thai shorts and a soccer shirt. He looked fit and healthy and happy to be there.

I was delighted. My trainer that I had been promised had arrived back early from Bangkok, which meant I wouldn't have to deal with the old psycho any longer.

The new trainer's name sounded like "Ame." His English was poor, but he was the ultimate professional, and he appeared to know exactly what he was doing.

22 days until the fight.

"Technique," Ame said as we climbed into the ring, making a slow and steady gesture to me with his hands. "Sabai, sabai," he said, which I knew to mean *relax, relax*. I'd be hearing those words a lot in the coming weeks. Indeed, they were highly esteemed words in the Muay Thai vocabulary.

Ame sat with me in the centre of the ring and wrapped my hands and took me through a light warm-up before I put the gloves on and got started with training proper.

Delighted to discover that I am ambidextrous, Ame spent the session talking at length about various set-ups I can employ to draw a defensive movement from my opponent on one side and strike elsewhere. It was an invaluable session and I learnt a great many new things.

I returned to the hostel to find Philly's bed vacant and her bags gone. She had moved on to someplace else in the world. I hadn't had a chance to say goodbye to her, but that's often how it goes. People coming in and out.

That same afternoon, I would meet a man who had been born in Isaan – a poor Thailand province – attended university in Sydney, and then just recently returned home to his rural village to be with his family once again. He was an exceptionally intelligent man, caught in the painful depths of a cultural divide, and he was in Chiang Mai on the backpacking circuit to further explore the country of his birth and come to learn more about his heritage. His name was Ruampol. Later that night, he took me to a local Thai restaurant, which was an extraordinary experience – one of the highlights of my entire Thailand trip.

The sole white person in the large, busy establishment, I followed Ruampol around like a baby duckling following the mamma duck as he bartered in Thai to get us onto a table. A Thai worker brought us out a ceramic pot with a stove plate on top of it and with red-hot coals burning underneath. We would be cooking our own meals that night. There was an extraordinary buffet of raw produce in the centre of the room, from which a mass of crowded, bustling humanity was selecting the ingredients they wanted for their meals.

Ruampol selected a wide range of meats, vegetables and spices, and we sat down at our table with other Thais pressed in around us. Ruampol proceeded to make a range of dishes, from soups to curries, whilst I barbecued the meat on the hot plate. The Thais around us would occasionally lean over my shoulder and pluck a piece of cooking meat right off my hot plate. I quickly learnt that this was acceptable behavior, and I too got inquisitive about what my neighbours were cooking. An elderly man smiled a toothless smile and gestured for me to help myself to his cooking. It tasted like fish, only infinitely more delicious than any other fish I had ever eaten.

The room was stifling as a seemingly endless flood of Thai people continued to sidle up to the buffet table and then proceed to sit themselves around the sizzling stove tops. Their happiness and conversation was infectious, and Ruampol kept a running commentary for me – relaying in English what was being said all around us. The conversations were all light and playful. Everybody was enjoying the food and the company of others. All of the people present were strangers to one another, but you never would've guessed it from the familiarity with which they engaged and interacted. I sat there amidst the turbulent scene, wide-eyed at what I was a part of. Nobody had made a single mention of the fact that I was a foreigner, and that I was white. Nobody had looked at Ruampol any differently for sitting with me. I couldn't help but feeling, in that moment, that western cultures still have so much to learn.

Afterwards, Ruampol invited me along to a Couchsurfing get-together which was taking place in a café on the far side of the city. I happily joined him, and we met more travelers and like-minded individuals from all

corners of the globe, come together in one place for no reason other than to acquaint themselves with other human-beings. Out front of the café was a barefoot western girl who appeared lost.
"Are you here for the Couchsurfing thing?" I asked her.
"Couchsurfing?" she said in a strong German accent. "Yes, I do this."
"Us too," Ruampol said. "Shall we go in and see everyone?"
The German girl shrugged and nodded. "Sure," she said.
Ruampol and I soon discovered that the girl had in fact been standing out the front of the café because she was waiting to catch a tuk-tuk, and she was only saying yes because she knew what Couchsurfing was, not because she had been planning on attending an event. Her free-spirited willingness was inspiring, and she was delightful company. She entertained us all by demonstrating the various yoga poses she had been learning at a meditation centre on the outskirts of Chiang Mai, and teaching us about the up and down energies at play in the world, and the importance of seeking a steady middle ground.
Ruampol and I got lost walking back to the hostel, and we ended up jumping a fence and running across a university campus to get to a place from which we could orient ourselves. A Thai security guard caught us climbing the fence and laughed and shooed us over encouragingly, waving his night stick at us mockingly in case we ever thought to repeat our poor behavior.
I was feeling utterly in love with Thailand on that night. I was feeling at home, and surrounded by joy and comfort and all of the overwhelming positivity that human-beings can emanate.
"Oh, hey. Have you tried these things yet?" Ruampol tapped me on the shoulder as we walked and pointed at a street cart. At first glance, it looked indistinguishable from any of the others that lined the streets at night, but upon closer inspection, I saw that the cart was laden with insects. Some of them were cooked – others were still crawling and hopping.
I recalled the insects scattered over Antony on my first morning in Thailand. "First time for everything," I said. I'd had a few drinks at the Couchsurfing gathering. Ruampol handed me a fistful of different insects and paid the lady.
I pondered for a moment the pros and cons of eating them all in one big group versus eating them one at a time. I decided that I wanted to experience them properly, and so I ate them individually. Each one tasted a little bit different, but they were all pretty much just crunchy and relatively tasteless.
I went to bed feeling as if I had finally had a proper Thai experience with Ruampol that evening in the Thai eatery. The place had looked like a shed, with a tin roof and wooden support posts sticking up sporadically throughout the room, but it had felt like a home. It had felt like the biggest

and friendliest family dinner I had ever had the joy of attending. Suddenly, as I lay there, staring at the ceiling, I felt as if my life back home in Australia had a huge hole in it. I felt as if there was no real sense of community – certainly nothing that compared to that of the Thai people. The way that total strangers had interacted so easily and comfortably with one another was breathtaking to me, and I experienced a yearning in my heart for a bond like that. I didn't feel as if the Thai people were the ones missing out on iPhones and wifi and electric toothbrushes. I felt as if *we* were the ones missing out on family and conversation and interaction. *Real* interaction, with body language and smiles and laughter. Not text boxes superimposed on a screen.

I felt a little sad for the first time since I had arrived in Thailand. Melancholy. Pensive.

I'm just here to be entertained, I thought to myself with a wry smile at the ceiling.

Someone had started up a bout of raucous snoring and there were quiet sighs of exasperation emanating from various parts of the dorm room. I laughed softly to myself and rested my hands behind my head. It was too hot in the room for sheets or clothing.

There's a sadness at the core of being human which we all feel. It comes from the intrinsic knowledge that we will all die someday. And from that knowledge, there stems a degree of nobility. Despite the acceptance of mortality, fragility and inevitability, we will get up each day and we live our lives. Noble creatures, human beings.

I found myself thinking about Daniela from Switzerland. Dead set gorgeous and full of life. I replayed in my head the conversations we'd had whilst walking home from that first night out. We were talking the way a guy and a girl talk when they're somewhat drunk, very attracted to one another, and acutely aware of the fact that they're going to be breathing the oxygen in different parts of the world at the same time the following night. There'd been an element of misty-eyed reflection regarding the nature of time and space, coupled with an aching acceptance that neither time nor space can be breadthed by desire alone, and that circumstance would inevitably drive us apart. And so, and with reckless abandon, we had dived deeper into one another, wildly investing our emotions, hoping that if we tied our ribbons tightly enough, they might never be untied.

Life is not something you're supposed to think your way through. You *feel* your way through.

That is the tragedy of travel.

I am forever falling in love and then having to say goodbye. It's the laugh you fall in love with. Forget the compulsion for bodily augmentations, perfect teeth and flawless skin. It's always been the laugh.

There will never be enough time.

The heart is an extraordinary machine. When a toaster breaks, it ceases to be capable of turning bread into toast. The heart, however, can be broken, stepped on and smashed into a million pieces, yet still it beats on, relentless.
Yes, the heart wants love, but above all else, the heart wants life.
Falling in love can be a scary business. Of course it's scary. It's one of mankind's most innate fears, that of falling. However, it's not the fall that you need fear. The fall doesn't hurt. It's exhilarating in fact, to feel the wind rushing past. It's the landing you ought to be afraid of. The landing hurts. So, why not simply keep falling…?

Let's know one another, See, my soul be right here;
Upon me Look closely, now, so's whispering near.
Rebellion it burns, yes, the monsters take Flight;
Just know me dear Girl, no, there's no need to fight.
Let's know one another, oh, like birds Know the trees;
And Fear me not, never, not my elbows or knees.
Can I come to know you? What? You've nothing to Share?
So Washed be the brain, God, she's not even there.

CHAPTER 5
ON PADDED SOLES

"Maybe ever'body in the whole damn world is scared of each other."
- John Steinback, Of Mice And Men

I love being inside a Muay Thai ring. I adore my time spent there. I have never felt so alive as when I am in a fight. I live for those moments. Those moments when nothing else matters. There is no drug more powerful or addictive than the effect that fighting has on the human species. Once you've experienced it, it's all that you want to do. In a Muay Thai ring, all of the bureaucratic bullshit and the paperwork and the nitty-gritty legalities and stresses of day to day living in the 21st century completely evaporate. It's only when you are fighting that nothing else matters. Concerns you may have held onto for months and years simply melt away. Fighting is such a beautifully simple thing. It feels like hitting the reset button. It feels like exactly what I am supposed to be doing. It feels natural, as if it touches an ancient and intrinsic part of our being. Human beings understand fighting. It's ingrained in our DNA, and it doesn't matter what language we speak, or how we were raised, people will always understand fighting, and absolutely anyone can do it. There is no advantage in the world of fighting that money or status can give you. There is no bullshit or grey areas. All is fair in love and war. There are no falsehoods and no smoke and mirrors once you are standing face to face with your opponent. Those people who can talk their way through any industry cannot and will not ever be able to talk their way through the world of fighting. It's as brutally frank and honest as it gets, and I just love that. It's a place where I can feel like a man, and I can feel a connection that reaches back through the ages to my primitive ancestors. They were fighting way back then, almost two hundred thousand years ago, and I'm fighting now. Men find their identities in the utilitarian aspects of living, and there are few skills more utilitarian than physical combat. The bond that I feel with my opponent and others that have the courage to step into a ring is unlike any other friendship, because it's based on such extraordinarily brutal honesty. My opponents cannot hide anything from me in a fight, and nor I, them. When we clinch and exchange knees and elbows, I can feel the exact moment when his spirit breaks. I can *feel* it. It's a very raw and personal experience, and it's one that all fighters know and understand, and when they shake hands and look each other in the eye, they're quietly acknowledging the depth of their knowledge about one another. It's damn near impossible not to like your opponent after a fight. You just love the guy, because you know him and you trust him, and you respect his courage, regardless of the result.

I sometimes wonder if stamping out physical confrontation amongst children is a negative thing. I wonder if removing the physical realities of life from someone's consciousness doesn't create the potential for greater disrespect amongst people. Remove respect for the physical world, bombard the consciousness with Hollywood bullshit, and you'll soon find that ego and self-righteous falsehoods will fill the vacuum. So often now, people bypass physical fighting, and a war of words turns into somebody getting shot to death, or stabbed, because tensions get to a point where they can no longer be diffused. Nothing teaches respect quite like a tough fight. Fighting is a form of communication, and like I said before, there is no form of communication more honest. We live in a world constructed from lies on top of lies, and manipulation and more lies, and tricks and games, and smoke and mirrors, and intricate interpersonal politics based on more lies. We live in a world where social status goes to the wrong people – people with camera lenses and a propensity for blowing their own respective trumpets. Again, it's all smoke and mirrors. It's all bullshit. Our society today revolves around lies. Clothing is a lie. Make-up is a lie. Photos are lies.

In a Muay Thai ring, it's as real and as honest as it gets. There are few things more refreshing than to have the veil lifted away, and few things will do that more effectively than having a punch land on your cheekbone, with someone's full and angry weight behind it. Nothing else will burst a bubble more effectively.

Ame had brought in a Thai friend of his for me to spar with. He was a former champion, and he was brutal. We smashed punches and kicks at each other for five minutes and then Ame called time.

We sipped at water and then went at it once again, laughing at each other as the heavy shots found a home upon the opponent's anatomy.

Now, this is living!

Ame called time again, and I realized that we had drawn a crowd down the alley to watch. The onlookers were entirely Thais, come to watch the action with delight etched on their faces. It was a free Muay Thai show, and the Thais whooped and cheered as round three began.

21 days until the fight.

We clinched for the last two rounds and exchanged knees and light, careful elbows. We were careful not to cut each other. Elbows are like knives, and there are few things that can derail a fight campaign quite like a deep cut over an eye that requires stitches. It was a good sparring session. One of the best I'd ever been involved in. The Thai was a former champion and was exceptionally skillful. Ame had patrolled around the ring and observed us whilst we sparred, joining in the cheers as we exchanged heavier shots.

I was feeling quite proud of myself at the conclusion of the session. I was thoroughly exhausted, but I had held my own against a former Muay Thai champion, and I felt as if I had even managed to grasp the upper hand for a few moments in the clinch battle. It had been a battle of skill more than brute force, and I walked back to the hostel yearning to unleash some full force strikes on someone in a real fight.

I was losing weight from the training, despite eating five or six times a day. Muay Thai training will do that. It shreds every last ounce of fat from your body. It finds and removes fat from places you didn't even know you had. Losing weight is good for speed, but losing too much weight can leave a fighter exposed to sickness, and so I spent the next few hours of the day eating and drinking as much as I could manage in an attempt to replenish my energy reserves.

A group of English guys and girls were passing through the hostel and invited me to go for a walk into the city with them, but I declined and instead packed a book and went out to catch a three-wheeler tuk-tuk with a Thai driver.

"Hey, can you take me to a waterfall?" I asked. "Somewhere nice?"

The driver repeated the request back to me and then nodded and I climbed into the back and reclined luxuriously as the tuk-tuk weaved its way nimbly through the traffic and the warm air breathed past my exhausted body. My clothes flapped in the wind and they dried out quickly after having showered in them.

We arrived at a lonely waterfall in the mountains, and the clouds parted to allow the hot sun to beat down upon the scene.

'Want to swim?" I asked the driver, nodding towards the waterfall.

The driver laughed and warmly fended off the offer. "I wait for you here," he said.

"Are you sure?" I asked.

"Yes. Sure." The driver was climbing into the back seat as he spoke and was laying himself down for a midday nap.

"Ok, thanks," I said. "I'll be back in a couple hours."

I climbed up past the waterfall, away from the road, and continued on into the jungle until I found an untouched waterhole that was open to the beating sun. The sounds of the jungle were all that could be heard at that spot, and I set my bag down and pulled my clothes off and slipped into the lukewarm water. I floated around, basking in the sun and letting the water lap against my skin, letting the tender spots ease as gravity released its grip on my body for a brief moment in time.

I listened to the rustling of the jungle and the singing of the birds for a while, and then I swam over to the edge and pulled my book out of my bag. Leaning against the water's edge, and with just my shoulders out of the water, I spent what must've been the most serene hour of my life, reading a book in an isolated swimming hole in the middle of the jungle in northern Thailand.

I returned to the tuk-tuk and my driver offered to take me back to the hostel via a snake show.

I agreed.

The place where the snake show took place had a photo of Sylvester Stallone out the front, posing in full Rambo attire with some Thai natives. My driver explained to me that it was the people from this snake enclosure whom had worked with Sylvester Stallone on the fourth Rambo movie, which had been filmed locally.

There was nobody else there to see a show, which didn't start for another hour, and so my driver introduced me to some of the snake handlers and they offered me a splash of Thai whiskey and we all got talking. Muay Thai, Australian snakes and wildlife, girls. Simple chit-chat amongst strangers. Then they offered to show me the snakes. I had seen snakes in Thailand before. I had even been bitten on the hand by a colourful python I was trying to pick up at a snake show in Krabi, during a visit to the southern islands of Thailand a couple of years prior. I was eager to get a private show, and so I fished out my little go-pro camera and agreed.

The Thai snake handlers were all crazy, happy-go-lucky characters, and they hissed at me as they pulled out three Cobras and someone threw an identical, *fake* Cobra into my lap. I froze for a moment as the snake landed in my lap before throwing it back in the direction it had come from before I'd managed to connect the dots and realize that it was a fake. The Thais roared with laughter and I joined in at my own expense. That had really kick-started the adrenalin.

One of the snake handlers stepped into the snake pit with the three Cobras and they raised themselves up to glower at him. He crawled around in front of them and occasionally tapped the floor with his knee, eliciting a hissing strike from one of the deadly snakes, which would narrowly miss.

"You want try, Australia?" the handler asked me, gesturing at the three swaying Cobras.

"Ah," I wasn't sure about that. I didn't want them to think I was scared though, obviously. It's a guy thing, perhaps. "Will they bite?" I asked, somewhat stupidly.

"Yes," another of the handlers said, deadpan.

"How long would I live for if one of them bit me?" I asked.

"If bite. Twenty-four hour," the Thai said. "Twenty-four hour. Die."

"Great," I muttered, eyeing the lethal snakes. My adrenalin was still coursing through my veins, mixing quietly with my smarting pride as a result of the fake snake trick. I thought about what it might feel like to know that you only had 24 hours left to live. "I can get a lot done in twenty-four hours," I decided, nodding to indicate to the Thais that I wanted to enter the pit.

They laughed and roared their approval and gestured me forwards.

I found myself thinking about how this kind of behavior would most certainly *not* be permitted in Australia.

I stepped into the pit and got down onto my haunches in front of the cobras, still holding my go-pro camera out to film the encounter. The snakes stayed upright, their cold, beady little eyes watching me, swaying occasionally when I moved to get more comfortable.

Working up the courage, I inched my hand forward – still holding the camera – and then quickly yanked it back when one of the Cobras lashed forward at me. The snake's open jaws hit the ground with a hiss, mere millimeters away from my hand, and then it swung back upright again with its two colleagues.

I released the breath I had been holding and then slowly stood up and backed out of the pit, much to the delight of the snake handlers.

I shrugged as coolly as I could to the Thai men, my calm countenance belying the sound of blood rushing in my ears and my heart thudding madly in my ribcage.

That will wake you up in the morning.

I stayed for another sip of the whiskey and one of the Thai men fished out his phone and added me on Facebook, and then I left again with my tuk-tuk driver. We returned to the hostel.

I decided my body needed a day off from training. My ribs had healed from the battering I had received on day one, but I was still battling several other nagging injuries, plus general soreness and fatigue. On the advice of a German guy, I went down to the front desk and booked an elephant trip for the next day. I bought toasted sandwiches from a 7/11 down the street and went to bed just as the sun was setting.

I awoke early, showered, and waited at the curb for somebody to come and pick me up. I'm not a huge fan of doing touristy things, but I'm not opposed to it either, and my battered body was crying out for a break from taking hits every day, and elephants are pretty cool, touristy or not.

A red pick-up truck pulled in to the curb and a window retreated.

"Michael?" a Thai man called from the driver's seat.

I nodded and clambered onto the back of the tray - onto which there had been welded some benches - and which had been covered over for protection from the elements.

The air rushed through the tray compartment as we drove through the narrow, maze-like streets of Chiang Mai. We were looking for the other travelers that had booked onto the tour. I had been the first person picked up, and so I sat patiently in the back and stared out of the narrow slots at the world rushing by.

We stopped in at a secluded, heavily foliaged resort. I leant forward and looked around with interest at the place. This was how the more well to-do travelers live. The group we were picking up was entirely French speaking. There was a French family with two younger boys, and a group of five French girls that looked to be about my age. We got the introductions out of the way and I discovered that only two people in the group spoke English - two of the girls from the larger group. I attempted to put to use some of the French that I had learnt in high school but it mostly came out in Spanish - which I can speak a little - so we quickly dispensed with that idea.

We drove for three hours up into the mountains and it started raining as we went. Thick, tropical rain. The scenery was spectacular, and I got a sore neck from staring around through the gaps as we climbed up through mist-shrouded mountains and valleys. The two English speaking girls asked me how my trip had been so far and we ended up talking for most of the journey. One of the girls was apprehensive about the experience, and spent a great portion of the drive telling me about how poorly elephants are treated. I found it difficult to listen to her. She wasn't wearing a bra, and her flimsy little shirt was doing an appalling job of containing what was a rather significant situation. The French girl didn't seem the least bit concerned about flashing her breasts at the whole group - a group which included two young boys and their parents. Europeans are more liberal about their bodies, I've been told. I was finding it difficult concentrating on politely averting my eyes and listening respectfully at the same time, but I got the general gist of things. Elephant riding equals bad, was all I really needed to know.

We drove past remote villages and spectacular mountain farmscapes. The rain continued to hammer down, but it was warm and humid. It felt like a scene from a movie that I couldn't quite put my finger on. The French girls *oohed* and *ahhhed* as we saw elephants lumbering across the valleys in the distance. Finally, the little red pick-up truck came to a stop at a remote village and we all clambered out, stiff and sore from the bumpy, cramped ride, but relieved to be finally at our destination.

Within moments, we were all soaked to the skin. The French girl's flimsy shirt was rendered completely obsolete, much to the amusement of our Thai welcoming party.

There were elephants there waiting for us, towering high overhead and standing patiently on padded soles. I went over to them and introduced myself, shaking the two big ones respectively by their trunks.

"Here, here!" one of the Thai guides pressed a large bunch of small bananas into my hands. The elephants immediately went to work with their trunks, trying to wrest the bananas from my grip. I stepped back and the elephants followed for a few steps, but then they abruptly stopped. Their back legs were chained to posts. I fed the elephants the bananas one by one, and the group of travelling French girls came over to join in. I handed them the rest of the bananas and stepped back to give them a chance.

I got chatting with one of the Thai guides, who seemed to approve very strongly of the French girls, and we bonded over a manly discussion about the virtues of rain and thin clothing.

"Why do you chain them up like that?" I asked the guide.

"Or elephant disappear," the Thai said with a shrug of his shoulders. "But no problem, aye. No hurt for elephant."

"It doesn't hurt?"

Head shaking.

I shrugged. That was good enough for me. There's quite a significant movement amongst the progressive-minded about the mistreatment of elephants in Thailand and how it's wrong for tourists to go and ride them, but I don't really subscribe to the thinking. It doesn't bother me. We chain up dogs by their necks to poles and think nothing of it, we ride horses everyday and think nothing of it, we raise cattle for the sole reason of slaughtering them to eat them and think nothing of it. Getting overly concerned about elephants who are fed, watered, safe, and whom provide a meager living for people eeking out an existence in a desperate part of the world seems like a slippery-slope way of thinking to my mind. If you follow that line of thinking right to the end, you end up becoming a vegan human-hater who lives with the constant guilt brought about by the knowledge that even the plants that you're eating were once living things and they're dead now because you're too selfish to starve to death.

Life eats life, it's the way of the world. All of the calories that have ever existed or will ever exist are already in motion on Earth. The energy simply cycles through different forms. It's the circle of life. The Lion King taught me this as a kid. Plants are every bit as alive as animals are. Life eats life. It's a desperate world, and elephants eating bananas on the end of chains is less than even the tiniest tip of the iceberg insofar as cruelty is concerned.

Personally, I've been to too many raw and dangerous places and seen too many acts of base brutality to allow myself to slide to the left. Any naïve, liberal ideals I may have once held have been long since stripped away by the coldness of the real world. It's a dangerous place this world of ours, and I have long since decided that I will not be someone's victim. Travelers are often of the love-struck, vegetable-eating, starry-eyed, progressive-minded hippy persuasion, but I do not count myself amongst their lot. My survival instincts simply won't allow it.

I was looking forward to an afternoon spent with the elephants.

We were provided with a home cooked lunch of various Thai dishes. As I was eating, a trunk slithered over my shoulder, trying to explore the food options on the table. I glanced over my shoulder to see that one of the elephants had pushed its head inside through a doorway. The lumbering creatures clearly knew where the food was.

"Anybody wish to address the elephant in the room?" I muttered to myself, nudging the trunk away from my food. After lunch we were given blue overalls to wear. It was time to ride the elephants.

With the rain hardening – hammering into the ground and turning the Earth into thick mud and puddles – we stepped up onto the front legs of the elephants and were boosted up to sit behind their heads.

The Thai *mahout*, which is the name given to the elephant trainer, was lifted up by the elephant's trunk and they assumed their places sitting on the gigantic skulls of the huge creatures. We were each taught various Thai commands to steer the elephants. Go, stop, left, right, back-up, kneel.

I was placed on the biggest elephant and I was soon joined by one of the young French boys who were travelling with their parents. He looked to be around ten or eleven, and he seemed plainly terrified of the elephant. I tried my high-school French on once again in an attempt to calm the boy, but it seemed to make matters worse, if anything. I patted him lamely on the shoulder.

We were all soaked through to the skin by that stage, as the elephants finally lurched out of the encampment and began to follow a trail up into the misty mountainside. Far below us on the right-hand side, there was a river winding through a valley. We could hear the sound of rain hitting the surface of the water. It was peaceful. It felt cleansing.

The elephants meandered along at a slow pace, occasionally stopping to tug at foliage to eat. The Mahouts either climbed up and sat on an elephants head or followed along on foot. The French girls were busily posing for photos and delicately passing their various technological devices across from elephant to elephant so that they could take photos of one another.

"If you look closely," I said to my French-speaking young companion in my best Sir David Attenborough voice, "you'll see the female in her natural habitat... Watch closely now as she exhibits her mating call, pushing her lips together in a manner not dissimilar to that of a duck, whilst carefully angling her phone to ensure maximum and yet incidental cleavage exposure..."

The young French boy ignored me.

The elephants continued their leisurely hike for an hour before angling off toward a steep, muddy embankment. The path led down to the river, but the heavy rains had turned the path into a miniature creek, and the elephants were having a hard time keeping their feet.

My French friend started clamoring to climb off when the elephant directly in front of ours slipped and fell onto its side. I laughed and grabbed the boy firmly whilst gripping the elephants neck with my thighs. Luckily, our elephant was a little more careful, and it took its time descending the dangerous path, occasionally slipping forwards a meter or two, but always managing to correct itself. The elephants were surprisingly flexible and agile creatures. Incredibly strong.

We finally reached the river and a few of the elephants trumpeted joyously as they splashed down into the water.

I gestured to the French boy that we could slip off now, and we both dived into the river, which was very nearly as deep as the elephants were tall. The rest of the group finally made its way down to join us by the river, and the French girls found buckets and started showering and bathing the elephants, before the whole situation descended into a gigantic water fight.

I watched mirthfully as the young French boy I had been with on the elephant ride tried to sneak up on one of the older girls, only to be flattened by a spray of water from an elephant trunk. He came up gasping for air and shooting furious looks at the huge, impassive elephant, much to the uproarious delight of the Thai elephant trainers and the French girls.

Finally, the elephants were finished swimming, and the red pick-up truck appeared on a road beside the river.

"Hey. Australia." It was the Thai guide, gesturing me over to the big elephant I had been riding. He was pointing underneath the big animal's belly. "Walk under elephant. Means good luck."

I stared. "You want me to walk underneath the elephant?" I repeated, a little disbelievingly.

The Thai nodded vigorously. "Means good luck for you. Maybe good luck for…" he gestured towards the French girls with a sly wink.

I laughed and shrugged. "Ok, I just walk straight under?"

"Yes. Walk under."

I offered a silent prayer that the elephant didn't freak out and stomp on me, and then bowed my head and strolled casually underneath the enormous weight of the elephant, hoping to be imbued with sudden and profound good luck.

20 days until the fight.

Muay Thai: Peace, At Last

The fearsome truth that less is more,
Are you prepared to go to war?
For less is more means oh, just that,
The heavy price of tit for tat;
The few that live can have it all,
The few that live can walk the hall,
So fight, we must, they have to go,
It's cold out there, you ought to know.

CHAPTER 6
THE STARS AT NIGHT

"The only people for me are the mad ones, the ones who are mad to live, mad to talk, mad to be saved, desirous of everything at the same time, the ones who never yawn or say a commonplace thing, but burn, burn, burn like fabulous yellow roman candles exploding like spiders across the stars."
- Jack Kerouac

I returned to the hostel to find more new people had moved into my dorm room. I got talking with a few of them and we quickly formed something of a group mentality. We all went out to dinner together and then someone suggested we go and look at the night market, which was a weekly Chiang Mai event.

The night market was, in a word, astonishing. I have never seen so many people crammed into a single stretch of roadway before. There were countless market stalls and vendors selling their wares. We walked the entire length of the market street, which stretched all the way from the eastern gate to the western gate of the "old city."

I nearly went crazy amidst all of the humanity. Despite it having rained all day, the temperature amongst the crowd was stifling, and the humidity, crushing. It was impossible to string two seconds together without touching someone else as everybody hustled and bustled along the street. I'm not much of a people person at the best of times. Here, there was simply no escape. No side alleyways to duck down and escape. I felt claustrophobic in there, and it was taking a considerable amount of my willpower not to start shoving people away from me to make some space. It took us the better part of two hours to walk the length of the street, and we had all seen enough by that stage. We split a tuk-tuk fare between us for the ride back to the hostel.

There was a tall blonde Dutch girl amongst the group named Romy. We got talking and realized that we were both going to be staying in the room together for the next week or so, which was an unusual amount of time for most travelers to stay together. She made a passing comment suggesting we take an overnight trip together in the coming days to Pai or Chiang Rai, both of which are other northern Thailand townships. I agreed that it sounded like a good idea and then forgot all about it.

I had training in the morning and that day was supposed to have been my day of rest. I had successfully, albeit narrowly, avoided consuming any alcohol for the day, and I wanted to cap off that achievement by getting a good night's sleep before delving back into the world of physical punishment.

I'm not very good at sleeping, which is a little bit strange given that all you need to do is lie down and close your eyes, but I guess it's not that simple. My brain doesn't stop running. I put it down to physics. The idea that things in motion tend to remain in motion and things at rest tend to remain at rest.

Here we are. Countless millions of young, restless human beings, and all we want to do is give our lives to something, but we don't know what. Advertising saw the hesitation and now it has us throwing ourselves at the latest products and fads, and all the while we are getting overweight and feeling dissatisfied with the returns on our many investments. Meanwhile, the answer is all around us, particularly here in Thailand. We ought to be giving our lives to each other. There is surely nothing more beautiful on Earth than our relationships and our connections with other living things. Yet the world has us lying through our teeth and smiling at people whilst we take their money. A litany of social pressures have us terrified of committing to the wrong thing, and so we commit to nothing. We float downstream like tiny, irrelevant pebbles in a flooded river, just waiting for something to come along and give us a sense of direction and purpose. We turn the TV on in search of answers and it tells us that we need to be buying this new phone with the fancy new buttons and this new toothbrush with the newer, more amazing bristles that will do exactly what your old phone and old toothbrush did. But that doesn't matter. You're invigorated by a new sense of direction and purpose in your life, and everyone else seems to be buying the new phone and the new toothbrush, and so it must be the sensible thing to do. Why should we question what the TV says? What do we know?

The torment of night.

Morning finally arrived, and with it, a new character in my story. Stuart was a middle-aged school teacher from England, and he had come to Thailand for five weeks to learn Muay Thai, and some wily tuk-tuk driver had dropped him off at my ring.

19 days until the fight.

We introduced ourselves before Ame arrived and the training started, now with two of us in the class. We ran and skipped and did pushups and drilled kicks and punches and elbows and knees and finished with a sparring session that was limited to just boxing. The sparring was one-sided, and I felt bad pushing him back against the ropes time and time again. I tried to go easy on my shots as they landed. Stuart had done karate and aikido for more than twenty years, he said, but karate and aikido are a poor match for Muay Thai. They're showy, intricate and ineffective. Fine motor skills are no good in a fight. When things get real, you can't catch a punch and then contort their wrist to perfectly offset someone's weight distribution. You just can't.

Between rounds we discussed the Ashes cricket series which was currently underway in England. Australia was losing, so I didn't want to talk about it too much.

I spent the afternoon resting and listening to music. Romy tapped me on the shoulder whilst I was napping and told me that she had booked a bus ticket to go across to Pai the following morning, and that I should buy a ticket from the front desk and join her.

I thought about Muay Thai training and decided missing another day or two wouldn't hurt. I was being complacent about my upcoming fight, but I didn't care. I was feeling confident. I went ahead and booked the bus ticket, without even knowing much about the township of Pai. I was just going with the winds of the world, and in this instance, my sails were being filled by a friendly girl from Holland.

The following morning, Romy and I went for breakfast together and then waited by the curb for the bus to take us to Pai. Romy had her bulky travelling backpack between her legs. I had asked her if she wouldn't mind squeezing my toothbrush into the front pocket, and she had kindly obliged. In addition to my toothbrush in Romy's bag, I had my phone, passport and wallet in my pockets, and I was wearing clothes and a watch. We were all set to go.

"How far is it to Pai?" I asked Romi as we climbed onto a small bus.
"I think maybe three hours?" Romy replied. "Four hours, maybe?"
"Ok."

The bus arrived at a bus station, where there were many more buses. Apparently we were to make a transfer. Romy and I crammed onto the front seat of another bus that was already full of fellow travelers. We re-arranged ourselves to try to get as comfortable as possible. The bus was hot and our skin was all sweaty and rubbing against each other, but we both did our best to ignore it. One of the Chinese travelers on the bus shouted out that he had forgotten his hat and that we should turn around to go back to his hostel to get it. The bus driver refused and the Chinese man glowered. This had the potential of becoming a longer than necessary bus trip.

"It's just a hat, mate," I told the Chinese guy with what I hoped to be a persuasive shrug.

More glowering, but the bus driver jammed the bus resolutely into gear and pulled out into the traffic, bound for Pai.

And what a drive it was!

Like a scene from Jurassic Park, the road wound its way through mist-covered mountainsides that occasionally separated to reveal spectacular jungle precipices and plunging valleys.

"A road of three hundred corners," Romy murmured at one point, looking a little pale.

I grinned and went back to enjoying the ride. My imagination was running wild as each sharp corner revealed a new scene. If you ignored the twisting ribbon of asphalt and the occasional thatched hut, it felt as if we were driving into a jungle wilderness that had been untouched since a time when gigantic reptiles ruled the Earth.

The Thai driver had put the air conditioning on and was playing soft Thai music over the speakers. Sitting in companionable silence with Romy and staring out the front windows, I could've driven that road back and forth all day long.

We arrived in Pai at around lunchtime to find that Pai was a sleepy little Bob Marley style community right on the Thai border with Burma. I was a little surprised to find that there were more tourists in the town than there were locals. In fact, it was almost like playing a game of "spot the Thai." There were stray dogs all along the main road, but they appeared harmless enough. It was a small town of cafes and bars set amongst a spectacular wilderness. There was a giant, white Buddha statue built on a mountain to the north, overlooking the village.

It was the silence that was most beautiful about the place. I felt as if somebody could've coughed a few streets over and I would've heard them. The peace and the serenity of the small town was hypnotic. Within minutes I felt as if it had seeped into my bones, and I felt so utterly relaxed and at ease with the world. Romy didn't look quite so comfortable as she lugged her gigantic backpack along the street. I would've offered to carry it for her, but she was a proud girl and I didn't want to insult her. I also didn't very much feel like carrying that bag. The thing was enormous.

"Let's find a place to have lunch," I suggested, looking at the array of cafes lined up on either side of the main street. We were spoiled for choice.

Lunch was a peaceful affair spent chatting, eating and drinking tea. I have many life rules revolving around tea and the consumption of tea and all things related to tea. There's Rule #39: If there's tea involved, I'm officially jealous. Or there's Rule #13: If you are kind enough to offer me tea, the answer will be yes. I like to have rules of my own. Men and women who live by a code can be trusted to behave accordingly. If you take the time to learn someone's code, what you're really doing is learning who they are. But of course, in the name of freedom and rebellion and growth, there always Rule#1: Don't hesitate to break the rules. That's an important one to me. Conformity – even to your own set of rules – is stunting. The ability to challenge your own thinking is what enables growth in a person.

"So, now what?" Romy wondered aloud after we had paid and she was once again faced with the task of lugging her gargantuan backpack around.

"Place to stay," I said. "Then you can put that bag down and we can relax a little."

The third place we tried met our hospitality criteria – it was cheap, serene, and had private rooms with double beds and bathrooms. There was also a pool, which was a bonus.

We set out onto the streets in search of something to do. There wasn't much. Fellow travelers told us that there was a canyon we could visit and some waterfalls and hot springs if we had the time, inclination and a scooter. However, it had just begun raining gently, and neither of us was in the mood for a road trip. Instead, we found a quiet bar with cushions in place of seats and a vacant pool table. It was still early in the afternoon, but to hell with it. We were free and we were young and we had nowhere to be and nobody to see. We ordered beers and got started on what would evolve into a pool playing and beer drinking marathon, disrupted intermittently by periods of lazy conversation on the cushions.

A big and ugly stray dog wandered into the bar and joined us on the cushions, curling up for a snooze with his giant head on my thigh.

"I think I could fit my head in his mouth," Romy said, staring at the giant dog as it began snoring contentedly.

I laughed. "No sudden moves. He might wake up and eat us both."

The afternoon in the bar soon became dinner, and then continued as darkness fell. The bar – which had been completely deserted all afternoon aside from Romy and myself – began to fill up.

Romy was beginning to look as if she may have drunk too much, and she was quick to agree when I suggested we return to our lodgings and turn in for the night.

Romy went straight to bed whilst I stayed up a while longer, staring up at the stars. I hadn't been able to see the stars in Chiang Mai, and I had missed them dearly. People would live very differently if they looked at the stars more often.

The humidity was still stifling at that hour of night, and so I stripped off, rested my beer bottle on the edge of the pool and slipped into the water.

The silence of the Pai night was breathtaking. The sound of displaced water lapping against the edge of the pool sounded almost deafening by contrast. And meanwhile, the night sky was putting on its own, private, *spectacular* show for me, or so it felt.

Do you ever have those moments in time where you feel as if the entire world exists for you? As if the entire thing is all a part of your own, personal narrative, that you alone have constructed? Is that some kind of huge, existential arrogance at work, or is it a misunderstood interpretation of the energies at play all around us? Or is it categorically correct, and I am simply too humbled and insecure to accept that the entire narrative of the universe was constructed by me, and for me? Or am I thinking too small? Perhaps the term *me* is where the misunderstanding begins... Perhaps the world really was created by me, and perhaps the world really does revolve around me, but perhaps *me* is in fact an all-encompassing energy – one which connects us all. Humans, plants, animals. Maybe it is our collective consciousness that wrote the story of the universe, and continues to write it.

It seems absurd to consider that all of this might just be random. This beautiful life of ours. How could it be that it bears no meaning or relevance to something? The meaning of life is surely the fact that it ends – an inevitable finality which teaches us to be grateful for the beauty within which we dwell – but can that be all there is? If we are only here for the sole purpose of enjoyment and gratitude, then why are we so driven to evolve? Why are we so driven by thoughts of progress and improvement? To what end are we careening so wildly, uncontrollably and inexplicably?

I climbed out of the pool and trotted off to bed, briefly cut adrift by the magnitude of the heavens and now safely ensconced once again in my fundamental philosophy of life: I am simply here to be entertained.

*

"Simon!... You there? Simon?"

I knocked on the old wooden door again, aware of Romy watching me curiously.

17 days until the fight.

"Coming."

A voice called from the far side of the door, and I smiled to myself upon hearing the familiar voice. I lived in Southern Thailand a couple of years prior, and it was in a place called Krabi – at a discrete hostel made out of shipping containers – that I had first met Simon. Simon is Australian, though he is of Vanuatu heritage. He is dark skinned and, when I first met him, he was a chubby, cheerful guy who was curious about the art of Muay Thai. I had talked him into attending a training session, and through intermittent contact with him, I had been thrilled to discover that he had competed in two victorious Muay Thai bouts since we had last parted ways. That had been two years ago, and now, as if the planets had aligned, he was right here in Pai, staying at a Muay Thai fight camp and training for his third professional Muay Thai fight.

The door creaked open to reveal a completely changed young man – totally different from what I remembered. The only things that appeared familiar were the Aussie accent, the cheerful countenance and the easy laugh. Otherwise, he was almost unrecognizable. Gone was the puppy fat, replaced by a body fit for the warrior that he had become. He was shirtless – as is so often the case in the heat of Thailand – and he appeared proud and confident of what he had achieved since we last met. We hugged with an unusual familiarity, given that we had only spent perhaps forty-eight hours together over the course of our lives. Yet still, we had so much in common, and we had a history together. Our ribbons of life had intersected on two occasions now, in two different places. He was an extraordinarily good-natured guy, and if the universe meant for us to meet again, well then I was all too willing to oblige.

"How's it going, mate?" I said, gesturing around at his room and the empty old pool out front and towards the gym in the distance. "Oh, this is my friend Romy… Romy, this is Simon."

They said hello and Simon took up the narrative, telling Romy how we had first met a couple of years earlier and how I had talked him into something that now held a preeminent position in his life. I was quietly hoping that Simon was just as pleased to see me as I was to see him. He's just one of those great guys.

Simon led Romy and I across to the Muay Thai gym, which was called Charn Chai. It's a gym popular with the tourists that run rampant throughout Pai.

"I was hoping Romy and I could join you guys for a group class," I was saying to Simon. "She wants to see what this Muay Thai thing is all about. Do you think you can hook us up?"

"Yeah, sure mate," Simon said easily. "Classes don't start until later but we can hang out until then. I'm resting up because my fight is coming up in about a week. I'm fighting in Chiang Mai, man."

"Ah, mate. I'll be there," I said eagerly. "Fight number three!"

"Yeah."

"Always a tough one, the third one."

We discussed the recent loss of Buakaw Por Pramuk – a Muay Thai superstar and a huge celebrity of Thailand – to a little known Russian fighter. I had watched it on TV at a bar.

"It's the frame, mate," I said, covering up my face and propping out an arm to indicate what I meant. "Buakaw always frames when he defends rather than using a forearm guard or footwork to evade… It's not a bad technique against another orthodox fighter because it protects you from the power shot, but against the southpaw it leaves the uppercut wide open and it leaves the elbow wide open, and you saw what happened."

"Yeah mate, imagine having only thirteen fights and then getting in there and beating *Buakaw* with an elbow!" Simon exclaimed.

Buakaw has had over two hundred and forty professional Muay Thai fights. Mind-boggling numbers which aren't unusual for career Muay Thai fighters. Here was Simon, training for his third fight in two years. I wonder if Buakaw can even remember all of his fights.

Romy pointed out that we wouldn't be able to stay for the group Muay Thai class because the bus back to Chiang Mai would be leaving too early, and so Simon wrapped her hands and lent her some gloves and shin guards whilst I found some Thai training pads. I climbed into the ring with Romy and spent forty-five minutes teaching her the basics of Muay Thai. She was a tall girl, and I was impressed with the power she managed to generate behind her knee strikes. It was a fun little play around session, and then it was time to be on our way if we were to catch the bus back to Chiang Mai.

"Good seeing you Simon," I said, shaking his hand again. "Let me know when you're fighting. I need to get a Thai SIM card in my phone or something like that. I'll definitely come watch your fight, mate, I can't wait to see it."

I would end up missing Simon's fight, which he lost on points after battling hard for five rounds with a superior Thai fighter. The Thai had a strong thip game, and he had made it almost impossible for Simon to close the distance and land his best shots. I saw a video of the fight, in which Simon continually marched forwards, ignoring the constant thip kicks to his torso and throwing potentially lethal elbows in an attempt to steal a knockout victory in the final round. It wasn't to be, but he displayed immense heart in the ring and a will to win, and that's as good as a tick in the victory column so far as I am concerned.

The bus drive back to Chiang Mai that afternoon was as equally spectacular as the virgin experience. In fact, I thought it was even better than the ride across, if only because I was listening to great music and because the return bus driver must surely have just concluded an epic *Fast And Furious* marathon. His driving style was intense, to put it mildly. He somehow managed to shave just over an hour off our journey time. It felt a little bit like we were participating in a vehicular version of the running of the bulls, only *we* were the bull, and we were trying desperately to gore some poor sucker on a bright pink scooter who was too far from home and who hadn't bothered to pay for travel insurance.

Along the way, it began to rain, and a strong wind whipped up, bringing the jungle canopy to life all around us as we hurtled through the mountains at tremendous velocity. Coming in to the traffic-laden streets of Chiang Mai, a Toyota pick-up truck cruised along next to my window, mere inches away from my head. I frowned as it drew level and then slowly pulled ahead. I couldn't quite believe what I was seeing.

Is that a tent?
Somebody had pitched a two-man tent in the tray of the ute. I could see young children clustered inside of it, with the evident aim being to avoid the rain whilst the vehicle thundered along the highway. Necessity is the mother of innovation. You see all sorts of things on the roads in Thailand, and a pitched tent was relatively mundane, in retrospect. I offered a quiet salute to the passing vehicle and its dogged passengers. Kudos to them. I wished them good luck in all their future ventures – tent or no tent.

Driving back into Chiang Mai felt depressingly like re-entering the developed world after a couple of days spent in Pai. Advertisements crowding each other for space. Advertisement on top of advertisement. I abhor advertising.

The human brain is often compared to a sponge. You hear it all the time. It absorbs everything, they say, whether consciously or by osmosis, whether we like it or not, and often with paralyzing outcomes. Take advertising. Simple enough concept, for sure. Present something at its absolute, photo-shopped best, and people will like it and they will want to buy it…
However, I'm curious to know if anybody ever considered the impacts and implications that this line of thinking may one day have on the countless sponges of the world? Did anybody stop and consider where this slippery slope might *end*? I look around the developed world today and see a world full of people who are completely obsessed with their image, and disconcertingly nonchalant about reality.

Human beings have become walking, talking advertisements for *themselves* – that person who only exists for the briefest period of time in the very late and very early hours of the day, when nobody else is there to see them.

Indeed, I believe that the only honest words are spoken during the late evening and early morning. That's when important conversations are best held – that is to say, conversations where honesty matters.

Muay Thai: Peace, At Last

Known nought of life's fears, nor Cared for your thoughts.
    He needs not your love, and he'll Think as he ought.
       Unbowed by time's wind, unbowed by the Rage,
    You'd best bring an army 'gainst the man of an age.
Unleashed be God's Thunder; his elbows and knees,
            You'll do as he says, and he'll do as he please.
        Hated, for sure; oh, despised for his Sin.
He needs not your love, there's no doubt who will win.

CHAPTER 7
SPARRING

"You have enemies? Good. That means you've stood up for something, sometime in your life."
— Winston Churchill

It's a common misconception in martial arts that kicking is done with the foot. A common mistake. A painful mistake. To kick with your foot is to break your foot. There are lots of small bones down there. The phalanges and metatarsals. If you must kick someone, it's best done with your shin. Much bigger and thicker bones in the shin. Not only will this hurt you less, but it will hurt the person you're kicking a whole lot more.

Stuart, my training partner from London, learnt this the hard way during our daily sparring session. In our few sessions thus far, he hadn't thrown a single kick. Finally working up the courage, I saw the kick coming about two minutes before he threw it.

"Checking" kicks is a huge part of Muay Thai. Checking a kick is the act of using your shin to block an opponent's kick, preventing it from connecting with anything softer and more vulnerable, like your liver, your ribs, or your soft, meaty thigh muscles. The dynamics of the shin bone is an important thing for a developing Thai boxer to learn. The shin bone is much tougher and more dense up close to the knee. Indeed, there's a sharp and incredibly dense piece of bone there at the front of your knee that is the perfect tool to use when checking kicks. A little trick that I have developed when checking kicks is to check wider than normal, which means that the dense part of shin connects with the lower, thinner, more vulnerable part of my opponents shin. And, if I'm lucky and my opponent is poorly skilled or too slow, I can catch an incoming kicker squarely on the foot. As Stuart can now attest, that is an excruciatingly painful experience for the person throwing the kick.

As you can probably imagine, broken legs are not unusual in Muay Thai. There are ways to lessen the chances of incurring such an injury.

Conditioning the bones of your body is a process that occurs according to Wolfs Law – a law which states that bones in a healthy animal or person will adapt to the loads under which they are placed. Thai boxers have taken the art of bone remodeling and toughening to another level entirely. They kick heavy bags, trees, posts, you name it – all so that they can toughen up their bones until they are almost as strong as iron and can be thrown at will, almost entirely impervious to damage. Through sparring and conditioning drills, they also harden up their forearms, wrists and knuckles, elbows and knees, and even foreheads for those competing in the old school version of Muay Boran, where head-butting was perfectly legal. Muay Thai defense is legendary. When you watch a fight between high level Thai practitioners of the sport, they seem to be almost immune to the strikes of their opponents – strikes that would render any normal, untrained person immobile and bed-ridden for weeks. Their level of conditioning is extraordinary.

The next way to prevent a broken leg is to learn proper technique, the most important part of which is to turn the foot that you're standing on. This turns your kicking leg at the hip, effectively ensuring that the kick lands horizontal, rather than diagonally or vertically. This is important because the shin bone is shaped a bit like a piece of 2 x 4, or a wooden ruler, like you would use in primary school. It's tough and dense in one direction, from front to back, and narrow, bendy and easy to break in the other direction, side to side.

Then of course, there's fight tactics. Knowing *when* to throw a kick is of critical importance. Muay Thai is an exceptionally technical art form. Identifying when your opponent rests his weight on his front leg is equivalent to a green light for throwing a kick at his thigh, because for him to lift his leg and block the incoming kick, he must firstly shift his weight back onto his other leg, which requires *two* movements and which takes much too long. Learning about weight distribution is an important part of developing effective fight footwork. That's a big part of the reason why boxers wouldn't last more than a couple of minutes in a ring with a Thai kickboxer, simply because boxers place almost all of their weight over an inwardly facing front foot. Thai kickboxers would have a field day throwing full force kicks at the front leg, crippling the boxer and providing him or her with a lengthy rehabilitation period – plenty of time to bury their head in the sand and have a good hard think about the wisdom of trying to fight a Thai.

Stuart howled and clutched at his leg as he hit the canvas. I stood there and laughed. My Thai trainers looked concerned for a moment, and then when they saw that Stuart wasn't badly injured, the too laughed at his expense. Stuart appeared surprised by how badly that had hurt, and that's what I found amusing, because it was all too common. Muay Thai and martial arts have become something of a commercially popular pastime in the modern age, and as a result, too many people have come to underestimate how much fighting can hurt.

I leant back against the ropes and waited patiently for the British profanity to stop, and for Stuart to locate his manhood.

They're supposed to be tough, those Brits.

16 days until the fight.

Stuart finally regained his footing and we touched gloves and started again. I recognized instantly that Stuart was now solely focused on protecting his foot, and so I feinted in that direction and followed through with an easy sweep kick to his other leg. A simple trap, baited and taken. He hit the canvas once again, looking furious now. Emotion had evidently kicked down the door and barged in to the frontal lobes. That would greatly affect his ability to fight, and so I engaged with him again, eager to teach my friend a lesson. He wanted to step into a ring and have his first Muay Thai fight himself before he returned to Britain, and he would lose if he was unable to disconnect himself from his emotions. The Thais watched on knowingly.

I allowed Stuart to let his anger bring him to me, and I caught him coming in with a front *thip*, which is a powerful push kick. Stuart's angry momentum carried him right into the kick, and I heard the air expelled from his lungs as he flailed backwards, just barely keeping his feet.

I followed through on the kick by marching forwards, chasing him across the ring.

Stuart looked edgy and panicky now, twitching hurriedly in response to my slightest feints and backing up towards the ropes.

"Sabai, sabai," I said to him. Relax, relax.

I threw a slow leg kick to give him a confidence boosting check and then backed off slightly, allowing a status quo to perpetuate for a while.

Fighting is much like dancing. It is a form of expression and communication. Through body language alone, a fighter can dictate who leads and who submits.

I am a pressure fighter. I walk forwards constantly. It feels unusual for me in a fight to stand still or to back up for any length of time. Perhaps contrary to what you may suspect, my aggressive style has developed out of an emphasis and prioritization I award to defense in my training. If you ever take a moment to observe a martial arts training session, you will see that almost 99% of the training revolves around offensive movements. Fighters like to hit things, basically. They invest huge swaths of their time practicing their combinations, their punches, their kicks, their elbows, their knees, their takedowns, their submissions, etc. In my opinion, not only does this detract from the entire point and purpose of self-defense, but I believe that it's not the most optimal way to train for a professional fight.

Fighting is a scary business. It's even scarier in reality than in your Hollywood fueled imaginings. I mention this so as to iterate that it cannot be overstated the effect that adrenalin has on the body in a combat situation. The fight or flight response is a powerful survival tool - and I think the term should be changed to include the natural "freeze" response that adrenalin can trigger. There are two ways to freeze. The first type of instinctive freezing is in fact a way for a human to play dead in the face of a predator. A good way for a fighter to utilize this knowledge and to make your opponent freeze up during a fight is to shout at them. It's precisely the reason why predators roar or scream. It causes their prey to freeze or hesitate. It was a technique often used by Muhammad Ali. The other way a person freezes is called paralysis by analysis. The brain goes into hyper drive and throws so many options at the frontal lobe that it's only normal to be struck dumb by indecision. In this regard, a fighter who has perfected and trained eight or ten simple fight moves can often be a more effective fighter in a high-stress moment than a fighter who has learned and trained hundreds of different movements. Another important effect of adrenalin is the removal of fine motor skills. You cannot tie your shoelaces, for example, whilst in the throes of a fight or flight reflex. It is for this reason why many intricate fighting styles such as Aikido are ineffective in a real fight. Muay Thai movements are all gross motor movements - movements which are helped by the influx of adrenalin.

The ultimate goal of combat training revolves around the body's response to adrenalin. It is not about learning and perfecting techniques in a safe and controlled, air-conditioned and stress-free gym environment. Effective combat training has to replicate the stresses of a real life or death situation. The whole point and purpose of combat training at its most fundamental, is to re-wire the human brain. To re-wire the flinch response. The US Marines describe it as running towards the gunfire, not away, and it's the same with martial arts. It's a silly idea to jump out from behind a dark corner at someone who has been effectively combat trained. Human survival instinct is to flinch *away* from a shocking stimulant. A "flight" response. A trained fighter will flinch *towards* the stimulant, and often leading with a clenched fist or an elbow. A "fight" response. Ingrained. Instinctive. A fundamental re-wiring of the brain.

The Thais understand this notion and so they train for fighting in the best and most effective way possible. By fighting. Thai children will begin their fighting career at the age of five or six, when their brains are still in their formative and most pliable years. Training adults to become instinctive fighters is much more difficult, and focusing entirely on offensive training is not the optimal way to get the job done.

Why isn't training for offense the best way to train for an aggressive response?

Because, as I mentioned before, fighting is scary. And if a fighter hasn't re-wired that fight or flight response, then regardless of how much offensive training he or she has performed, the fighter will instinctively look to curl up in a ball and shy away from punches when it comes time to fight for real.

It cannot be understated the effect of adrenalin on the body.

So I bring you back to the mass of fighters who train almost exclusively for offense, hitting heavy bags and pads every day with perfect combinations and timing. And then it comes time to fight and their offense is so perfectly ingrained that all they have to think about is protecting themselves from getting hurt. Unfortunately, the human desire for survival is so powerful, that the need for safety and defense will easily override all of those years of dedicated offensive training. Fighting is about not thinking. Or limited thinking, at best. As soon as the fight starts and the first engagement gets underway, a lot of fighters will feel their minds working overtime, trying to anticipate their opponents' movements so that they can defend themselves and avoid getting hurt or knocked out. The body doesn't understand that there's a referee there, especially during the early stages of a fighter's career. So far as your body knows, getting knocked out or injured is tantamount to getting killed and eaten, because your body doesn't know that the referee is going to step in and stop the fight. That doesn't happen in nature, and so our fears will so easily take over in the midst of a fight, despite our best rational efforts to the contrary. There will be so much going on in a fighter's head that most of it won't even get processed and a fighter's defense will often more closely resemble a child in the foetal position, because their thinking can't keep up and they've had to resort to pure instinct. They do this because they haven't trained properly for defense.

So then, what is the most optimal approach to training? What is the best way to re-wire the brain to be best suited for a fight?

Well, instead of constantly hitting things now when I train, which is fun, I ask my trainers to put on gloves and shin guards and attack me, which isn't so fun. I tell them that I won't strike back, so it's not a sparring session, I just challenge them to hit me and then keep on hitting me. That way, I can practice my defense. After all, as I have mentioned, the whole purpose of martial arts is self-defense. What is the point in being able to throw a perfect one-two-three combination if you've already been knocked out and then killed and your body has been taken home to be eaten for dinner? I believe that every professional fighter's first aim in training should be to develop the ability to *survive* any fight, for however many rounds. Only once that is assured, then offense and the ability to hurt someone in return can be trained as a bonus. I train my defense to the point where it becomes ingrained and it overrides my instinct to curl up into a ball. Then, come fight time, I can relax and control the flood of adrenalin in my body, knowing that I am safe defensively and I'm not going to get hurt. If my opponent attacks, my body reacts instinctively and I stay calm. There's no reaction lag or processing time either, which means my defense is very fast. It simply happens, because I've trained it to. I've also trained myself not to blink when punches get thrown at my face, so that I can watch and observe how my opponent retracts his punch, because that's where the best opening for counter strikes are. If I flinch and blink when he throws his strikes, I might miss critical openings and holes in his technique that I can exploit the next time he attempts that movement. Then, in that calm head space, I can dedicate my precious thinking time towards thoughts of attack and aggressive offense.

By training defensively, I have made myself into a very aggressive fighter.

By training myself to remain calm, I have made myself far more dangerous in a fight.

Stuart's eye was beginning to swell shut, and so the trainers called an end to our sparring session and an end to the day's training.

I glared at the dwarf as I walked back past him. He nodded to me, and I thought I saw a glimmer of respect there from him. I hadn't gotten it all out in training that morning. I wasn't done yet, but that's sometimes the way it goes.

After a few days apart whilst I had been in Pai and he had been exploring Chiang Rai, Carter and I met up once again, and together, he and I went out to find a place to have lunch, and I asked the Thai waitress if I could have a cup of tea with mine.

My tea arrived and Carter looked at it, affronted.

"You drink that shit?" Carter asked, glaring at the cup of tea like it had said something offensive about his mothers cooking. "Real men drink coffee," he proclaimed.

I half expected him to jump out of his seat and start singing Star Spangled Banner.

"Do they?" I said, for lack of anything else to say.

"You bet your ass they do!"

The British love their tea and the Americans love their coffee. The British are self-deprecating and sarcastic, and the Americans are ego-centric and dramatic. Australians are like the confused love children of the two western Empirical powers. Some Australian people were raised by their parents and grandparents and inherited British values and mannerisms, whilst others were raised by Hollywood and MTV and inherited American values and mannerisms. We Aussies are the Frankenstein's of the west.

I was tempted to point out that coffee lowers fertility, and thus infer that coffee drinkers wouldn't be real men for very long, and thus infer that Americans are pussies, but instead, I sipped at my English Breakfast tea and kept my thoughts to myself.

I wasn't in the mood for it.

It was a beautiful day and I was enjoying myself.

Did you know that there are only twenty-two countries on Earth that the British Empire hasn't yet invaded? America has some catching up to do. Not that invading countries is necessarily a good thing. I'm just thinking out loud.

I figure that there are 24 hours in a day. How we choose to spend those 24 hours is really the most defining measure of our existence and of our character. Most people presumably sleep around 8 hours a night, so that leaves 16 more hours, during which our lives can be spent in a manner of our choosing. Most people presumably spend 8 hours at work, and then the remaining 8 hours relaxing with their families and friends and enjoying themselves. Work, rest and play – 8 hours apiece – a balanced lifestyle. I've just now come to the realization that the vast majority of my 24 hour block currently revolves around learning, training, practicing, thinking, recovering and perfecting the art of hurting people as badly as possible. Using my very own reasoning about the correlation between choices and character, I can't help but wonder if my current chosen lifestyle makes me a bad person…

"You wanna get a drink tonight?" Carter asked.

I shrugged. "Sure, I guess."

"Reckon there's a place in town where you can buy Foster's?"

"You do know that nobody in Australia actually drinks Foster's, don't you, mate?"

"For real?"

"Well, I've never even tasted it before, and I'm Australian, so…"

"Yeah, but you're a pussy," Carter said.

"Ok then."

The afternoon moved along and Carter and I chatted to some girls and I wandered off to find a quiet spot to read a book and write in my journal and listen to music.

The sun had come out and the mercury was climbing rapidly after lunch. It was burning hot.

I took a cold shower and then went back to the room for a nap. I was still feeling a little raw and aggressive after training. I wasn't entirely sure why. It was probably the first time since coming to Thailand that I wasn't feeling exhausted and injured and drained. I was still humming with a furious energy. I wanted to fight, basically. The training was beginning to take hold over my mind. My testosterone was responding, and I was craving a fight. I just wanted to compete.

It's lucky that people cannot be convicted for what goes in their minds, else we would all be criminals. It's easy to forget that humans still have an evolutionary drive, the same way that animals do. It's a little bit absurd to call instinctive behavior evil, when it simply isn't. Greed, gluttony and lust, pride, envy, and fury. These aren't bad things to feel. These aren't evil things. They're perfectly natural things that have all evolved in tune with our binary reward system, and for a perfectly good reason. That reason is survival. Humans are innately creatures of survival. We all have a "dark" side. An animal side. A primitive side. We *must* survive, and we *must* win. Mother Nature demands it of us.

Survival instincts are the basis for all politics. Love and fear are both survival instincts. One is for child rearing, the other is for preservation of self. Neither is better or more appropriate than the other. They both serve a survival purpose. It's a violent world. This much I know. Survival or not, there's real evil in the world. I've heard it said that money is supposedly the root of all evil, but that doesn't make sense to me. Money was a creation, so it cannot be the root of anything… No, I believe the idea of property to be the root of human corruption – of true evil. That's precisely when we started putting our own welfare before the welfare of the community. That's where communism versus capitalism started, with the idea of property.

It is said that human beings are the most intelligent creatures on Earth. Unsurprisingly, it is human beings that make this claim. I can't help but look around at all the dying forests and the nuclear bombs and wonder if we aren't the stupidest creatures on the planet.

I worry about the state of humanity sometimes. Often, actually.

We are going through a capitalism-driven era of people telling other people not to care what others think. *Just do what's best for you,* we say. *Just worry about yourself.* What an abhorrent thing to tell someone. Parents raise their kids to be indifferent to the thoughts, wants and needs of others and then they wonder why there's a bullying pandemic in our schools. Teenagers watch music videos of Kanye West and Kim Kardashian spruiking their brand of narcissistic selfishness and then they believe that this kind of behavior must be a good thing because famous people are doing it. *If you care and invest solely in yourself, then maybe you will become a celebrity someday and then you can perpetuate the cycle of self-infatuation!* Self-infatuation is masturbation. The word "selfie" pretty well sums it up. Celebrities have raised an entire generation of self-obsessed boys and girls and it's the kids that look up to and aspire to be like these celebrities that are paying the price. With the likes of Facebook and Twitter to act as stages for grandstanding and attention-seeking, social pressures and competition is greater than it has ever been before. If you're not a wannabe model with a thousand Instagram followers, than you're worthless and nobody likes you. Competition, particularly amongst young women, is crushing. Body image issues, self-esteem problems, stress, eating disorders, you name it.

Who do we blame for all of this?

It's easy to blame the celebrities, but they're just cogs in a wheel. It's not their fault. The problem lies with the speed of our technological and cultural evolution. Our bodies, by contrast, are extremely slow to evolve, and have not yet evolved to understand the modern world that we have created. Our biological reward systems are all confused. Attention is a good thing. It means improved status for mating, first pick of the hunt, improved social status, and so on. Once upon a time, attention was earned by being the most resourceful, the most intelligent, the most courageous. Now, however, attention is garnered by those with a camera lens and a lack of self-respect. It's a self-fuelling cycle of bullshit. A perfect storm. A slippery-slope of a culture in decline. Our biological constitution simply doesn't understand the modern world that we have built for ourselves.

Sex is the currency of the day.

Sex sells, we've discovered.

The hyper-sexualization of popular culture is destroying families and relationships. Family, belonging and relationships are high on Maslow's Hierarchy of Needs – that which most powerfully drives the human machine. Behind oxygen, water, food, sleep and safety, the human need for family and belonging is incredibly strong. By placing self-gratification (which is at the very bottom of the Hierarchy) before a relationship, the culture that we have custom-designed is turning our innate human values upside down and rendering them obsolete. As a result, more people than ever are going to sleep at night feeling broken-hearted and lonely and wondering what they're supposed to be doing with their lives. We have capitalism to thank for that. Advertising and celebrities. Damn celebrities. If you had to name the most unstable and dysfunctional group of people in our society today, you would probably say: celebrities. At the very least, celebrities would make the top two or three, and I can't really think who might top them... And then, if you had to name the most influential group of people in our society today, you would probably say: celebrities. I don't know about you, but if I stand back, cock my head to the side and squint a little, I can see a bit of a problem with all of that. I'd love to see the likes of Kanye West or Justin Bieber in a Muay Thai ring. I've said it before; a Muay Thai ring is the great equalizer. No amount of money can save you in there. Good looks won't help. Expensive clothes are just fabric. Money is just an idea.

Elbows are as real as it fucking gets.

The guilty are caged whilst the sinner goes free,
The truthful despised as own' truthful can be,
The liars are loved and adored for their lies,
The world's to the rich who can laugh as it dies.
In life as it is, where we steal as we're taught,
The only thing left is to never get caught...

CHAPTER 8
TROUBLE OUTSIDE THE RING

"But I've bought a big bat, I'm all ready, you see.
Now my troubles are going to have trouble with me!"
— Dr. Seuss

I lay on my top bunk and stared up at the ceiling. I felt my stomach growling.
I was getting hungry.
I wondered where Carter had gotten to, the lazy buffoon. He'd asked me to wait for him before going to dinner.
I located my phone and sent him a message.
Hey mate. I'm hungry.
He replied instantly.
Where do you feel like eating?
I'd already made up my mind.
That place at the back of the night market. I like it there.
Carter replied.
So let's go then?
I frowned.
Sure, just as soon as you get your stupid American self back to the room so that we can go. Unless you wanna meet there at say, 9?
There was a pause.
Michael I'm on the bed beneath you.
I frowned again and listened to the vibrations of the room. I could've sworn I was alone.
Bullshit, I texted back.
Michael. Look. Under. Your. Bed. Dickhead.
I rested my phone on my chest and stared up at the ceiling some more.
"Carter?" I said finally. "You there?"
"Yep," was the deadpan reply.

"Ready to get dinner then?" I asked as casually as possible.

"Yep."

"Night market place?"

"Yep."

"Now?"

"Yep."

"Ok then." I swung myself off the top bunk and led the way to the door without so much as glancing at Carter. "Man, I'm hungry."

Carter bought us both drinks throughout dinner, and so I was feeling comfortably buzzed by the time we were finished.

"Let's go to a bar and kick on," Carter said enthusiastically. "Know any good places?"

I shrugged. Sounded good to me. "Sure. I know a rooftop bar just round the corner from here."

The place was called THC bar, and it was all cushions and soft flooring with reggae music, a cracking view over the city at night and the pervasive smell of marijuana hanging in the air.

Carter kept the drinks flowing and we struck up conversations with everybody we met. It was a friendly atmosphere, eased further by the heavy penchant for drug use.

I got up to go and buy the next round of drinks and struggled to get my legs under me. I was very drunk by this stage, but I was having a good time. I was just starting to get my balance sorted when Carter rushed over – seemingly out of nowhere – and grabbed me by my shoulders.

I thought for a moment that he was trying to kiss me, but the reality was even more terrifying.

"Mick, did you hear!" he shouted at me.

"I dunno, maybe?" I said.

"Do you know the US President?" he asked.

"I know *of* him," I said, not wanting anybody to think I was with the CIA or anything like that. A natural concern when I am drunk. I wasn't sure at this point whether or not the room was swaying, or if Carter and I had started dancing.

"I just saw on the news that Obama got attacked on Air Force One. The President's dead!" Carter shouted in my ear.

I felt my knees go weak. I felt as if my stomach had plummeted and ended up someplace just south of my hamstrings. I cast about for something to hold onto and tried to comprehend the enormity of this news. "Jesus," was all I managed to say. I was staring at my knees, as if maybe they had all the answers.

The President of the free world had been killed.

That was problematic.

This changes everything, I thought. I immediately wanted to go and contact my parents. I knew that the world would be in turmoil – in fact, I was surprised by how calm the situation in the bar was. Obviously, this was still very fresh news and nobody else in Chiang Mai had heard about it just yet.

What if the airports get closed down? What if borders get closed off and I can't get back to my family?

In this, the most terrifying moment of the 21st century, my only thoughts were of my family.

Instantly, my mind was racing through the planning. First choice was an airport, but what if they were locked down? Plan B… I had to get down to the Malaysian border as quickly as possible, and from there I could make my way south and east along the archipelago and island hop from one to the next until I found a boat or a tourist with a yacht that was capable of getting me down to mainland Australia. That became the critical thing in my head. I *had* to find an Australian yacht in an Asian port and I had to do it pronto – before they all got the hell out of dodge. Hell, even if I had to steal a yacht from someone, then so be it. This was a matter of survival now, and my family would need me. Time was of the essence. Public transport couldn't be trusted. I'd have to steal a motorbike. That would be optimal.

I looked back at Carter. "We need to move," I said as quietly as I could, and I started dragging him as surreptitiously as I could manage towards the exit. "Quickly, whilst we've still got a head start on this thing."

It was at about this time that I realized Carter was roaring with laughter, and I put two and two together at a reasonable pace. "You bastard," was all I could say. I was almost entirely overcome with relief. The President wasn't dead after all.

"Come on," Carter said, steering me along. "This place is closing in a few minutes. These joints all have to close at midnight. It's a military thing. Let's go to Zoe's."

"Ok then." I had heard of Zoe's In Yellow. It's apparently the hip, go-to nightclub for foreigners in Chiang Mai. It was probably worth checking out. And besides, in light of the news that the world was still clinging on to some semblance of normality and peace, I was in the mood for celebrating. We caught a tuk-tuk to Zoe's and arrived to find the pavement already throbbing to the sound of loud music and hectic revelers.

"Looks half-decent," Carter observed, bobbing his way into the crowd and weaving towards the bar. I followed him along with my head on a swivel, looking at the eclectic mix of Thai locals and foreign tourists all crowded together on the various dance floors.

At the bar, Carter and I found ourselves standing next to a pair of German girls who were staying in our dorm room back at the hostel. We all whooped and cheered drunkenly upon seeing each other, like monkeys spotting bananas, and then we took our drinks and charged out onto the dance floor to administer dancing lessons.

Indeed, I have mastered the art of dancing as if nobody is looking. Most unfortunately on this occasion, people *were* looking, but that's just how it goes sometimes.

The night wore on, and as night melted quietly into morning, I found myself drinking at an isolated table and chatting with Carter. We were discussing our best apocalypse plans. The President-getting-assassinated thing was still firmly at the front of my mind.

"Best thing to do is to get a sailing boat," I was saying. "Get yourself some simple water distillery set-up, like rednecks use to make moonshine, and there you have it, mate! You can sail around from place to place, travel the world, catch fish out of the ocean to eat and distill seawater into freshwater and basically have a great time of things."

Carter was shaking his head vigorously. "You gotta get your hands on some heavy weaponry," he said. "Assault rifles, shotguns and revolvers need to be your first priority. Otherwise you're fucked, even if you get yourself into some nice sailing boat or whatever, someone else is just gonna come along and whack you, so there's that, man. And crossbows are the way to go if you can't get guns. They're quiet and powerful. Like sniper rifles."

"It depends on the scenario," I said, shrugging. "Ammunition won't last forever, so I reckon the best way to go, if you wanna talk militarily, is the old fashioned ways. Raise up an army Ghengis Khan style, on horseback, with bows and arrows, which are way faster to draw back than a crossbow, and you can even just make more of them if they break, and then with shields, spears and swords for your infantry soldiers. Shields and spears have been the best weapons for close-quarters combat for centuries. Swords are way too messy, man, same as knives. If you get that close that you're in a sword fight or a knife fight and you don't have a shield, then the fat lady is already singing, mate. Spears give you some *distance*."

"Fine, whatever dude. What do you think the most important *skill* is for when the zombies come? It's gotta be something like archery, right?"

"Nah, the most important skill is public speaking I reckon, mate," I said. "The fellas that thrive when the zombies come will be the ones that can band together under a strong leader who can speak well and give direction. Humans are tribal creatures. It's unnatural to plan for these sorts of things thinking that you're going to be on your own the entire time. That's counter-productive. You gotta raise up a strong community, and that will require a strong leader."

It was at this point that one of the German girls' shrieking shattered our little world and Carter and I both spun at the sound.

There was Francesca, clearly stuck between trying to get our attention and trying to keep an eye on a situation that must've been unfolding elsewhere. She was stuck in the middle. Indecisive. Panicked.

I shared a concerned frown with Carter before we both picked up our beers and rushed over to the panic-stricken German. This looked somewhat serious.

"What's up?" Carter asked hurriedly.

Francesca pointed frantically. "*Leah!*" she exclaimed desperately. Her English appeared to have eluded her for the moment. Adrenalin can have that effect. Her friend's name was Leah.

Carter and I followed as Francesca hurried back through the crowds and into the back of a neighbouring bar. There was a live Thai band playing to a thinning crowd. The bar opened up to the night sky at the rear, and it was there that we found Leah, looking close to unconsciousness, and with four Thai men all gathered around, shaking her and shouting at her.

At first, I thought that they were concerned for her well-being, but then the situation came into better focus and my alcohol induced haze cleared in an instant.

"What the fuck is going on here?" I shouted over the music, wanting to make sure I was heard by everybody present. Sometimes, the mere invoking of a scene of confrontation can be enough to make people melt away into the background, but not these guys. They appeared furious about something and they rounded on me.

"She steal from us!" one of the Thai guys shouted in my face, pointing accusingly at Leah. "Video! See?" he pointed at a security camera behind the outside bar. "She steal from bar. Now pay!"

I threw a grim look at Francesca and walked over to Leah, doing my best to ignore the Thai guys breathing down my neck. "Is she ok?" I asked Francesca, gesturing at Leah. "How much has she had to drink?"

"We drink the same amount," Francesca said, turning to confront the Thai men, clearly emboldened with fury. "They spiked her drink!"

"SHE STEAL! SHE STEAL! WE HAVE VIDEO! SHE PAY! NOW!"

I shoved the Thai guy back, "shut up," I said.

I quickly realized my mistake.

The four Thais all stepped in closer and one of them came right up and pushed his forehead against mine.

"Hey, hey, whoa!" Carter said, leaping in to separate us. He put his hands up defensively and submissively. "Let's all just take it easy here!" he said.

I was suddenly acutely aware of the glass beer bottle in my hand, and I braced myself in case anyone approached me again.

The leader of the Thai outfit pointed angrily at me now. "*You* pay."

"Did you drug her?" I asked, pointing at Leah, who had passed out now. Francesca was attending to her. "What did you put in her drink?"

"We call cops!" the Thai responded. "You wait here! We call cops!"

I shrugged, "go right ahead. Nobody's giving you a damn cent."

I noticed that one of the Thai guys had taken his rubber thong off his foot and was holding it in his hand, as if he were about to throw it at me. I wonder if they teach that move to the Special Forces guys. The ol' thong throw. I somehow doubt it.

The tension in the air was palpable.

I could hear my heart pounding, as if it had somehow found its way into my skull.

The leader had pulled out his phone and held it threateningly in the air. "You pay now, or we call cops," he said, trying again.

I knew what was going on. I had seen it before. This was a simple shakedown. These guys wanted a bribe. Tourists are easy money. Give them a fright, threaten them with police and demand their money. Drunk tourists are even easier. Simple economics.

Suddenly I had a decision to make. If I repeated my demand that he go ahead and call the cops, then the ball was in their court once again, and there was no knowing what might happen. For all intents and purposes, the cops may have arrived and *increased* the price of the bribe. For the moment, he had given me a move, and I needed to use it.

I took a few steps forwards and parked myself resolutely in between Leah and the four Thai men, and I eyeballed the leader of the pack.

I'm a good speaker, but I didn't have the slightest clue what to say, and so I said nothing. Nonetheless, the message was abundantly clear. I was offering this guy violence if he decided to approach, and now *he* had a decision to make, but he hesitated, as I'd hoped he might.

"Carter, get Leah and Francesca back to the hostel," I said, turning to look earnestly at Carter. He moved immediately, gesturing frantically for Francesca to help him with Leah. They got her moving and headed for the exit as quickly as they could manage.

I eyed the Thai right up until the last moment, daring him to take me up on my offer, and then I followed my friends out onto the street. I was acutely aware of turning my back on these guys, and my every sense was screaming at me with the slightest brush on my arm as I walked through the crowd. But I made it to the door unmolested, and I released a breath I had been holding. My heart was thudding painfully in my chest. I wasn't angry. I was scared.

Sometimes, the best move is not to call a bet, but to raise it.

It had paid off, but I shuddered to consider the myriad number of ways in which that could have gone differently. We had gotten very lucky.

I found Carter waiting for me on the street. Francesca was nearby, bundling Leah onto a tuk-tuk.

"Alright?" Carter asked.

I nodded, trying my best to look cool and impassive, like it was nothing. Like I did this kind of thing all the time. Like I was in control. None of those things were true, but appearances matter. Maybe I could even convince myself of one or two of those things. "Where are they going?" I asked, nodding after the German girls in the tuk-tuk as it sputtered along and disappeared down a side street.

"Taking Leah to find a hospital," Carter said. "Do you reckon she was drugged?" he asked.

I shrugged. "I didn't get a good look at her," I said. "It happens though. This is Thailand."

There was no question that I wouldn't be returning to this part of the city for the remainder of my stay. But that didn't really bother me. I hadn't much liked it anyway. Too crowded, too noisy, too many tourists, too many working girls. Not really my scene.

"Are we done for the night?" Carter asked. He appeared rather shaken by the encounter with the shady locals.

I shrugged and nodded. "Let's walk. I'm supposed to have training tomorrow morning. Walk it off. Will do us good."

Carter agreed and we began our slow and steady stroll back across the city. Away from the nightclub scene, the city was quiet. Almost silent, in fact.

"Those guys could've been Mafia, you know," Carter said warily, glancing back over his shoulder. "There's a big presence here in Chiang Mai."

"They weren't Mafia," I said.

"How do you know, man?" Carter asked. "We need to be careful, dude. We should probably catch a tuk-tuk back or something. These sorts of guys have eyes everywhere, man."

I sighed inwardly.

Americans.

Drama-queens.

I bumped into a phone booth that I thought I was going to be missing by a foot or so. Maybe I was still more drunk than I'd first thought.

It was then that I noticed that I was wearing a hat, and I frowned. "Hey, Carter," I said.

"Mm?"

"Was I wearing a hat when we left our hostel earlier?"

Carter glanced at me, and then he noticed the hat and burst out laughing. "You kept that!"

Evidently, he knew something I didn't. "What do you mean?" I asked, taking the hat off to inspect it. It was a nice enough looking hat. Some kind of bowler hat type of deal. It was black, with a white stripe running around it.

"There was some dude from Iceland wearing it, remember?" Carter asked. "He bought us a drink... You took it off him and said you were gonna give it back!"

I frowned. I vaguely recalled something like that happening. "Well, shit," I said, eyeing the hat in my hands. "Should we go back and try to find this guy?"

Carter laughed again. "Good luck, dude," he said. "My feet are too sore. I'm not walking back."

I realized that my feet were rather sore as well. "Well now I feel a little bad," I said, putting the hat back on my head. "Be rude not to wear it I suppose."

Carter nodded seriously. "Seven years of bad luck to steal a hat and then not wear it."

"Really?"

"Of course, dude. Here, come here." Carter took the hat from my head and we stopped walking. "Repeat after me," Carter said, holding the hat between us like it was some kind of precious jewel. "I will forever wear this hat."

"I will forever wear this hat," I repeated.

"As a mark of my shame."

"As a mark of my shame."

"So help me God."

"So help me God."

Carter placed the hat delicately onto my head once again, all pomp and ceremony in the middle of the dark street. We were silent for a moment, absorbing the scene and pondering the implications of the oath.

"You know," I said thoughtfully. "I'm pretty sure there's only like eighty thousand odd people that live in Iceland, or something like that. There aren't many of them, anyway. I could probably just travel there and ask around and I'd probably find the guy that owned the hat."

Carter nodded seriously. "Otherwise, you have to wear the hat forever," he said ominously. "As a mark of your shame."

"Yes, yes. I get it," I said. "As a mark of my shame." There was a stray dog sniffing around a full bin liner nearby.

"Come on then," I said, and we resumed our stroll. "I have training in the morning."

We walked on in silence for a while.

I was thinking about the confrontation back at Zoe's. I couldn't quite shake the incident. Indeed, it appeared to have shaken *me*.

"You alright?" Carter asked after a while.

He must've noticed I was a little quiet. Humans can be strongly intuitive creatures at times.

I sighed and decided that honesty might be the best policy. "You know that happy feeling that people sometimes get?"

"Yeah?"

"I think I've lost mine," I said.

Carter nodded understandingly. "Motherfuckers, right?" he said. "Filthy, lying assholes."

I nodded in agreement.

"Don't worry about it," Carter said. "Just pray like fuck those guys weren't Mafia is all I'm saying."

I sighed again. This wasn't helping. Maybe honesty wasn't the best policy after all. "I'm fine," I said. "Don't worry about it."

"We should go back to the night market," Carter said, suddenly sounding eager. "They had knuckle-dusters and knives and shit there… And I can probably get us a gun, too."

I grimaced and shook my head. "Hell no."

Weapons are a strange temptress. They feel like a refuge. It's natural, perhaps. Humans have an inclination for tools. However, I don't consider weapons to be of much use defensively. Fights are don't-blink propositions. Adrenaline is billing over-time hours, which means fine motor skills no longer exist. It's damn near impossible to reach into a pocket, extract and open a folding-knife or slip on a pair of brass-knuckles in a defensive situation. And it takes time. Time you don't have, unless you can get it done quicker than your opponent can blink, which you can't, unless you're a ninja, which you're not. Fixed blades on a sheath are probably best if you insist on carrying weapons, but they're still a terrible idea. Bad because weapons will raise the stakes to a point at which neither side can back down if it starts. It might not have been life and death a moment ago, but as soon as you pull a knife, now someone has to die or be terribly injured before the situation is finished, and it's just as likely to be the person that drew the weapon. If you carry a knife, you're far more likely to get stabbed than someone that doesn't carry a knife. That's a fact. If you carry a knife and lose it, you're going to get killed with it. If you hadn't been carrying the knife, maybe you would've walked away with a few bumps and bruises. I thought again about how I had handled the situation at Zoes, and I knew for sure that I had handled it poorly. Incorrectly. I had endangered all of us with my own pride and stupidity. The key to surviving a real fight is the art of de-escalating. You want your opponent to *not* feel threatened by you, and that's critically important. Now, even if a fight does come to blows, there may be a few punches thrown and then everyone nods at each other and decides that it's not worth it and walks away. However, if one or more of the parties concerned feel that their lives are threatened and that they're backed into a corner, the fight won't stop at a few punches. There's no knowing what might happen when people believe that they're fighting for their lives. It's only natural to assume that being big and scary and intimidating is a good defense, as it may deter people from wanting to fight you, but the truth is that those big, scary and intimidating people are far more likely to wind up being killed or injured should the fight eventuate, because their opponents are scared of them, and if there's more than just two people involved in a fight – which there usually is – then the big and scary individual is going to be savagely targeted and outnumbered. My advice is to take a leaf out of the book of the Thai fighters. These guys are brutal fighters, but you'd never know it. They don't have torn sleeves over their biceps and barbed wire tattoos around their throats, and that's exactly my advice in regard to everyday survival situations. Don't make yourself a target. Sun Tzu, the famed war philosopher and author of *The Art Of War* says to "appear weak where you are strong." Do the training, learn the skills, but never think yourself so superior as to show them off, and never try to intimidate others with them. No posturing. Posturing looks good in the movies, but it's not a good idea in a genuinely dangerous environment. And if you haven't done the training and don't have the skills, then *definitely* don't attempt any posturing.

There's no need to carry weapons. Should the going get tough, and should someone else raise the stakes for you, then almost anything can be used as a weapon. The belt around your waist or your t-shirt on your back can be used to strangle someone. Hard surfaces such as concrete walls and bitumen roads are more dangerous and unforgiving than fists will ever be. There are tools around us at any given time. The real weapon that humans possess is the brain. Carry that with you at all times and you'll keep yourself far safer than if you carry a knife or a knuckle-duster. Those weapons are for fools.

I was angry at myself, thinking about how I could've handled the situation better. I was angry at the German girls for being so stupid as to get themselves into a situation like that.

My pride had nearly gotten us all into a lot more trouble than the situation was worth, but I don't like bullies. Quietly, despite all my insistence to the contrary, I knew perfectly well that I was just angry I hadn't hit anyone. I'm a damned fool sometimes.

Michael Goodison

When peace can be waged with the flags in the streets,
Demanding the death of the warmonger cheats;
Give us world peace or you'll never survive,
We'll eat all your children and then burn you alive.
The right is to left as the left is to right,
If only they knew what awaits in the night.
Fight for the peace, and demand it, be tough.
You're funny, you lot, but enough is enough.

CHAPTER 9
THE DATE IS SET

"We were the people who were not in the papers.
We lived in the blank white spaces at the edges of print.
It gave us more freedom. We lived in the gaps between the stories."
— Margaret Atwood, The Handmaid's Tale

"You want fight?" Ame asked me, giving me the type of caring, earnest look that only Thais seem to be able to give.
I nodded grimly. "Yes," I said. "I want to fight."
Ame looked at me for a good moment longer. I felt as if he were studying me – his gaze piercing my very soul. Finally, he nodded, seemingly satisfied with whatever he had observed. "Ok, you fight," he decided. He turned and pointed to the back office where I had first been introduced to the lawyer-turned-fight-promoter upon arriving in Chiang Mai. "See here. Speak," Ame said, gesturing to the office. "You want fight, you speak."
I nodded and got gingerly to my feet. It had been a bruising session, not made any easier by my being hung-over. I needed to get a grip on my partying. The hostel atmosphere was exceptionally infectious, and I knew that I risked going into my fight under-prepared if I continued this habit of getting caught up and swept away with the culture of the backpacker hostel.
The lawyer's daughter was inside the office and she smiled warmly when she saw me. Her Thai countenance clashed with her slightly Australian-accented English. "Hi," she said, reclining in her chair. "You want see my dad?" she asked.
I nodded. "Ame said to see him about organizing a fight for me," I said. "I am going home on the 19th of this month, so I need the fight to be before that date."
The girl nodded. I hadn't caught her name. "You want fight?" she asked, giving me that same look of earnest concern that Ame had earlier awarded me.
"Yes," I said, almost on the verge of exasperation.
Of course I want to fight! That's the whole point and purpose of my being here!

"You learn of Thai boxing?" the girl asked.

I nodded again, gesturing back at the ring where Ame was sitting patiently. "Yeah, I've learnt a lot," I said. "I'm ready to fight whenever you can get me onto a card."

"How feel?" she continued, looking at my body studiously. "How power?"

"I feel good. I feel strong," I said, nodding and bouncing my shoulders a little to affirm my point. "Fitness is no problem. I'm ready."

"You fight Thai," the girl said pointedly, pointing at the walls where there were posters of ominous looking Thai fighters holding belts and glaring back at me. It sounded like a warning.

I shrugged nonchalantly. "Yes," I said, nodding again. "I'm ready to fight a Thai."

Thai, Chinese, Caucasian, Tasmanian, why should I care? I'm not a racist. I'll fight them all. Everybody bleeds the same colour. The Muay Thai ring is the great equalizer.

The girl gave me a searching look and then relented. "Ok, you fight fifteen," she said.

"Fifteen?" I asked.

"Fifteen August."

"Ok, 15th of August. Got it," I nodded. "Good."

I was trying to figure out how far away that was.

Today is the 1st day of August, mate... So, the 15th would most probably be 15 days away.

"Two weeks," I said aloud, nodding. Two weeks felt like a long time away. I wanted to fight *now*, but I didn't get to decide that. And besides, another two weeks of training wouldn't hurt. It would do me no good to get impatient and fight before I was entirely prepared.

"Do you want to get a drink later?" I asked the lawyer's daughter before I had even realized what I was saying.

Where did that come from? I wondered, looking at the Thai girl as if seeing her for the first time. *She's super attractive, and she seems nice enough. Sure, drink sounds like a good idea. Good thinking, pal. A little consultation wouldn't hurt next time, though... Better hope she says yes now.*

"Drink?"

"Tea, coffee," I shrugged. "I'd like to buy you a drink. Talk to you... You can tell me about your time at Uni in Sydney?"

"Why you want drink with me?" she asked, frowning suspiciously.

Oh, boy. Not quite what you were going for I presume then?

"I'm writing a book," I said, thinking quickly. "I'm a writer... I want to talk to locals. Ask them about their lives. Things like that... And you're pretty cute, so..." I trailed off and shrugged. "What do you say? I just need to go back to the hostel and have a shower. I'll meet you back here at twelve?"

I've been told that Thai girls are very different to the Australian girls I'm familiar with. Unlike westerners, Thai girls like and respect a man who makes decisions for them and who can be assertive. The present situation seemed like as good a time as any to test out the new approach.

"What's your name?" I asked curiously.

"Opangji," she said.

"Sounds like Jumanji," I observed. "It's a nice name," I explained, anticipating the confused expression. I turned to leave, talking over my shoulder. "I'll meet you back here at twelve."

"Ok," she called after me.

I smiled to myself as I returned to Ame.

His face was a question mark.

"15th of August I have a fight against a Thai," I told him.

Ame nodded appreciatively. "Two week," he said. "Training."

"Training," I agreed.

It hadn't been the best session. I was hung-over and fatigued and it had shown. I'd taken every possible opportunity to do the bare minimum that was asked of me, but I was feeling ok. Morale can get low after a session like that, but I rationalized it away and blamed the drinking. I knew that if I stopped drinking and knuckled down for the next two weeks, there would be no way my opponent would come into the ring fitter than me.

I was eager to fight.

I hurried back to the hostel to have a shower and get ready to meet Opangji for our date.

Finally, the date has been set. 15th of August. Two weeks away. Two weeks of really hard and proper training. I need to concentrate. I'm getting easily distracted. I haven't actually experienced any moments of anxious energy in my training, and that bothers me a little. I just can't seem to get scared for this fight. I know that fear is an extremely powerful motivator, and I was relying on fear to improve my training intensity, but I just can't seem to switch it on. I'm too relaxed, too content. Am I over-confident? Probably. Is that a bad thing? Possibly. I wonder who my opponent will be. I doubt I'll meet him before the fight. I wonder if he even knows that our tracks have just been overlaid and we are now on course to collide. I wonder if he can feel it. He has an opponent now, and I can damn well guarantee that he's never had an opponent quite like this one before. I need to get angry. I'm not angry yet, and that's bothering me. I'm not scared, I'm not angry. I'm calm and relaxed. Calm and relaxed is good, that's how I fight at my best, but I'm feeling lazy. I'm in no rush, and I'm spending more time thinking about all of these backpacker girls than I am thinking about my upcoming fight. Does something need to change, or should I just maintain this complacency? Being calm has always been my approach, after all. It just feels somewhat strange at this point to not have any real intensity bouncing around inside my head. Oh well, we'll see how it goes. I just want to fight someone, just for the sake of fighting.

Opangji was waiting for me right on time, and she had even changed her clothes. She had changed out of her shorts and a singlet and opted for jeans and a shirt.

"You look very nice," I said, gesturing at her get-up.

"Thank you."

We strolled out back along the alley toward the street, past the glowering dwarf. "Does he ever wear a shirt?" I asked, gesturing back at the little Thai.

Opangji laughed. "No size for him," she said. I wasn't sure if she was joking or not.

"He has cool tattoos," I commented. *I wonder how angry he would get if I snuck in here one night and poked tiny holes in the bottom of all his cups...* Indeed, there was something about that dwarf that elicited a yearning – a compulsion, no less – to braid his hair with little beads in it and then have him arrested for conspiring to usurp the king. Thais are very sensitive to anything inflammatory or insulting directed towards their king. Most Thais have framed portraits of the king situated in their living rooms or over-looking the dinner table. This is something of a contrast to Australians and their general feelings towards political leadership. Most Australians would rather munch on their own socks than have to look at a photo of a Prime Minister.

Opangji led the way to a small café that she knew. It was a back-alley place that rarely saw foreigners, and so we were greeted with raucous cheers from the workers as I entered with Opangji leading me by the arm. The girls working at the café clearly knew Opangji and they wasted no time diving into a conversation in fast Thai, flicking sly glances my way without any attempted guise.

"Hey, Australia," one of the girls finally spoke to me as she slid onto the bench beside me and patted my shoulder. "You fight Thai boxing?"

I nodded. "Yeah. 15th of August is my fight," I said. "Do you want to come and watch?"

The girl poked my stomach. "How many sit-up you do?" she asked.

I grinned. "All of them," I said with a wink.

There was club music playing in the little café, and the girls seemed more than eager to show off their dancing skills. There were purpose built poles joining the bar to the ceiling, and they took it in turns climbing up onto the bar to dance around the pole. They tried to pressure Opangji into having a go, but she did what I took to be the Thai equivalent of a blush and steadfastly refused.

It was a fun little place. There was no one else in the establishment, just the working girls, Opangji, and myself. The rules regarding customer service are all a bit different in this part of the world to those in Australia. There's nobody suggesting to the girls in hushed whispers that they speak with courteous professionalism and efficiency. Instead, hospitality establishments all seem to want workers that just want to have fun. It's a playful culture, and I like it a lot. Not as stiff and cold as what I'm accustomed to. More human. More personable. Just a hell of a lot more fun and amusing, and after all, I exist to be entertained!

Opangji and I had a few drinks, though it was less of a date and more of a gathering, as the three working girls insisted on being a part of the scene, which was fine by me. They were outgoing and a great laugh to be around. Their energy was seemingly never ending. Finally, Opangji had to return to work, and I walked her back to the entrance to the stadium. I thanked her for the time spent together and we parted ways.

I'd see her again in the morning.

She was always there in the office next to the ring.

I wandered back to the hostel and found Carter waiting for me. I told him all about my date with a Thai girl and he was furious I hadn't taken him along as well.

"I've always wanted to try dating a Thai girl," Carter said, sounding a little wistful. "They're super cute, don't you reckon? And I don't think I've ever seen a Thai girl that didn't have the fittest legs I've ever seen."

It was true. Thai people all look extremely lithe and fit when stood next to your typical westerners, and the girls can be quite spectacular.

"Just so long as they're really girls," I said pointedly.

"Ah, yes indeed, my good man," Carter said, slapping my shoulder heartily and adopting a strange, posh accent. "One must forever fear the dreaded penis-girls of Thailand."

"So, what are you up to then?" I asked. "Have you had lunch?"

"Breakfast, you mean?" Carter chortled. "Yep, I'm all caught up. Want to get a pair of scooters or something and go for a ride?"

"Scooters?"

"Sure, why not? We can just cruise up into the mountains or something, I dunno. Follow the signs, try to find something cool. What do you think?"

I shrugged. "Sounds like fun. Let's do it."

And so, Carter and I strolled down the road until we found a place leasing out scooters. They cost us 250 Thai Baht for twenty-four hours, which was around $8AUD. Cheap as chips for our own, personal mode of transportation.

Traffic in south-east Asia is infamous, and it's a reputation of notoriety that is well deserved, although Chiang Mai isn't too bad, comparatively. The lines on the road don't appear to mean anything, scooters cluster together and move about like schools of fish, all squeezing around bigger vehicles like the ocean crashing over rocks. Driving in south-east Asia is tremendous fun, just provided you're armed with the knowledge that, truly, anything goes.

What I fear a lot of people fail to understand is that we don't live in a legal world. There's no law in nature that ensures humans obey human rules and regulation, and Thai roads are just one such prime example of this. We live in the real world, with a whole series of cleverly designed, *artificial* worlds superimposed and overlaid on top. The business world, the financial world, the political world – these are all simply overlays. In other words, don't be offended when somebody careers through an intersection, comes to a screeching halt in front of your garishly-coloured scooter, brandishes a knife at you and demands that you hand over the mangoes. Those sorts of people live in the real world, and you live in a fantasy. It's up to you, though. We created these fantastical worlds and overlays for a reason, presumably.

Carter and I spent half an hour or so having a great time weaving through the outrageous Chiang Mai traffic before we turned off and headed vaguely north, towards the mountains.

We took a few turns at random and found ourselves climbing and weaving into heavily forested hillsides.

There were signs pointing towards village home-stays and we continued to turn off onto smaller and smaller roads, until the bitumen gave way altogether and was replaced with dirt and gravel tracks. I doubted our little scooters – mine was bright purple – were designed for tracks like those, but we persisted, getting ourselves thoroughly lost in a spectacularly foreign landscape. We passed tiny outposts where Thais rested in bamboo huts with no walls. Cooking smoke filtered out onto the road occasionally, and Carter and I soon stopped at one little hut where there was a clear drum of gasoline and a hand-pump.

Nobody out there in that neck of the woods spoke a word of English, and so we were down to hand gestures and body language, which was more than sufficient to get our tanks filled and a few mangoes and bottles of water to share.

We got on the bikes again and continued our weaving climb. The dense forest soon gave way to huge vistas. We were a surprisingly long way up by then, and the view down over the valleys were breathtaking. The mountains were steep, and I was astonished to see the distinctive broad brimmed hats worn by Asian farmers moving about, way up on the side of the mountains during the heat of the afternoon.

Carter and I were exchanging eager points and gestures all afternoon long, making sure we each saw and appreciated the world that we were driving through. We saw wild elephants lumbering along on a distant hillside, huge, terraced rice fields, little farm huts, surreal shades of green, and Thai farmers, all working their fields way up there in the middle of seemingly nowhere.

We were truly a long way from any kind of developed civilization by then – if not geographically, at least. Chiang Mai was only a few hours away, but the nearest electricity pole or phone line could've been on another planet for how isolated it felt out there in the mountains.

The few people that we saw all stopped what they were doing and turned to watch the garishly coloured scooters winding past along the ancient, rutted paths. It must've been quite a bizarre sight to them. I easily assumed that they had never seen another tourist on a scooter in that particular part of the world.

Carter and I stopped on the side of a mountain to watch the sunset, and we were pleasantly surprised when a local man called out to us and waved us up towards a track that led to his house. His wife and children were inside and the smell of cooking pervaded the air. There was no easy way to communicate. We spoke no Thai and they spoke no English, but the warm gestures and expressions were made with clear intent.

We were officially invited to dinner.

Carter and I were delighted to accept the offer, in the middle of nowhere, high up in the north Thailand mountainous jungle. It felt ancient. It felt as if we had stepped into another time – one long lost to industrialization and modernization and development and innovation.

Even out there, however, I noticed that one of the young girls was wearing Nike sandals on her feet. They were dirty and old, but nonetheless, American consumerism had still managed to find its nagging way into that tiny countryside abode.

A peculiar little part of me wished that I was out there experiencing that on my own, without Carter. There are beautiful places in northern Thailand, and I had found a new favourite.

I really love serene places. Quiet places. Solitary places. I place a high value on time spent in my own company. I rarely feel lonely. I have my own thoughts for companionship, and, when they have gone quiet, I have the trees, the animals, the insects, and the ghosts of history to keep me company.

I value the peacefulness.

The modern world can be a deafening place, and it's all too easy to get swept along in the tide of white noise and be utterly carried away. Lines can become blurred and then disappear altogether. Returning to myself in the natural world is a little bit like hitting the reset button. Re-grounding myself. Re-identifying the distinction between that which is superfluous and that which truly matters.

Dinner was difficult to pin down. There were potatoes and lots of different kinds of vegetables and plant-life. The meat was impossible to say. It was delicious, however. Too spicy for my liking, but I could still appreciate the consummate skill of the cooking.

The Thai family seemed content to chat amongst themselves whilst Carter and I stared around the dwelling. There was a single car battery that was powering the sole ceiling light and turning a small fan. I got up and traced another electrical cable out the back door and found that the battery was being charged by a small, hydraulic wheel, sitting neatly in a little stream.

It was a delightfully simple little setup. Self-sufficient and tidy.

Saying thank-you and goodbye was an awkward process, but the Thai smiles seemed to indicate understanding. We all bowed to each other and high-fived the kids and then Carter and I got back on our bikes and puttered off again into the fast-encroaching darkness.

Darkness comes quickly in the tropics.

It wasn't yet 8 o'clock, but the stars were already out on display.

"Know where we're going?" Carter asked after we had followed the driveway back onto a track that we recognized.

I shrugged. "Downwards," I said. "So long as we are heading downwards and south-east, we should find a major road or some signs that point to Chiang Mai."

"Ok then." Carter sounded doubtful, but I was reasonably confident. It can be an intimidating feeling being lost in a foreign country, particularly being lost so far from a civilization that we were familiar with, but I had long since become accustomed to the feeling. A couple of years prior, I had trekked alone for four weeks through the Nepalese Himalayas. I got lost on numerous occasions and slept in the snow in the most extreme wilderness I had ever encountered, but I had survived then, and I would survive now. At least on this occasion we were warm, we had each other, and we had scooters. Getting lost is where the fun starts. It's character building.

I've taken it upon myself in my life to proactively seek out suffering. It's a big part of the reason why I love to fight so dearly. It's not so much about the fighting, it's about teaching myself to appreciate the times when I'm *not* fighting. It is the same for anything. One cannot really appreciate warmth until one has been cold. One cannot really appreciate drinking fresh water until one has been on the verge of dying from thirst. One cannot appreciate the warmth and comfort of a mattress and blankets until one has slept on the cold, hard ground in bad weather.

Suffering is one of life's most important teaching instruments – one which the modern world has largely weaned itself off of. Suffering teaches appreciation for what you have, and it ingrains within you the most important attitude of all – that being gratitude. There is no emotion more healthy in life than gratitude. Not love or joy or happiness. Being grateful trumps the lot, and if you can develop just such an attitude through time spent actively suffering, then you can learn to always find things to be grateful for, even in the most dire of circumstances. It is for precisely this reason why I have always found that people who we might consider to be "worse off" in life, are always the kindest, most compassionate, and most grateful. It's extraordinary to visit a place so poverty stricken and to realize that all the people residing there are more contented and happier with their lives and have less to complain about than people living in the developed west. Capitalism teaches us to always want for more – the complete opposite of that which gratitude teaches us. We have built a society upon foundations of greed and inherent complaining.

The not-so-simple cure for our western greed is suffering. It's also the greatest test of a man's character. I find myself incapable of trusting those who haven't walked into a few good punches in their time and come out smiling on the other side.

Up ahead, I saw Carter applying the brakes on his scooter and I followed suit, wondering what he was doing.

We came to a stop in the middle of the road together. The only light was provided by that of our headlights – small pinpricks in the otherwise oppressive darkness.

"Ok, where in the known universe are we?" Carter wondered aloud, staring around at the densely forested surroundings. It felt like a scene from a movie. Animals were making their respective sounds. I imagined I could hear monkeys rustling about in the canopies. It was entirely possible that I wasn't imagining it.

I wasn't too concerned about being lost. I can usually visualize where we are on a map in my head and figure it all out. My sense of direction is typically uncanny.

I pulled up the trusty map in my head and consulted it. I spun it this way and that and consulted it some more.

"Asia," I concluded.

Carter was quiet for a moment. "You're sure?" he asked, deadpan.

I consulted the map again. Rustled it around and squinted at it. Zoomed it in and then zoomed it back out. I thought about the villages and landscapes that I knew and I plotted their locations on the map. I pictured the distinctive mountain peaks and the petrol stop and the waterfalls. I located all my points of reference and then used them to triangulate our position.

"90% sure," I concluded.

Carter sighed and turned his engine off.

The headlight automatically turned off with it.

I followed suit.

The silence and darkness was sudden and oppressive.

There was no denying it any longer. We were completely lost.

I climbed off my scooter, took my helmet off and went and leaned against a tree. It was back to the drawing board. The sun had completely set, so I couldn't use its location to figure out where North lie. I could've found South using the southern cross if I was in the southern hemisphere (multiply the length from the two furthest stars by a factor of four, go directly downwards and your facing South!), but that wasn't much good to me now. I'd heard about the North Star in the northern hemisphere. Apparently it precisely identifies north in the night sky and it never moves. Polaris, I believe it's called. Feeling suddenly hopeful, I looked up at the sky. My hopes faded immediately. There must've been millions of the damn things up there. No way of knowing which was the North one.

I listened intently, hoping to hear the sounds of civilization carried on the breeze. Perhaps there was a farming village nearby that grew rice and maybe I'd be able to hear chopsticks clinking against each other and the dull vibration of human speech if I listened closely enough...

Nothing.

Jungle noises.

Nothing else.

"Well, this road has to lead somewhere, right?" I reasoned.

"I'm just about out of petrol," Carter said. "And I don't want to walk in the dark."

"Well, when you run out you can just jump on the back of mine," I suggested. "We'll just follow this road for hours if we have to until we find something."

"And what are we going to do about the scooter?" Carter asked. He didn't sound too pleased with the situation. He sounded like he thought it was my fault, which was a definite possibility.

"We'll come back for it in the morning," I said.

"It will get stolen."

"By who?"

"Look, I'm not just going to blindly follow some fucking road. It could take us to fucking China for all we know."

I consulted my map again and then shook my head in the dark. "I don't think we've got enough petrol for that." I was pretty sure I could find our way back. We had been riding for maybe 8 hours, averaging perhaps 30 kilometers an hour, roughly. That meant that we could've potentially travelled almost 250 kilometers, so we probably *could've* been in China already, but I doubted it. Most of our travelling had been in loops and circles and twists and turns and we had doubled back on ourselves on several occasions. And I figured the borders with Burma and Laos would come with checkpoints and armed guards and stamps and paperwork, and we hadn't seen anything like that. No, we were still in Thailand. Somewhere in Thailand. Northern Thailand, most presumably. Somewhere west and north of Chiang Mai. I wasn't sure whether we were further to the north or further to the west, but we were definitely somewhere in that quadrant. Unless we weren't. But we were, I was confident of that. We needed to be heading in a general south-easterly direction, and then chances were good that we would see a sign or encounter a major road. The problem now was that, with the sun having set, I couldn't tell which direction we were heading in. The roads were twisting relentlessly and the terrain was studded with mountains and the road folded back on itself constantly as we weaved our way nearer to ocean level. Quite simply, we were lost. Yet still, I didn't *feel* lost. I couldn't really rationalize it or explain it, but I felt like we were close to getting ourselves back on track.

"Let's just push on a little further," I said, grabbing my helmet again. "We know we have to get down out of these mountains, so that's a start, then we can figure it out from there, but I reckon we're going the right way."

Carter shrugged. "If you say so," he said, starting up his engine once again. Onwards we rode.

The hunter's lot, the lonely night,
The darkened, heavy skies.
For life or death, the hunt begins,
Remorseful, anguished cries.
Kill he must, or be himself;
Hunted dusk til dawn.
An ancient field, a killing floor,
The hours crawl 'til morn.
Lace the shoes and draw the sword,
A legacy is hewn.
He asks but one of favours owed,
Arise: the hunter's moon.

CHAPTER 10
THINGS ARE LOOKING ROSIE

> *"If you even dream of beating me,*
> *you had better wake up and apologize."*
> – Muhammad Ali

Carter and I eventually found our way back into Chiang Mai. We limped into a petrol station and then we were back on our way. It was almost 11pm and I was more than a little hungry.

We got the quickest food we could find and then collapsed into our beds in the dorm room. It had been a long, weary day. My eyes were sore and stinging.

I knew that Carter was leaving early the next morning but we never got around to saying goodbye. Such is how it so often goes. He had been a fine companion.

I was asleep in moments.

At training the next day, Stuart and I were surprised to find that there were now *two* trainers waiting for us. We soon discovered that Ame – despite being a former Lumpinee Stadium champion – wasn't the pinnacle of Thai trainers. Ame had found a friend of his and asked him to come along specifically to help train me for my fight. The new trainer's name was Lek, and he was a beast of a man. Powerful, strong and uncompromising, he was to be my new trainer from this moment on. Ame would train individually with Stuart.

Things were starting to get real.

Lek trained me with an excruciating eye to detail. Every technique was drilled and drilled relentlessly until it was perfect, and then it was drilled some more. We clinched together and I quickly learnt that there are levels to clinching, and I wasn't even close to being as good as I had previously thought that I was. I'd been able to manhandle Ame around the ring – a former champion – and yet Lek was like an immovable tree stump. The strength in his neck was positively freakish, and I couldn't have felt any more humbled by his presence. Here stood a real warrior. As real as it is likely to get. As real a Thai warrior as I am ever likely to meet. The man was a machine, and I cannot overstate that fact.

Emboldened by the presence of my new alpha trainer, I threw kicks hard and heavy, and he returned them with interest. His style was a unique blend of evasive, light-footed defense contrasted with utterly uncompromising offensive power and aggression.

After ten minutes in the ring, Stuart and Ame decided that it would be best for them to exit the ring and train outside the ropes, giving Lek and I the full run of the place so that we could throw each other into the ropes and slam jumping knees into one another with reckless abandon. Indeed, I've never encountered a human-being so utterly invulnerable to physical damage as Lek. I'd get into my positions in the clinch and I would blast his rib-cage with the most savage knee strikes I had ever thrown, and the man wouldn't bat an eyelid.

I would've given anything to see him in action. I couldn't imagine any man ever besting him. Perhaps Lek could've succumbed to a points defeat from time to time, but surely nobody had ever felled him to the canvas. Even with every positional advantage that I could muster, I just couldn't move the guy off his base.

He was as near to my idea of what a perfect fighter would look like as I've ever seen before, and I was lucky enough to share the same ring with him. Short, fast and stocky, with incredibly powerful legs and hips, with a relentless, uncompromising attitude and a fighter's brain that knew the inside of a Muay Thai ring better than the back of his own hands, Lek was a kickboxing God. The Mike Tyson of Muay Thai, if only a few years past his athletic prime. Hell, this guy would've kicked Mike Tyson clean in half if Mike were stupid enough to get into a ring with him.

I was in awe of this man.

The training session ended and I was embarrassed to lie in the ring and have Lek massage Thai boxing ointment into my legs and chest. But I needn't have been. Nothing was below Lek where the wellbeing of his fighter was concerned. I belonged to him now. I knew that as well as I knew that night follows day. I was Lek's fighter, and there are few things that I have accomplished that have made me more proud. I had passed his battery of subtle Muay Thai tests, and now I had him in my corner, and if I knew anything about this man after two hours in a ring with him, I knew that he was utterly immoveable.

Surely, nobody could beat me now.

I returned to the hostel feeling ready and eager to train hard again tomorrow. Training needed to be my first priority now. Leisure time needed a certain criteria – something that had been lacking thus far. From here on out, I promised myself that my leisure time needed to be relaxing and restful. If it was otherwise, then I owed it to myself and to my Thai trainers to say no, and instead stay at the hostel proactively recovering, reading books, writing, eating and drinking, etc.

Easier said than done, to be sure, particularly in certain company.

Later that afternoon in my dorm room, I met Rosie for the first time. Hailing from the Isle of Man, she was intelligent, gorgeous and down to Earth.

There are certain "types" of people in the world – those whom naturally feel most at home in each other's company, as if they are simply operating on the same wave-length. Rosie was my type of person, and we hit it off immediately.

She suggested meeting up later for a drink and I agreed without a second thought. So much for my newfound promise to take it easy. I was silently praying that all of this drinking and socializing wasn't going to come back to haunt me when it came time to fight. I rationalized it all away with my typical shrugging attitude.

I'm feeling fine in training. Fit and strong. She'll be right.

But the feeling of unease followed me out onto the street that night when I decided to beg off company and go to dinner on my own. I promised Rosie I would be back to catch up for a drink after dinner. I was feeling a little unsure of myself for the first time in a long time. The formerly rock-solid answers to all of my self-imposed questions were suddenly feeling empty and dishonest. What was I supposed to be doing there? What was I trying to achieve?

There are moments in life when a certain energy invested in the universe seems to compound, and certain things align all at the same time to present to the right kind of mind, a brief, critical moment of enlightened thinking. Such was the case on that evening, whilst I was eating dinner alone on the curb, and it wasn't a very positive moment.

Sometimes, when I am travelling to poorer countries, I have light-bulb moments where I fully comprehend that I am a jerk. I am a part of all that is wrong in the world. Me, with my mobile phone, my iPad, my branded sneakers, my camera, my sunglasses, my backpack and coca-cola bottles. I would completely understand if the Thai people hated me, but they don't seem to. Their tolerance of the western lifestyle is a humbling experience and it makes me feel like even more of a damned jerk. Some people in this world live hand to mouth, in a way that we of the developed world can scarcely imagine, and they do it every single day of their lives and they do it without complaining. Me, on the other hand – I complain all the time. I whine and I say how life is unfair. I am an asshole and I know it. Travel always reminds me of this little fact. It reiterates the fact, over and over again, like someone banging cymbals inside my head. I spend long moments lying awake at night or staring out of windows on bus trips, seriously considering renouncing my materialistic, spoilt-brat existence and going to live as a monk somewhere, perhaps in a cave, relying on fish from a nearby stream for sustenance. I've given it real, serious thought, and purely as a result of guilt. Deserved guilt, it must be said. It's easy to try to justify my behavior and my way of life by saying that everyone else does it, it's just the way of the world; I was born in Australia and therefore I am entitled to this life whilst the people living in poorer parts of the world deserve their life because the place into which they were born hasn't developed yet. Sometimes, I even postulate that I am pretty *good* for a tourist, and that there are plenty more western tourists that come to countries like Thailand that must be far more spoilt and far more ignorant and far more rude than me. It's bullshit and I know it. It makes me feel better about myself for a while, but it's still bullshit nonetheless. People that make excuses and find ways to justify unfairness are all a part of the problem, and I am one of those people. Nobody likes to consider the fact that maybe, just maybe, I am a bad person. So we justify ourselves to ourselves. We stroke our delicate little egos and then we go and perpetuate the cycle. The guilt weighs on me often and heavy. It is crushing. Sometimes, I cannot help but feel a little relieved to return to Australia, so that I can be surrounded by other spoilt, ignorant, selfish people and so that I can convince myself that, see, everybody behaves this way, so therefore it is ok and therefore I am a good person.

Bullshit.

Perhaps you're wondering why I was feeling this way on that particular occasion… Well, there were beggars on the street where I was eating, and suddenly I was at their level, and I got a long, hard and sobering look at them. I actually *looked* at them for the first time. I had seen them before – the same beggars out on the same street each night in the same spots – but previously I had ignored them with my typically hardened, experienced-traveler, seen-it-all-before-and-not-impressed expression plastered across my face. On that night, however, it was different. It just was.

I sat there on the curb and watched the foreigners walking past along the street, dressed to the nines in their novelty t-shirts and hefting shopping bags with brand names on them. Some people glanced at the beggars, but almost all of them quickly averted their gaze and quickened their pace. I sat there watching for an hour, and, in that time, two people stopped to give coins to respective beggars on the street. Both of those people were young, western men, walking on their own.

I stared at the people that ignored them entirely.

I was feeling a little bit like crying, more out of helplessness than anything else. I wasn't angry at those tourists in particular. I had walked past these same beggars many times now without giving a cent. I'm no less guilty than anybody else in that regard. I was just angry at the entire system of greed that we had created. Perhaps I wasn't entirely mentally prepared for the task

Muay Thai: Peace, At Last

of sitting and observing beggars on the street. These poor, crippled human beings are just a few of the infinite manifestations that are as a result of the pyramid scheme that is capitalist enterprise.

I got up to leave and emptied all of the remaining Thai currency in my wallet into a small cup being held by a man with legs that ended at the thighs. He smiled gratefully, and that made me feel even worse. I walked away, feeling furious at myself, and furious at the world.

Fuck every billionaire in the world.

Fuck everyone who has the power to make a difference and yet does nothing.

I returned to the dorm room and wrote in my travel journal. It was barely coherent, yet it all boiled down to a massive *fuck you* to the unfairness of the world, and a massive *fuck you* to myself, for not being capable of affecting change.

The world depresses me on occasion.

Not my life. I love my life and everything about it. I just hate the world sometimes. The vanity and the greed. The selfishness.

But hey, whatever.

The world keeps on turning, regardless of how I feel about it, apparently.

Rosie and I went out to the familiar THC rooftop bar and we had a few beers together and chatted about life and relationships and anything else we felt like talking about. It was a conversation that is almost certainly familiar to anybody who has been traveling, particularly those who frequent the backpacking scene, and it felt nice to chat peaceably with a sweet, intelligent woman who was on the same page as me. She felt like a real companion – like her problems were my problems, and mine, hers. Even when the conversation lulled and we sipped at our beers whilst the music filled the silence, I was just glad to be with someone else who understood me.

14 days until the fight.

I had the following day off training, so I didn't feel too bad about having a few beers. Rosie had an incredible story to tell. The recent Tunisia terror attacks had hit close to home for her. A female friend of hers had taken a bullet up through the jaw and out through the eye socket, taking the eye with it. That same woman had also lost her husband in the attack, defending her with his body. Human bravery knows no bounds. Courage is the greatest value possessed by someone, so far as I am concerned, and it's something I look closely for in other people. I have a rather strange rule, for instance, when it comes to making friends and trusting people. That's Rule # 4 in my mental rulebook: Never trust someone whom everybody likes. You see, I am of the belief that someone who is liked by all is someone who flits about from side to side, and who is lacking in their convictions. A lack of conviction means a lack of courage, and how can you ever trust someone who is lacking in courage? It's simple, really.

Naturally, with such stringent criteria, I've always been wary of befriending people, and so I can count my real friends on a single hand. In my opinion, that's excellent. Like anything else in the world, the value of my friendship will dilute if I hand it out to anyone who wants a piece. My friendship must be earned, and it's earned with courage and selflessness.

That is part of the reason why I have so much time and respect for Muay Thai fighters. Nobody can ever question the courage of a man or woman prepared to step into a ring to engage another person in a violent fight – one that can end with debilitating injuries. Courage is the quality that enables all others. Without a foundation of courage to rest upon, everything else in a person is fake – their values, their beliefs, their words, their promises, everything.

Nothing elicits respect the way an act of bravery will. And in order to know bravery, you must first know fear. Without one, you cannot have the other.

Martial arts are such incredible instruments of character-building. Few things in life can act as more powerful a catalyst for change as can real, competitive fighting. Humans are built to fight, and for a very good reason.

Rosie and I strolled back to the hostel and it was off to sleep.

Early the next morning, Rosie brought me tea up to the busy dorm room before she left and went on her way to find the next story in her traveling adventure. She had flitted in and out of my life, like flicking a switch on and off, but we would stay in contact and I would come to count her as a friend.

The rest of the day was spent resting, reading and listening to music. There was as much eating and non-alcoholic drinking undertaken as I could manage. Proactive recovery. I watched old Muay Thai fights on YouTube and dedicated as much of my thinking time as possible to visualizing and studying my upcoming fight. Visualizing is an important tool in a fighter's arsenal – for any athlete or performer, really. Your nervous system controls your movements and your mind controls your nervous system. Muscles have only secondary roles to play in the game of movement. Visualizing helps to train the nervous system, making the scenario seem as real as possible in your mind and then imagining, *visualizing* your own physical actions. Repeat as often as possible until your responses become ingrained, by mental repetition alone. It's a huge part of training, and it's one that I am particularly good at. Visualizing the fight before it happens can also help a fighter stay calm, because, having already envisioned the fight a million times, he won't be entering into the unknown come fight time. It's important to note that your opponent is going to be doing the same thing – visualizing a positive outcome of the fight, and so there are tactics that I like to employ early in a fight that will shatter those pre-conceived notions of success in the mind of my opponent – effectively bursting the bubble and exposing them once again to fear, and all that comes along with that

most powerful of emotions. One of the things I like to do is talk to my opponent and say whatever I can think of to throw him off guard. Of course, I've already *visualized* myself saying these things, and so it has no effect on me, but it can seriously unbalance an opponent if you do something they're not expecting. I also like to suddenly and sharply alter my behavior in the opening round. Maybe appear relaxed, smiling and friendly when we touch gloves and for the first few engagements, and then completely change tack and throw an unrelenting assault of elbows strikes into their face and growl and shout at my opponent like some kind of deranged animal. Whatever it takes to catch an opponent out from their pre-conceived plan and get them fighting *reactively*, effectively handing control of the fight over to me.
There's a more simple term for these kinds of tactics.
Mind games.
I absolutely love mind games, and I feel that they are underused at the most elite level, so much so as to almost appear negligent. Go and ask a lion if they think their roar is an effective hunting tool. Well, humans also have voices for a reason. Fighting is the furthest form of communication, and our voices can be extremely potent weapons when deployed correctly. Similar to a lion's roar, the human voice, when used correctly and aggressively, can instill in others the powerful *freeze* response that I've mentioned previously, where the brain simply stops thinking cognitively.
The best fighters in the world are the most intelligent.
I value intellect in the ring more highly than strength.
And so I spent the day with my eyes closed, watching the fight unfold, watching the various positions and responding. I listened to the crowd and I felt the heat and humidity in the centre of the ring. I felt the rough touch of the canvas floor on my bare feet. I saw the referee out the corner of my eye.
Over the course of the day, I must've played the fight in my head more than a thousand times, and in every single instance, I emerged victorious, with my arm raised to the cheering crowd. Naturally, I was in a terrific mood when the sun began to set. The mind is an amazing thing. True freedom exists solely in the mind. I don't think there's ever really any such thing as complete, physical freedom. Nature has her own laws, but the mind has none. I believe that the only people to ever have experienced real freedom are those who are insane, or perhaps on drugs.
I went to bed that night feeling more ready than ever to fight. I was craving that fight. I was yearning for my moment in the ring. Sleep was slow in coming.
13 days until the fight.
Burning myself out wasn't a concern. I've heard that it's all too easy for fighters to burn themselves out, be it emotionally, physically, or both, in the

lead-up to a fight, but I've never encountered it. Mine is a cold fury. It simmers, it rarely boils. In fact, that is something that I was craving for this fight. In my prior fighting experience, I had never fought with rage-fuelled abandon. My fights have always been relatively calm affairs, for me, anyway. I'd had seven professional Muay Thai fights up to that point, and they had almost always ended in the 2nd round, by way of knockout, and I've never gone away from a fight feeling like I couldn't fight again the next day if I wanted to. Mine is a patient style. Precise. Calculated. Calm and easy. Efficient. And I was tired of that style. I wanted the rage to reach a boiling point. I wanted to find the edge and then cross over it. I wanted to throw all caution to the wind and lash out blindly at anything and everything. I wanted to go a little bit wild, and I wanted this to be the fight in which I would do it.

Strangely, I wanted fighting to be *more* stimulating. It might seem bizarre, perhaps, but I suspect that this phenomenon is one understood by all problem gamblers, drug-abusers and adrenaline junkies. Once you've had a taste, you just want more, and you want it harder and faster and more dangerous than ever.

I am aware of my youth and of its fleeting nature. I am aware that someday my drive and my desire and my passion for fighting will inevitably peter out. With my own mortality front and centre, I want to make the most of an impassioned youth. I want that bloodlust and that passion in my life. I am sincere in the belief that the meaning of life is that we die, and with that in mind, I make it my all-consuming mission to live as vividly as possible. I want to really taste food, I want to really love and I want to be really hurt and I want to know that I am alive. We can hide from our feelings as much as we like, or we can live. It's a personal decision, and I choose to live. I want to be as alive and as vibrant as it is possible to be. If I'm going to die regardless, I might as well live a little whilst I can. All too often, abstract desires to live a fulfilled life are trampled by the everyday realities of law and order, regulation, database registries and paperwork. Few things are more frustrating to me than the lack of stimulation offered in a regulated society. Invisible chains are everywhere, always *preventing* life from transpiring, and never enabling it.

And so there dwells a rebel in my soul. But rebellion is a lonely thing. By definition, it has to be. Conformity becomes inevitable when people gather in groups to rebel. Bikie gangs have completely missed the point. To join a gang is to seek companionship and validation, not rebellion. Perhaps they ought to rebrand themselves. Loneliness is the price of rebellion. The price of conformity, however, is boredom, and I consider that to be a torture of a far greater magnitude. Show me to my lonely place in the world. No, actually, never mind. I'll find it myself.

People are leaving the System in never-before-seen numbers, throwing off the society we designed to seek out self-sufficient hiding places amongst the birds and the trees. Oh, the things it says about our System…
Maybe someday it will all fall apart, and then life will truly begin.
Or maybe, in a fit of boredom, we'll burn it down ourselves.
We built it, after all.

Michael Goodison

Who'd dare to live a life of crime,
    when Hell awaits those few?
Best we all had shut our doors
    and cower from the view.
Indeed, sometimes, in certain lights,
    that Hell looks awful fine.
But don't be fooled, they swear, I'm told;
    it's dancing, sex and wine.
Every day and endlessly,
    'til never comes around,
The pirates steal, the fighter's fight, and lovers go around.
I'd hate to think what hellish times
    those poorly suffer there,
In Heaven they could play the harp
    or breathe the hallowed air.

CHAPTER 11
WHEN ALL ELSE FAILS

> *"Tension is who you think you should be.*
> *Relaxation is who you are."*
> – Chinese Proverb

"Ok, sparring. Three minute. Change. Ok?"

There was a new guy at training, taking our little gang from two members to three. I didn't like the new guy. He was a bodybuilder type of guy from France. Brash, arrogant, bullying. He looked down his nose at the Thai trainers and sneered at myself and Stuart.

Finally, after doing all the pad work and skipping, the three of us got a chance to do some sparring.

There was only two pairs of gloves, and Stuart and the Frenchie were wearing them, so they took centre ring and went first. I leant against the ropes alongside the two Thais and observed.

The Frenchie had no talent at all, and he went completely berserk as soon as the Thais said to begin, throwing heavy punches at Stuart, who backed up and defended haplessly. After three minutes, the big French guy was heaving and dripping in sweat, but he looked delighted to have had the chance to beat up Stuart for the full round. I glanced at the Thais and they nodded me into the centre of the ring. Stuart was pulling his gloves off and cursing under his breath. I knew how he felt. The bullying, talentless Frenchman had no class about him, and clearly possessed no understanding about the purpose of sparring.

I pulled on Stuart's gloves and took centre ring, facing the Frenchie. Up close, he really was a big guy. Maybe 190 centimeters tall and nudging 100 kilograms of fake tan, muscle and tattoos. He was a regular bad boy, and he was sneering at me. "I thought you said you guys had been training for weeks?" he goaded in that silly French accent.

I sneered back. I hate bullies. Can't fucking stand them.

"Three minute. Sparring," Lek said as way of a green light.

The Frenchie banged his gloves together and marched forwards, and I loaded up and slammed an angry, full-force kick into his forearms, which backed him up slightly and halted his advance.

"You're allowed to kick in Muay Thai," I said to him, mocking his battery of punches that he had thrown at Stuart in the prior round. I followed the roundhouse kick with a stomping front kick to the abdomen, forcing the burly Frenchman off balance and bouncing him off the ropes.

The Frenchman responded to my jibe by grunting snidely and then heaving into another barrage of punches. I covered up and stood my ground, letting the punches slam into my arms and shoulders. They were heavy, cocky punches, and a couple of them managed to take my breath away.

There's something about getting hit that further enrages the male brain. It does mine, anyway. Frenchie had hit me and he had hit me hard, and now I wanted to kill the arrogant clown. But I also wanted to do it with Muay Thai. I didn't want to engage him with wild punches and brawl with him. I didn't want to descend to his level.

I pushed away from the barrage of punches and plastered a bored, is-that-all-you-got look across my face. "Kicks, remember?" I said to him pointedly. I feinted with the next kick, drawing his eye and forcing him to cover up, and then I stepped into the space created and initiated the clinch, which I immediately used to throw an enraged series of knee strikes at the torso. I've always been of the opinion that the fastest way to a guy's heart is directly through the rib cage. I had backed him up against the ropes now, and I hit him with another quick series of knee strikes. There are levels of power in the world of fighting, and knee strikes take the crown. The Frenchie doubled over and went down to his haunches and clutched at the rope. I backed off with feigned concern on my face.

I can be about as competitively stubborn as they come.

The Thai trainers stood there silently, watching the Frenchman with disinterest. There was still time left in the round and nobody was coming to stop the bout. There's nowhere to hide in a Muay Thai ring, and least of all when you're hurt and you're losing and you're humiliated. The Thais, perhaps more than anyone else, understood the importance of respect in the ring, and I was willing to bet that they would've stepped in themselves for round three of sparring with the Frenchie had I not managed to beat him down myself.

Frenchie got to his feet and did exactly what I expected him to do. He launched himself at me with furious abandon. Sometimes, offense is the best defense, but not on this occasion. Standing in my natural southpaw stance, I braced against my legs and extended my right glove firmly into Frenchie's face, stopping his advance and effectively blinding him at the same time, and then I threw a couple of easy, distracting left punches at his arms and face, which he hurriedly blocked. He threw his left arm and chest into a wild hook across my right arm, trying to bat it away from his face, which was exactly what I was waiting for. I allowed my right arm to come down, pulling his right glove down with it, whilst his left whistled across uselessly in between us.

There it was.

The opening.

Huge and beckoning, right down the middle.

Stepping out slightly forwards and to the right to establish some momentum, I bunched my left thigh and launched my entire bodyweight behind my left hand, which connected clean as a whistle, catching the Frenchie as his weight was transferring forwards, *into* the punch.

I've heard it said that horses can fall asleep whilst standing up. Well, humans can do it too. The Frenchman's oversized head snapped back violently, and that was all she wrote.

Big, burly bodybuilder-man crumpled to the canvas and didn't move an inch.

I growled in my throat and exhaled.

Motherfucker.

Some people just deserve exactly what they get.

Nobody was in a hurry to go to the Frenchman's side. After a moment, Ame nudged himself off the ropes and strolled forward to roll the Frenchie onto his side and ease his mouth guard out of his mouth so that he didn't suffocate to death.

Thailand can be a rough place to the unsuspecting.

"Nice one," Stuart said into the relative silence.

I just nodded and bit into the Velcro straps on the gloves, sliding them off my hands. That punch had felt bloody satisfying.

I caught Lek's piercing gaze and held it for a second. There was silent approval there, I was sure of it. Pride, even.

12 days until the fight.

Stuart and I left the Thais to tend to the Frenchman. We walked back down the alley, past the dwarf, feeling like two conquering avengers. I was still angry, and I cooled off in the showers. My temper receded along with my temperature and everything slowed back down again. I spent the rest of the day battling flare-ups in my mood. The testosterone was starting to really pile up as my body anticipated the coming fight. I was chomping at the bit to get back into the ring with an audience assembled and put on a show.

Stuart had two black eyes at training the following morning, and he seemed proud of them. Brits are an interesting lot. They cop a proper battering and they say thank-you.

There was no sign of the Frenchman and nobody even mentioned him.

I trained with Lek again. We worked on catching, evading and blocking body kicks and then counter-striking. It was a good session – highly technical. I felt as if my cardiovascular ability had markedly improved as a result of my training now. Where before I was struggling to complete the 2 hours of training, now I was breezing through it, throwing all of my strikes with full power behind them. Clinching was still exhausting, but I was learning clinch techniques that would force a stalemate and give me a chance to rest and catch my breath for a moment if I felt I needed it during the fight.

"You fight, win," Lek said at the end of the session, nodding his approval. He sounded confident. "You fight Thai, no problem for you. Strong IQ. Strong kick. Strong punch."

I nodded gratefully. A little confidence boost from the coach doesn't hurt from time to time. Thais aren't usually big on feedback, so I appreciated the pep talk. Lek thought I was ready, and that was important. Thais tend to know what they're talking about when it comes to the game of fighting.

I did extra training on my own in the afternoon. I ran around the old city walls of Chiang Mai and then did pushups and pull-ups using the shower stalls as gym equipment.

11 days until the fight.

I was sleeping well. I hadn't touched alcohol in a few days. I was injury free. Everything was feeling good. I felt fast, fit and strong. Even the act of climbing into the top bunk felt athletic and lithe. I tried to plan what I wanted to achieve from the next week and a half of training. I wasn't sure if my fitness could improve much more, of if it even needed to. I could easily last five rounds of a Muay Thai fight now if I had to. I didn't want to learn too much more now, either, for fear of overloading my mind too close to the fight. Now, I just wanted to drill what I already knew, and then drill it some more. Repetition and then some more repetition. That's what makes good fight training. A re-wiring of the brain. Most importantly of all, I had to avoid getting injured in the lead up to my fight. Nothing would infuriate me more than tweaking a muscle or bumping an ankle or overextending a shoulder. Maintenance of the body and repetition in training. That was the plan.

I woke up the next day feeling sore and fatigued. I wasn't sure why. Perhaps I had overdone it with two training sessions the day before. I had slept for at least 10 hours and yet still, I was exhausted.

I decided that what my body needed at that point was rest. I wondered down to the stadium and found Opangji there in her office. I asked her to tell Lek that I was taking the day off training to rest, but I would be back again the following day. She promised me that she would pass on the message.

Knowing that I didn't have to train that day, I immediately felt my mind and body relax. I hadn't even noticed that I had been tense, but now I understood why I was still so tired. I was burning out my mind. Despite all my confidence to the contrary, I was simply being too intense. As I ought to know all too well, intensity is a bad thing in fighting, but it can sometimes be difficult to avoid. As surprising as it may sound to those already well-acquainted with hard training, it's better to listen to reggae music than heavy metal music during your time off. Passive energy expenditure is every bit as important as active energy expenditure, and you can exhaust yourself by not switching the intensity off in between training sessions. I decided that the best thing for me on that day would be to not think about fighting. No visualizing anything, no mind conditioning work, no training, just resting and distracting myself.

I had heard about something people were calling the "Grand Canyon." Apparently it was a swimming hole nearby to Chiang Mai, at which you could jump off of cliffs into the water. It was supposed to be a very nice place. The sun was burning hot, as it so often is in Thailand, and so, after breakfast, I stuck my hand out, got on a tuk-tuk, asked to go to the Grand Canyon, and reclined luxuriously as the warm air rushed past my face.

It didn't disappoint.

The Grand Canyon turned out to be an old, open cut mine of some kind, which was now half-filled with deep, perfectly turquoise fresh water. There were sheer cliffs rimming all around the water, with a sole narrow path leading down to the water's edge. If you couldn't be bothered making the walk down to the water level, you were encouraged to simply jump in via the cliffs.

There were only a couple of other people there when I arrived. My tuk-tuk driver gestured me towards the cliffs and laughed and then said that he would wait for me.

I snapped a few quick photos before strolling down to the edge of the water. I'd been a lifeguard for five years in an earlier life. I wasn't quite silly enough to jump into foreign, unknown waters without testing them first. I stripped down to my shorts and eased into the water. It was delightfully lukewarm. Perfect temperature. You could swim in it all day long. And it was fresh and tasted faintly of minerals that had seeped into it from the surrounding rocks. Down at water level, I realized that the canyon was deceptively large. It was huge, in fact. It might've been as much as four hundred meters across to the far side, and then there were small gaps in the jarring walls that would lead an adventurous swimmer out into another pool on the far side. I spotted old, Thai houses situated on the far cliffs overlooking the water. They would've had a spectacular view from their vantage point.

There were small, bamboo rafts attached to ropes meandering aimlessly out in the middle of the water, and so I swam out to one of them and lay on it, like a lizard basking in the sun, half in and half out of the water.

I watched a small snake darting across the surface of the water, looking panicked about something. The scene was incredibly peaceful. After a time, I looked back up at the cliffs and tried to gauge their heights. The lower cliffs might have been three or four meters above the water level. The higher ones were closer to twelve or fifteen.

How could I say no to something like that?

I strolled back around and then edged out along the cliffs, heading straight for the highest point I could find. The place was deserted now. I had the entire canyon to myself. My own, private, playground paradise.

I stepped up to the edge of the cliff and gazed down at the water far below. As always, it looked a lot higher from the edge. I knew that the water below was deep and clear. There was nothing in the water that I might hit, and I wouldn't be able to get even close to touching the bottom.

The sun was shining down hot upon the scene, and I could feel a slight breeze licking around my shorts. I felt so far from anything up there. So utterly and beautifully isolated. No rules, no one to stop me or supervise. They treat people like adults in Thailand. Accountable for your own actions and your own stupidity, should it come to that.

The whole canyon felt still.

In fact, for a brief moment in time, my entire world fell still and calm. Completely silent.

10 days until the fight.

I breathed deeply and stepped out off the edge before I had even realized what I was doing. The surprise was almost more thrilling than the fall, and the fall was even further than I expected. An extra split second that feels like an eternity when you're falling.

Then I hit the water. The lukewarm liquid enveloped me and quickly halted my descent, like an old friend welcoming me back with loving arms. I hung there in the depths of the lake for a little while, suspended in the middle of nothing and enjoying the sensation. I felt so *free* in the middle of such a vast expanse of clear blue water. Surfacing, I swam back across to the path and found a nice grassy place to read my book.

My body – so heavy and lethargic that morning – now felt light and invigorated once again. Exchanging training for adventure and intrigue felt like a weight off my shoulders. Training can be tough, there's no two ways about it. That's the entire point and purpose of training, after all. Getting into the water and allowing the effects of gravity to release their hold, even momentarily, felt exceptionally good. Water is a beautiful thing.

I returned to Chiang Mai in the middle of the afternoon and turned my focus towards eating and drinking. I returned to the small café that Opangji had taken me to and the girls there served me fish and rice, which I ordered three times over. I ate and drank until I could consume no more and then I returned to the hostel to sleep.

I awoke just as others in the dorm room were starting to go to bed. It was dark outside now, but I was feeling fully recharged, rejuvenated, fresh and energetic. I laced up my shoes and strolled out onto the warm night streets to go exploring. It was a nice night for a walk, and I'd been hoping for weeks now to find a cockfighting event. I had heard people talking about them before, and I'd even seen a sign in Thai that appeared to advertise cockfights, but I had seen no other clue. The politically-correct liberals of today might very well call me a barbarian, but I find it entertaining to watch two animals fight for sport. It's an awful lot more entertaining than turning on the evening news or watching some Hollywood bullshit. How narcissistic are we as a species to close our curtains and allow ourselves to be entertained by mirrors when there are animals and stars outside, putting on an eternal show in front of empty seats. I find art to be an interesting study. What people watch or listen to or choose to consume often says a great deal about them as individuals. I don't accept, for example, that children become adults when they turn eighteen, as prescribed by Australian law. Rather, I contend that children become adults when they cease to find entertainment from mirrors, and instead seek out windows. Hollywood, MTV, commercial radio stations, pop culture songs – they all present their audiences with a mirror; something by which the audience can see *themselves* in. Mature artworks, however, present their audience with windows. A child becomes an adult when they cease looking inwards, and find themselves instead looking outwards, and being entertained by what they see. Listening, instead of speaking.

I am here to be entertained.

I didn't find any cockfighting on that night, and I wouldn't find any during my time in Thailand, which was disappointing. Instead, I found three naked British people, swimming happily in the gross waters of the Chiang Mai moat. I got chatting with them and quickly stripped down and joined them in the water. It wasn't remotely as nice as the canyon earlier in the day, but it was a new experience with new people. Skinny dipping in the Chiang Mai moat. The novelty wore off immediately the moment one of the British girls spotted an enormous rat on the bank near our clothes, and we hurriedly got out and dressed ourselves and said goodbye. A brief moment shared with random people. I never even caught their names.

I went back and showered at the hostel to get the smell of the moat out of my nostrils, and then I tiptoed back into the dorm room and napped on and off throughout the remainder of the night.

Training the next day was a relaxed, casual affair. Opangji had told Ame and Lek that I was sore, and perhaps they had taken that to mean that we were over-cooking things. It was entirely possible, but I was feeling much better after my day off. Staying away from alcohol was proving helpful.

Ame and Lek eased Stuart and I through some slow-motion technical training, practicing techniques and discussing fight strategies, and then the four of us walked down the street and into the air-conditioned comfort of a Thai massage parlor. I was yet to visit one of these famous Thai massage joints on my journey. I don't mind massages or being touched by strangers, I just don't really like being touched when it's as hot, humid and sweaty as it so often is in Thailand. Lek knew the girls working in the massage place and they seemed happy to acquiesce to my requesting to use their shower out the back before laying on one of the mattresses laid out on the floor. Stuart, Ame, Lek and I all lay next to each other and relaxed as the girls went about their massaging, whilst soft flute music permeated the air and the smell of incense and scented oils floated delicately throughout the room.

The gym was paying for us apparently, and so the four of us got the better part of three hours on the mattresses. There were brief moments when the massaging resembled a sports massage, whereupon the girls would elicit some kind of pain out of our muscles, but mostly it was just a relaxing experience. I was feeling deeply relaxed and lethargic by the time we left the parlor, and judging by the silence and the body language of the other guys, they were each feeling the same.

Suddenly, Muay Thai training didn't seem so tough after all.

After lunch, I decided I would go and pay a visit to one of the countless Buddhist temples that dotted the Chiang Mai cityscape. I was feeling a little soft and gooey after the morning massage, and some kind of spiritual experience felt like just the right thing to do.

I walked for about twenty minutes and passed several temples before I found one that I had walked past on a prior occasion and liked the look of. It had a grassy entrance and it felt peaceful. Once inside the walls and away from the noise of the street, the serenity of the interior was sudden and beautiful. There were monks in orange robes strolling peacefully around and I caught the eye of some of them and we exchanged respectful head inclinations. The temple itself soared up into the sky; covered in intricate carvings and inlaid with colorful patterns and depictions. There were statues everywhere you looked. Lord Buddha in various positions – seated, lying down, cross-legged, standing – apparently there were seven distinct Buddhist positions, one for each day of the week. Tradition has it that the day on which you were born is represented by a Buddhist position. I was born on a Friday, which the temple shows is represented by a standing Buddha, with his hands folded over his chest. It's called the "contemplating Buddha" position, and people born on a Friday are supposed to be fun-loving, friendly and ambitious, probably an entertainer or public figure. Their lucky day is Tuesday and their lucky color is pink. Their unlucky time is Wednesday night and their unlucky color is light green. I considered this all to be very profound and chord-striking, particularly because I've never liked those light green lollies.

According to the stories, Buddha assumed the Pang Ram Pueng (contemplating Buddha) position shortly after the enlightenment, whilst under the Banyan tree. He claimed at this time to feel disheartened and discouraged from teaching people to attain enlightenment, because the ordinary person is too attached to material things to ever be able to realistically see this truth – namely, nirvana.

I walked up the entrance steps to the temple and removed my shoes, as per the custom, and I entered the realm of the Buddha.

There was nobody inside.

I strolled around, looking at all of the statues and the various carvings and artistic depictions on the ceiling and walls. It was an impressive construction.

I waited patiently, hoping that a monk might feel some disturbance in the balances of the universe and come inside to talk with me and tell me something profound and enlightening – to intimately acquaint me with all of the known wisdom of the universe. Surely, that sort of thing would be helpful before my fight.

Nothing happened, and so I wandered back outside and found a gaggle of monks seated on the grass beside a small water feature. It looked like a nice little spot, and so I approached them and gestured at the ground, asking if I could join them.

There were nods of approval, and so I sat.

They continued to talk in Thai amongst each other, effectively ignoring me. Then, one by one, they got up and left, leaving me alone with the very last monk. He was young – probably younger than me. Maybe just a teenager. However, he spoke English, and so his companions had apparently nominated him to stay and talk with me.

"How's it going, mate?" I asked, extending my hand.

The bald monk smiled and shook my hand.

9 days until the fight.

Michael Goodison

A painter's dream; a canvas blank,
        a world afresh and new,
Imagine what we'd do, old girl,
        with colours green and blue...
Nothing written, nothing drawn,
    nor sculpted, sung or sewn,
No televisions, radios,
    no rules, no lies, no phones...
          A life to live and games to play,
        and nothing in the way,
      Food to eat and girls to meet
      And life can start today...

CHAPTER 12
SPARRING LEK

"I wanted you to see what real courage is, instead of getting the idea that courage is a man with a gun in his hand."
– Harper Lee, *To Kill A Mockingbird*

Although the monk spoke English, it wasn't very good. It was a great deal better than my ability to speak Thai, but communication between the two of us was challenging. Nonetheless, I had come seeking answers, and I am if nothing else, stubborn.

I asked him about what it means to be a monk and why he decided to become a monk. I forgot to ask his name. He told me that he became a monk as a very young boy because he was homeless. He told me that many homeless children in Thailand come to call a temple their home, because Buddhist temples are sustained by the goodwill and donations of their local Buddhist communities. It seemed as good a home for a young person as any. He told me that being a monk is all about balance, calmness and inner peace. It is about controlling and diverting negative emotions and physical desires and learning to control your mind and the energies that you put out into the world – those which can so powerfully affect your surroundings and other people around you. Being Buddhist is about connectivity to other living things, he explained in a round-about type of way, and an awareness of your place within an intricate ecosystem.

I like Buddhism. I've liked Buddhism for a long time. I like what it stands for and I like the values and beliefs that they uphold. I like that there is no praise for some narcissistic deity or God type figure who looks like a Californian surfer. It strikes me as being a very organic, intrinsic religion, based more on feeling than on thought.

However, despite my love for Buddhism, I wasn't learning anything new from this monk, and so I delved deeper into the questioning. I asked him what his thoughts were on Muay Thai and physical fighting. I asked him if there was any kind of wisdom that he wished all westerners knew. And I asked him if he thought I would win my upcoming fight, just on the off chance that he could predict the future.

As it turned out, there was nothing particularly profound that the monk could tell me. He said he didn't know if I would win my fight, he said westerners ought to learn peace and contentment, and he said fighting was not part of Buddhist teachings, but Thailand's culture strongly supports both Buddhism and Thai boxing and he reassured me that the two can co-exist in a single person.

Later that afternoon, I met a dark-skinned guy from Holland. His name was Darryl and he was a fun guy to be around. He was obsessed with every pretty girl that he saw and he spoke a lot about what he termed, "pick-up artistry," but I figured that was probably fair enough. It's the meaning of life, is it not, to fall in love, have kids, etc. Darryl and I spent the evening exploring the streets and sampling different foods from the myriad street vendors that populated Chiang Mai. We soon started drinking beer, and it was at about this time – as we were strolling past one of the exclusive, elite, high-roller, skyscraper motels that are popping up in Thailand's tourist hotspots – that Darryl suggested we go inside and take a look at how the other half live.

I wasn't sure we would be able to get past the front desk, but I shrugged and agreed. I was curious to see inside one of these behemoths of luxury and opulence.

Deciding that a conspicuous, care-free attitude would be the most conducive to success, Darryl and I strolled right up to the front entrance to the nearest luxury motel, still sipping at our beers. The doorman glanced at us briefly and we both ignored him, and he quickly opened the door for us. I was trying not to laugh as we passed into the sudden air-conditioned comfort that belonged to the rich and successful. The lobby was stunning, with enormous artworks on display, lush carpets and rugs, staff members wearing perfectly tailored suits. Meanwhile, standing amongst this not-so-subtle display of wealth and grandeur, Darryl and I were wearing our crappy travelling clothes and sipping at the cheapest beer available from the nearby 7/11, with expressions of supreme indifference plastered across our faces.

"Elevators," Darryl whispered out the corner of his mouth, leading the way across the lobby.

I nodded casually to the gorgeous Thai girl working behind the reception desk, hoping that my confidence was sufficiently belying my somewhat haggard, unwashed and decidedly rural-Australian appearance.

We got into the elevators with a family of Chinese people wearing suits and expensive watches, and it was there that we hit our first snag. The Chinese were looking at us curiously, and their curiosity grew as Darryl and I quickly discovered that we needed to swipe security cards before we could enter our floor number – of which we had over 60 to choose from.

Muay Thai: Peace, At Last

"Oh, you're on 58 as well?" I said, looking at the number that the Chinese family had chosen, right up near the top. "Yeah, us too. Not a bad floor, eh?"

There were polite nods all round and Darryl and I waited silently as the elevator moved excruciatingly upwards, steadfastly avoiding each other's gaze.

The elevator arrived at level 58 and Darryl and I soon discovered that this level held only a single entrance to what must've been an enormous suite or apartment. The Chinese family glanced over their shoulders at us as they closed the door firmly in our faces.

With a *ping*, the elevator doors closed behind us and Darryl and I were left staring at each other.

"Are we stuck?" Darryl asked, hurrying back to the elevator and hitting the call button. The elevator was descending back to the ground floor.

"Must be stairs or a fire escape," I said, glancing around. There was nothing.

Eventually, the elevator returned and we found, to our relief, that we could press the button for the ground floor without needing a security card. Trying not to break into a jog, we strolled back across the lobby floor, nodding again to the pretty Thai girl and ignoring the doorman and then bursting into laughter once we were outside the premises.

"Let's try another one!" I said, looking around eagerly at the skyline and spotting another luxury motel building nearby. "That one!"

We strolled into the next building and were surprise to find that we could easily negotiate this one. The security was minimal and there were plenty of staircases leading every which way. In fact, we soon discovered that the place was much bigger than we had anticipated, and it was a veritable maze. In near darkness and total isolation, Darryl and I explored conference rooms full of chairs and podiums, theatre production suites with half – made stage props and hastily thrown gowns and costumes. There was an unmade mattress on the floor in a dank storage room behind a kitchen, which was surprising. Someone was sleeping there? We made our way to the very top of the building and found ourselves on a huge, sweeping space that was clearly designed for entertaining of the garden-party variety, with decorative bulb plants, statues, and even a stage for a performing band or production of some kind. Most impressively of all, and much to the delight of Darryl and I, there was an outdoor pool. The entire place felt abandoned. Indeed, during our explorations of the building, we had barely encountered another soul, nor heard voices or footsteps. Where was everybody?

It didn't matter. From the rooftop pool, we had an extraordinary view out over the city. We stripped off and dived in, feeling like sea otters in a new ocean playground. The water was freezing and it took our breath away, but it was worth it for the experience. Upon getting out of the pool, we realized that foresight was not our strong suit. Neither of us had a spare change of clothes, nor anything resembling a towel. With a shared shrug and a renewed sense of being invincible – or invisible, even – Darryl and I strolled back out to the elevators in our dripping wet shorts, with our hair all tussled and carrying the rest of our clothes in our arms, and we strolled right back out through the lobby and back onto the street, leaving puddles in our wake.

*

8 days until the fight.
Strangely, my muscles were sore after the massage, but there would be no slacking off in training the following day.
Lek worked me hard with the pads, completing fifteen excruciating rounds before we took our gloves off and clinched with each other. Then, for the first time, Lek told me to put the gloves back on and asked Ame and Stuart to clear the ring.
Lek wanted to spar with me.
I wasn't sure what to feel as I pulled my gloves back on and allowed Ame to strap a shin guard onto my right lower-leg. Between the four of us, we only had a single pair of shin guards, and so we decided that Lek and I would simply wear one each, on our respective right shins.
I was nervous. Lek had nearly 200 professional fights to his name, and they had been almost entirely triumphant experiences. I glanced at his left shin – exposed and lethal, with no shin guard on it to soften the blow should he hit me with it. I didn't want to get kicked with that leg. Anybody who has been hit by a Muay Thai roundhouse kick will understand what I'm talking about. It feels like being hit by someone swinging a baseball bat, only baseball bats aren't sharp in the way that shin bones are.
Ame had his phone out to time the bout and he indicated that we should begin.
I leaned back against the top rope and pretended to stretch out my chest, buying a tiny bit of time so as to get my composure and ready my game face. This would be a lot different to sparring with Stuart. This was against a master tradesman, and Lek's trade was that of inflicting pain.
Lek waited for me in the centre of the ring, which was polite of him. He wasn't pressing the issue too much, which I quietly appreciated, though I felt my pride stinging ever so slightly. We started out slowly, as sparring usually does, prodding forward with easy range-finder jabs and thip kicks. We rocked back and forwards, easing the weight across both feet, prepared to switch our weight at any time to either defend or attack. Balance is critical, and I was focused intently on my weight distribution. I knew Lek

would be watching for any mistakes. If my weight got too far over my front foot, he would hit my thigh with a leg kick I wouldn't be able to defend. If I got too far back on my rear foot, he would press forward with punches that I wouldn't be able to answer. Whilst Lek was watching me, I was watching him with equal care. We were feeling each other out.

Sometimes I wonder if the human body might not be better suited to deal with life and combat were it equipped with three legs instead of two. Three points of contact just seems better, I think…

Lek struck a lightning fast thip to the front of my left hip, though I saw it coming and leant my waist back slightly, catching only the last inch or so of momentum before firing back with the exact same kick. It was like a chess match. He moved his pawn forwards and I mirrored him precisely.

Back to you, sir.

I was standing in the orthodox position to copy Lek, though I usually prefer to stand southpaw to favor the power in my left hand. He telegraphed a leg kick and then changed suddenly halfway through the move and instead threw a front, stomping kick. He was aiming for my chest, but I knew this move better than the back of my hand, having seen Lek employ it so often during our pad work together. He adored that tricky little move. The idea was to draw a check on the leg kick and then use the off-balancing to push me onto my butt, but I countered the move by stepping backwards out of orthodox and easily into southpaw, and the stomp kick slid harmlessly off my sweaty torso. Most importantly, however, Lek had made a mistake! It was an over-confidence mistake. Evidently, he had expected the kick to land and had anticipated using the force of the connection to correct his balance, but instead, he had met with no resistance and so he fell forwards ever so slightly, and suddenly we were in a clinch and wrestling fiercely.

I preferred this kind of battle, particularly against a lethal kicker like Lek. He couldn't kick me whilst we were clinched up, and I most definitely didn't want to get drawn into an extended kicking war with him, because he would win, simple as that, and I genuinely feared getting injured against him. I couldn't afford anything worse than a minor injury this close to my actual fight.

We exchanged knee strikes politely, using the inside of our thighs rather than the point of the knee. I saw a few openings to throw an elbow, but elbows are frowned upon in sparring. Lek managed to outwork me, and, just as I was gearing up to throw another knee strike, he countered my momentum and swung me around onto the canvas. I rolled back up to my feet in an instant and was ready to march back into the fray when Ame called time on the first round.

Stuart poured water into my mouth. "Having fun?" he asked.

"He's bloody strong," I said.

"You were doing alright earlier on, I thought. Before you started clinching."

"You think so?"

"I think he's wary of your punches."

"I don't want to kick with him though, so I thought clinching would be best."

Stuart shrugged. "Try it on with your punches a little more. If he whacks you with a few kicks just go back to clinching for the rest of the round. Take it one round at a time."

"How many rounds do you reckon he wants to do?"

Stuart shrugged and laughed.

Ame indicated it was time to start again.

Stuart slapped me on the shoulder. "You're up, champ."

Lek was waiting for me in the centre of the ring again, rocking back and forth like a praying mantis. Perfectly balanced and ready to strike.

I eyed his gloves. He was holding them high and extended. Defensively. Maybe Stuart was right. Maybe Lek was giving more respect to my punches than I had expected.

Deciding to favor my punches instead of my kicks, I assumed the southpaw position and grinned at Lek, flexing the psychological muscles ever so slightly. He responded immediately by slamming a right kick high into my forearms. I blocked the kick, which was poor form. Lek had been training me to either lean back and evade the high kick or to catch it. Both of those options offered me a counter-strike capability, whereas blocking the kick with my forearms offered me nothing I could use offensively. I'd just given him a free kick and an easy point and I hadn't scored back. Even a shin block would've been better. I could've switched off the check into a return high kick. I'd chosen the worst possible option and that was annoying.

The force of the kick had been stunning. Even though I had managed to fend it with my arms, it felt as if the kick rattled my entire existence. It was disorienting, though I disguised it with a look of indifference etched across my face. I'd never been kicked like that before. It was lucky Lek had kicked me with a shin guard on, else I might've broken an arm trying to block the kick.

It was a sobering lesson.

From then on, evasion was the name of the game where kicks were concerned.

Just don't get kicked… Just don't get kicked… Just don't get kicked.

Knowing that Lek was watching for my punches, I feigned forwards with a jab and used the momentum to skip into a right leg kick to his lead leg. It's one of my favorite go-to attacks from the southpaw position, and I felt a grim satisfaction as my padded shin buried into the meat of Lek's thigh.

The satisfaction didn't last long, however. Quick as a flash, before I had even managed to retract the leg and put it back on the ground, Lek had fired in a slashing, powerful kick aimed at the inside of my thigh. The kick connected with the inside of my knee and it spun my leg away from its intended position underneath my bodyweight, and so I toppled to the ground. I was duly impressed and humbled. Lek had executed a perfect sweep counter-attack, and now it was two rounds in a row that I had been sent to the canvas.

I got back to my feet and decided to forget about the kicking game altogether. Lek was simply too good. It wouldn't matter how intently I focused or how clever I thought I was, I just couldn't hope to best him. And so, I adopted my Mike Tyson glove position and waded forwards whilst throwing a battery of punches.

Predictably, Lek countered by fending me off with a thip kick – a favorite and obvious counter employed by Thai boxers against boxers – but I tensed up hard and managed to rebound the force of the kick, forcing Lek further back and off-balancing him. I coiled up over the power in my thighs and used them to throw several quick, explosive and powerful right hooks to the body and to Lek's gloves and arms as he covered up to protect his head. Punching power comes from the legs and the back, not the chest and the arms, as one might easily assume. When punching with your right hand, instead of thinking about pushing your right shoulder forwards, you want to be thinking about driving through your legs and pulling your left shoulder back. That's where real knockout power comes from.

Seeing that Lek was covering up blindly with a vertical forearm guard, I tried throwing an uppercut which I hoped would split right between his forearms and catch him right on the chin, but Lek saw it coming and countered by framing with his arms, fending me away, and the punch sailed clean in between us, as if I were aiming at the ceiling lights.

Ame called time on the second round and I returned to Stuart and his waiting bottle of water.

I was determined to get Lek to the ground. That was my measure of success now, I decided. If I could just get him to the ground, no matter how ugly it looked, I would consider myself victorious.

Rounds three and four were clinching battles, and although I managed to keep my feet in a relatively even round three, I ended up on the canvas twice more in round four, and Lek was the clear and dominant winner.

Ame decided that four rounds was enough, and we took off the shin guards, gloves and hand wraps and then the four of us eased into our stretching cool-down. I hadn't managed to get Lek to the ground, but I had survived the encounter, which gave me a slight confidence boost. I can't understate how much of a monster that man was in the ring. I knew that he had taken it easy with me. He could've slammed a battery of unanswered kicks into my body for four straight rounds if he had wanted to – and probably kicked me clean in half – but he hadn't, and that had given me a chance to be somewhat competitive.

I replayed the encounter over and over again in my head whilst I recovered in the shower, trying to figure out how I could do better if I was to face Lek again.

If you wish to win consistently in the ring, you must be prepared to lose consistently in the gym. That's a lesson for life in general. Losing will build a champion far more effectively than winning – provided one can deal with regular defeat – and if you must lose to improve, it's better done in the gym than in the ring.

The best fighters in the world get excited at the prospect of meeting someone who can beat them, because there is an opportunity for learning. Like anything else in life, the act of failing is by far and away the most effective form of schooling. By extension, I'm of the opinion that there are few things more important than developing a healthy attitude towards failure. Sticking within the safe confines of your comfort zone is a fantastic way of ensuring that you never improve.

I have to get better at the kicking game. I play too much towards my strengths of clinching and close range boxing. I rely on clinching. If I ever face someone who I can't close the distance against and they can force me to play the kicking game, I'm going to be in real trouble. I can't forever rely on the clinch to win my fights, as much as I would love to. It's a good strength to have, but now I need to improve my long-range skills and strategies. If I can evade and counter with kicks, then I reckon I can hold my own in a straight kicking war. I can always be faster, of course. Speed is king. Speed is king.

I hung out with Darryl in the afternoon. He told me that he would stay in Chiang Mai longer than he had been planning so that he could come along to watch my fight. I was chuffed that he would give up his time and disrupt his travel plans just to watch me. He didn't have to do that. It was very kind of him.

Training the following day was entirely about fitness. Focus on technique would become almost non-existent now in the days leading up to the fight. Now it was simply about making sure my body was in the best possible condition for the fight, and so there was a mountain of running, skipping, push-ups, sit-ups and heavy bag work to be done.

7 days until the fight.

I found myself thinking more and more about fighting as the days wore on closer and closer to the fight. I am a student of the art-form, after all, and I know that making the transition from student to professor or from apprentice to master was by thinking independently and coming up with new ideas and philosophies that are entirely your own. Bearing that in mind, I often find myself wondering what unarmed combat might've looked like between primitive humans. I've come to the conclusion that fighting between two humans in an animal state of combat would look almost nothing like what we see today, even in the world of mixed martial arts and cage-fighting. MMA would have you believe that it's the most pure and honest form of what fighting should look like, and certain styles have been demonstrated to be most effective in the MMA proving ground – Muay Thai, wresting and Brazilian Jiu-Jitsu being the premiere fighting styles – however, when I think about primitive fighting, I believe that many of our staple MMA movements wouldn't be at all effective or desirable, simply because primitive humans would've fought to the death, and fighting to the death means that they would've gone straight to the throat with their teeth, and they would've head-butted each other, and they would've ripped out the vulnerable genitals and gouged at the eyes. The use of the forehead and the teeth would be the two most damaging weapons, in my opinion, and it would be those two weapons that would most drastically change what MMA would look like. Suddenly, Brazilian Jiu-Jitsu positioning and strategy would have to change almost entirely, because from any position on the ground, the two competitors are going to be looking to rip the throat out with their nails and teeth and bite into any exposed flesh they can get their teeth into. Nails and teeth would probably be jagged and sharp tools of combat, owing to being forever broken and snapped in the tough grind of primitive life. There are no manicures for primitive man. Also, they would've had long hair and beards, which would've meant a lot of hair pulling – they wouldn't have cared that hair pulling is supposedly reserved for girls. Long, thick hair is as powerful a handle and steering tool as anything else available on the human body, and so it most certainly would've been used. They probably would've fought running battles, alternating between brief bursts of violence before one of the competitors broke free and tried to run away, only to be chased and the fight to resume again, and so running and running strategies and fighting whilst on the run would've all been important skills for the primitive fighter to learn. Knowing and utilizing the terrain, also – being able to run efficiently over an uneven surface or past trees and other obstacles. Tools and weaponry such as rocks and sticks would have been the obvious choice in a primitive fight to the death, but there would've been hand to hand combat on occasion, and it is that which I study and ponder. The more I think about it, the more I've come to the conclusion that running ability would almost certainly be the deciding factor in a primitive fight under natural conditions. The person who can run the most powerfully but also the most durably would be able to dictate the fight. If the better runner was also the better fighter, it would spell certain doom for whomever was the prey on that day, but if a powerful and durable runner was confronted by someone who was better at fighting, no fight would ever eventuate, save in the event of a clever ambush, for the runner would be able to escape the clutches of the attacker. Running, therefore, is the most important combat survival skill for a man in the wild. In particular, running using the lactic acid energy system, which is the one in the middle, between sprinting and marathon running. Aerobic marathon runners would've been easily captured in a sprint, and sprinters would've been easily overran over long distances, and so the most well-advantaged primitive humans on the savannah would've been the fast middle-distance runners – probably tending just slightly towards power than endurance (endurance is no good to anyone if you can't hold your own during the initial sprint) – with good fighting ability thrown in as a bonus.

It might seem strange, but I think about these sorts of things a lot.

The world carries around three days' worth of food in reserve, and a society is only ever three square meals away from a free-for-all. I'm a writer. Sometimes I can't help thinking like that. I shudder to think what the FBI would make of my internet search history.

There's task at hand, the soldiers told,
To each, one final ask.
Theirs not to know or reason why,
To die is not much to ask.
To thund'rous hordes, the soldiers march,
They march because they're told.
To death and blood the soldiers march,
Peace is for the old.

CHAPTER 13
TIME'S UP

"The nation that will insist on drawing a broad line of demarcation between the fighting man and the thinking man is liable to find its fighting done by fools and its thinking done by cowards."
– Thucydides

6 days until the fight.
Darryl wanted to hire scooters. I had already hired them out once before with Carter and I'd loved them, so I was more than willing to do it again. There was a British guy and two German girls who had all arrived in our dorm room overnight. The three of them were all very young – just teenagers, barely past adulthood – and so they seemed to form a natural bond. Together with Darryl and I, we rented three scooters and decided to ride them up the hill to Doi Suthep temple. This was another thing that I had already experienced earlier in my trip, but to me it was an excellent excuse to give the scooters a real workout.

We all went out to dinner together and the new British guy attempted, brazenly, yet poorly, to strike up a spark with one of the pretty German girls. The situation worsened later in the evening, when we were all in bed and I was trying to sleep. All the lights were out in the room, but that evidently wasn't clear enough a sign that people were trying to sleep, and that general quietness should ensue.

Nope, the Brit went and sat on the German girl's bed – the bed beneath mine, no less – and they started discussing some of the more deep and meaningful aspects of life, such as who had more "crisps" crumbs on their side of the bed. They seemed to be getting terribly excited about this little quandary.

I know exactly what you're thinking.

Who had more crumbs, then?

Well, that all depends on who you ask.

The British lad insisted that he had more crumbs on his side, but the German girl seemed to be willing to do a crumb count in order to prove once and for all that *she* had more crumbs on her side of the bed. The confidence in her assertion was impressive, but the Brit was stubbornly insistent.

This went on for close to ten minutes.

Just when you thought the whole crumb business was about to reach some kind of a climactic conclusion, a new and interesting twist would be introduced, such as a new, previously undiscovered cluster of chip crumbs, and the whole debate would begin again with renewed vigor.

I stared at the ceiling, silently biting my tongue. *How is it possible to discuss chip crumbs for ten minutes? And how is it possible to be so thoroughly excited and engaged by chip crumbs? Am I missing something here? Has the world gone mad? Do these chip crumbs symbolize something that is beyond my comprehension? Do I really care?*

It was excruciating.

I was just about ready to jump down from my bed and count the chip crumbs myself when the discussion turned towards all things Facebook. Now they were going through each other's photos on their phones and discussing whose photos had more "likes."

"This climate doesn't help my hair. And I'm not photogenic at all, so you have an advantage there. I definitely look better in person. I've always thought that photos don't accurately represent how I really look, don't you think?"

That was the British guy saying that. He was off to join the navy when he concluded this trip, apparently. He followed that announcement by demonstrating his marching ability, marching up and down between the beds, counting out loud and giving himself orders to stand to attention, and then obeying them.

The marching mercifully stopped and the conversation resumed, bouncing about relentlessly between chip crumbs, Facebook, and which country's military uniform looks the best.

"Hey, guys," I said finally, unable to stand it any longer. "Is there any danger of getting some silence, maybe?"

There were relieved murmurs of assent from around the room.

"Ah, sorry, sorry," they both mumbled, as if they had only just become aware of the others in the room.

The British lad slipped off the bed and darted across the room as if he had been scalded by hot water.

I felt a little bad about breaking up the bonding session, but the two of them would've been there for weeks at the rate they were going before one of them either died of starvation or got up the nerve to go for a hand hold.

Life is measured in minutes, and I wanted to sleep.

5 days until the fight.

After training the next day, and reveling in the liberation provided us by our scooters, Darryl and I decided to treat ourselves to lunch. We rode our scooters down to a busy intersection and decided to start our search for food there. Seeing no obvious parking places, we decided to leave them parked in a white, painted section in the middle of the intersection that nobody appeared to be using. It seemed like a decent place at the time.

Returning from lunch, however, Darryl and I were shocked to find our scooters chained together by the wheels and with white notices taped onto our seats. The notes were written in Thai, but the chains were a decent clue. We were in trouble.

Darryl showed his Thai note to a passing tuk-tuk driver who laughed and gestured for us to climb aboard. We were headed to the police station to sort things out. I thought about the lawyer's card still in my wallet in my pocket and decided to keep an eye out for a hardware store along the way. If we came across a decent shop before we arrived at the police station, I figured we could simply buy ourselves some bolt-cutters and solve the problem ourselves.

I was worried about corrupt police looking to exploit the naïve tourists. It's an all-too-familiar story in Thailand, though I've been told the situation is improving.

Indeed, corruption is rife in many parts of the world, as it is in the human condition. A lot of people have an innate mistrust of authority, and I, personally, struggle to trust law enforcement officers – even those in Australia – and I'll explain why… Can we agree that a boxer is most capable at throwing a punch? Can we also agree, therefore, that a boxer is the most capable of *avoiding* a punch? Can we agree that a bank's security force is also the most capable of stealing from it? Can we agree that a King or President is in the position to be the most capable of destroying their nation? Can we agree that a medical practitioner is capable of causing the most pain? You can probably see where I'm going with this… It's only natural, having considered these things, to fear those entrusted with the task of enforcing the laws of the land, when they are also inherently the ones most capable of subverting them. Corruption is a part of human nature, and I trust human nature far more than any regulatory watchdogs or oversight committees.

My fears were misplaced, as it turned out. The Thai police officers at the station were quite amicable and were even happy to pose for photos with Darryl and myself and offer us coffee. We bartered our fine down to 100 Thai Baht – about $3AUD – and then we were driven in a police car back to our scooters, where they were duly unchained and we were sent on our way, much to our bemusement.

"That was an interesting lunch," Darryl observed.

Interesting, indeed.

4 days until the fight.

There was a girl at training the following day, and none of us – not Stuart, Ame, Lek or myself – really knew how to respond to her being there. In a

Muay Thai: Peace, At Last

charged, male, physical environment, it was just unusual for a girl to be there. She was young and she was from Austria, and she wasn't bad in the ring. She told us that she had been training for years, which was impressive.

The promoter came down to watch us train and called me over to have my photo taken for the brochure.

"Not a bad change of scenery," Stuart commented quietly as we leant against the ropes and watched the Austrian girl going through a round of pad work.

It was certainly a refreshing change from the three sweaty blokes I'd been sharing the ring with for the better part of the prior month.

I posed for the photos and then thanked the promoter for having me on his show. He spoke poor English but he seemed to understand. He was grateful to me for appearing on his fight card. Foreigners are always a big draw card in tourist areas like Chiang Mai. He was expecting a big crowd for the night of the 15th, which was a Saturday night.

At the end of the session, Lek instructed me to go to a pharmacy and buy tape with which he would wrap my hands for the fight, and Thai boxing ointment, which gets mixed with Vaseline to make a slippery, oily mix that gets smeared all over the body and face of a fighter to help prevent nasty cuts.

There were more newcomers in the dorm that night, and most of them would be sticking around to watch my fight in a few days' time. There was an Irishman named Clark, two British girls, and a Welshman named James. I was eager to fight in front of them. I like showing off from time to time as much as anybody.

Training the next day was an intense affair, which I found surprising. I had expected the intensity to tailor off approaching the fight, but Lek had brought along two of his Muay Thai buddies and he seemed delighted at the prospect of unleashing them on me.

We sparred for a full hour, with Stuart, Ame, Lek and the two other Thai boxers forming a circle around me and then taking it in turns to step forward and spar with me. Occasionally, two or three of them would fight me all at once. I didn't get a moment's rest for the entire hour, and I was utterly spent by the end of the session. I can't think of a harder training session I've ever been put through. I was properly exhausted, battered and bruised, and I was bleeding from a small nick in the corner of my eye from a wayward elbow.

The other guys seemed to be having a blast. Nobody was too concerned about my physical state.

"Tomorrow, no training," Lek said, much to my relief. "You come next day, learn Wai Kru, uh?"

I just nodded meekly. It was all I could really manage at that point.

2 sleeps until the fight.

I returned to the hostel and spent the day hanging out with James and the two British girls. One of their names was Rhiannon, but I can't recall the other's name, much to my regret. They were lovely girls, very friendly and warm, and I was glad that they were going to be there in the audience for my fight.

Sitting down to drink tea that night, I found myself perusing a local newspaper. Parts of it were written in Thai and other parts of it were written in English. I wondered how they decided on which bits to write in the respective languages. There was a tiny article on page eleven about a suspected Mafia homicide in Chiang Mai which had occurred the day before. So far as I could tell, it happened just a couple of streets over from where I had been sleeping. The victim had been found with small caliber bullet holes in his knees, his feet, his hands, and then a line of bullet holes had been drawn across his forehead. Altogether, he had been shot fifteen times. Evidently, the guy had pissed someone off at some point in time. Either that or he knew something that someone else wanted to know. I couldn't help picturing the scene in my head. Scary stuff.

It was a dark night that night. Darker than usual. And my dreams were correspondingly dark. Blood spurting and bones breaking. They were the dreams of men from centuries past, floating through a subconscious eternity, snagging in the minds of those daring and jagged enough to protrude from society. Oh yes, fight time was looming ever closer.

The day before the fight.

I decided to attend training the next day simply to watch. Lek wasn't there. It was just Stuart and Ame in the ring, training hard. I sat down in one of the ringside seats that had been set up in anticipation of the fights the following night, and I just watched. Opangji must've seen me sitting there and she slid onto the chair beside me.

"Hey," I said in greeting.

She just smiled in reply and sat there beside me, watching the two men in the ring as they went through their paces. It was a sad smile. Solemn, perhaps. I pondered the meaning of it for a little while before I was distracted by the training once again.

I invested a little time trying to make myself nervous for the fight. I told myself that I'd be in that very same ring the following night and that there would be strangers sitting in these seats and I would be fighting against a Thai person who I had never met before and the lights would be on and the Thai klaxon music would be playing and the bars that encircled the ring would all be doing a roaring trade. The alleyway would come to life and I would be right at the centre of it… Try as I might, I just couldn't find a way to make myself nervous, and so I gave it up. That blasé attitude was bothersome to me. Why couldn't I get myself excited or nervous for this fight? It was entirely possible that I was overconfident, but I wasn't sure about that, either. My body was aching from the battering I had received in training the day before, although the cut next to my eye had turned out to be miniscule and was already almost entirely healed over. I wasn't feeling as ready to fight as I knew I could potentially be, but then I had felt ready and willing to fight two weeks earlier. I certainly couldn't be bothered doing anymore preparation for this fight. I just wanted to get in there.

Just a little bit longer, I told myself, over and over again. *Just wait a little bit longer. You'll get your chance tomorrow night. Just be patient. Enjoy the moment.*

I strolled back to the hostel feeling a little bit lost. Normally, I would be dedicating a good portion of the afternoon towards recovery, but having not trained that morning, I didn't really have much to do or to think about. I decided to pass the time by reading in the sun, and I was soon joined by James and the two British girls.

"Have you guys seen Darryl?" I asked.

"He met some girls," James said. "He's gone to their hostel I think."

"Ok." Darryl sure loved his pick-up artistry.

"Ready for your fight tomorrow, Mike?" James asked.

The two girls stopped what they were doing and turned to hear my response.

I suppressed a laugh as I realized that I had become something of an elephant in the room. It made sense, I supposed. It's probably only a minority of people who will ever experience a professional fight in their lifetimes. Fair enough that these people were intrigued by what I was experiencing.

"Yeah, I'm as ready as I'm gonna be," I said, doing my best to appear warm and welcoming of further discussion if they wished to pursue the topic.

"Aren't you scared?" Rhiannon asked. She looked genuinely concerned for me. It was touching.

"No, I'm fine, thanks," I said. "I don't think fighting is too scary... There are probably other sports that are worse."

"I can't think of many other sports where people are trying to kick you in the head," James commented. "I watch Muay Thai on TV back home all the time. These Thai guys are brutal, Mike. They start fighting when they're just little kids. Crazy stuff, man. From another world, almost."

I nodded. "It's the beating heart of Thai culture," I agreed. "Be almost rude for me to come all this way and then not compete in Muay Thai, don't you think?" I was joking around.

"Well, I just hope we aren't taking you to the hospital tomorrow night and sitting at your bedside," the other British girl said seriously.

It was a sobering thought, but nothing I hadn't considered before. I was eager. I was impatient. I wasn't scared.

Later that night, and as per the travelling custom, James and the girls wanted to go out for a drink. I decided to join them on the condition that I wouldn't be drinking. I trusted my self-control on the night before a fight. Nobody was in the mood for any intensive partying, and so the girls produced a pack of cards and we wandered around the corner to the THC reggae bar, where we found a little table and sat ourselves down to play cards. I love a good card game. I'm not very good at them, but I think playing games with other people is a huge part of what it means to be human. Watch animals in the wild and you'll notice that they all love to play with each other, and they dedicate a huge amount of their time doing exactly that. Humans are very much the same. Playing together is a bonding experience and a means of powerful interaction. And it's fun, obviously.

The others drank beers and cocktails whilst I sipped on soft-drink and water. It was a small price to pay. I didn't feel like drinking anyway, regardless of the occasion.

Being a reggae bar, the smell of drugs was ever-pervasive, and on this occasion it seemed that more than a few of the other patrons were partaking heavily of one substance or another.

"Aaaaayyyyy, yo, yo, yo," someone proclaimed loudly behind my head before, to my surprise, I found someone's legs on either side of my head, as if they were looking for a shoulder ride.

"What in the name of…" I muttered, shoving the legs away and turning to appraise the situation.

There was a guy rolling around on the floor, unable to stand himself back on his feet after being shoved from my shoulders. "Yo," he said after finally stopping the rolling and deciding that the floor would suffice. Then he said something in a European language that none of us could understand. It might've been Dutch. James spoke two languages – Welsh and English – but the rest of us were just English speakers.

"Bit like that, isn't it?" I agreed, turning away from the guy as dismissively as I could manage. Drugs aren't very conducive to accurate body language interpretation, and before I knew it, the guy was back trying to sit on my shoulders again. "Come on, mate. Knock it off, would you?" I shoved the legs away again. "You smell like someone's pissed on you."

And with that, the guy ripped his clothes off in a panic and threw them off the edge of the balcony. We were on a rooftop bar, and so the clothes would've sailed a long way down before reaching ground level, and now there was a naked guy in the bar. Nobody appeared too bothered by this development. He seemed harmless enough, sure, but I was most certainly not allowing him anywhere near my shoulders again.

The naked guy returned to our little group and slumped down against the wall, looking suddenly lethargic, as if a nap might be in order.

"How did we get so lucky?" James mused at my side.

The girls were laughing.

I soon begged off another game of cards and returned to the hostel. My mind had fixated firmly on the fact that I was fighting the following night, and I was keenly aware of anything even remotely resembling tiredness.

I had propped myself on pillows next to my reading light when James returned and clambered onto the bed next to mine. "What are you doing?" he asked. "Feeling nervous?"

I shook my head. "Writing up my next of kin details before I forget," I said. "A guy I've been training with has said he'll take care of them for me."

James nodded. "That's pretty morbid, man."

"It's just what you do."

"I'm not going to be able to make your fight unfortunately," James said. "I'm going across to Pai tomorrow."

"It's beautiful over there," I said. "I'm thinking I'll go over that way again on Sunday. The day after my fight. Get some R&R before heading home."

"Otherwise I'd offer to take a copy of those details for you," James said, nodding at the note I was writing to Stuart. "Just in case, you know."

I nodded and glanced over at him. "Yeah, thanks mate. No worries."

"It would actually be a pretty cool travel story to tell my parents I had someone's next of kin details just in case they died in a fight," James laughed.

"It's not in case I die," I said, grinning. "I don't think people die in Muay Thai... It's just in case I get injured or something and there's some kind of insurance drama or something like that, just so that people can get in touch with my parents or whatever. It's not really a big deal."

James bobbed his head in agreement. "How are you feeling? You must be getting a little nervous now?"

I shook my head again, though I felt a small, nervous pang shoot through my abdomen for the first time. "I'm fine," I said. "It's pretty easy to rationalize."

"How do you rationalize it?"

"Well... I guess I figure that human beings are all pretty much the same... Given the same set of circumstances, most people would respond in a select kind of way. The only real difference in a professional fight is the amount and quality of training that the two guys have done, and I'm confident in my training."

"So you think you'll win?"

I nodded. "Yep."

"Are you gonna film it?"

"Oh yeah, that reminds me," I grabbed my bag and rummaged through it, searching for my little go-pro camera I had brought along. I plugged it into a charging socket. "Stuart told me he would film it for me. I've never seen myself fight before so I'll be interested to watch the footage, actually."

Whilst I had my backpack on my lap, I also pulled out my mouth-guard and the hand tape and Thai boxing ointment that Lek had told me to buy from a pharmacy. I piled it all into a plastic bag and then set the charging camera on top of the lot. That would be my little bag of stuff I'd need to remember to take along to the fight the following evening. I can be awfully absent-minded when it comes to small details, and the camera and the mouth-guard and the Thai oil and the hand tape were precisely the sorts of things I could easily forget.

"Can you send me the video when you get it?" James asked. "It would be cool to see it. I've been putting together some videos of my trip."

"Sure, I can try," I said. "I'm not really sure how to do that, but we can meet up again over in Pai in a couple of days if you're still going to be there."

James nodded. "Yeah, I'm going to be there for a week. I've booked into a backpackers called Spicy Pai, which is supposed to be an epic place. I'm going to make a real time of it. Let me know when you're coming over and we'll meet up. I think the British girls are headed over that way as well after they watch your fight. We can reunite the gang and celebrate you still being alive!"

I laughed. "Sounds good to me, mate. I'd like that."

The Irishman, Clark, popped his head up from the bottom bunk. "You're fighting tomorrow night?" he asked. At least, that's what I assumed he said. He had a very thick accent.

"Yeah, mate," I said. "Just down the road here."

"Are you going?" Clark asked James.

James shook his head. "Nah, I'm going to Pai. But those two British girls are going. You can go with them."

"Those two?" Clark asked, pointing at the two vacant bunks opposing ours.

James and I nodded. "Yeah," James said. "They're really cool. Go along with them."

"Cool," Clark agreed, and he disappeared from sight once again.

I turned to James. "I'd better try to get some sleep now," I said, putting my hand on the light switch.

James nodded. "I'm leaving early in the morning so I probably won't see you," he said, extending his hand across the divide between our beds. "Good luck to you, my friend. I'll see you in Pai on Sunday."

"Thanks mate." I shook his proffered hand and then flicked off the light switch, plunging the room into darkness.

Muay Thai: Peace, At Last

When there're no cities left for to burn,
To where's a man then s'posed to turn?
For men are Gods of fire and flame,
Gods, are men, of swords and pain.
Angered souls, aimed from above,
Where there're no rooms or halls of love.
Break the chains, unleash them all,
And weep for cities, they'll burn and fall.

CHAPTER 14
READY

"And those who were seen dancing were considered insane by those who could not hear the music."
– Friedrich Nietzsche

I awoke early in the morning feeling refreshed and momentarily disoriented. For the first time since arriving in Thailand, I'd dreamt of home, and I was caught briefly off-guard by the relatively unfamiliar surrounds of the dorm room.

James was shuffling about quietly, trying not to wake anyone. I watched him zip his bag shut and sling it over his shoulder before easing out the door. He was on his way to catch the bus across to Pai. I was momentarily jealous. That was a spectacular drive through the mountains, and getting to see it in the early morning light would be a special experience for my friend from Wales.

The sun hadn't come up yet but I was wide awake. It took a few moments before I recalled with a tiny pang of adrenaline that today was the day of the fight. The fights were due to begin at 8:30pm later in the evening, and I was the second last fight on a card made up of seven fights. I still had a significant amount of time before I would be stepping into the ring, and I wasn't sure exactly what to do with it. Twiddling my thumbs seemed like a legitimate option, and it was high on my list of possibilities until I decided that eating, drinking and proactively relaxing and loosening up would be the most optimal use of my time. I thought about James again, riding the bus across the jungle-covered mountainside. Our respective ribbons of life – briefly intertwined for a few days – had taken us in two very different directions for a brief, twenty-four hour period. Whilst he would be relaxing with other backpackers in Spicy Pai, reading books, riding scooters, drinking beer and swimming in cool waters, I would be stepping over the ropes and into a professional Muay Thai fight in front of a baying, blood-thirsty audience. Life can take us to funny places.

Worst case scenario in the lead-up to a fight can be the much dreaded "adrenalin crash," which can leave your limbs feeling heavy and immovable, your brain ceases to function on anything other than instinct, and fine motor skills become a hilarious idea. I attribute this physical response to the "freeze" instinct that I've mentioned earlier. Confronted by a predator, real or conceived, it's not abnormal to freeze up and play dead. I've never been to that extent before – I get around this little psychological hiccup by always visualizing myself as the predator – but I've met plenty of fighters who have experienced the dreaded crash. Controlling your adrenalin is critical in the lead-up to a fight. For most fighters, they have a very useful distraction in the days prior to their fight, which is the weight cut. They have to focus on dehydrating themselves so as to meet the appropriate fighting weight when they step onto the scales. However, this was Thailand, and so there was no weighing of the fighters or any kind of approximate match-making. If there were two fighters respectively who presented themselves to a promoter and said that they wanted to fight, they were hurriedly thrown into the ring together and best of luck to them. I was one of those fighters today, and later that night I would finally be meeting the other guy who had put his hand up.

Adrenalin can be a life-saving chemical, but it can also do awful things to the body if allowed to continue for too long. The body speeds up metabolism, raising blood sugar levels by stimulating the liver to change glycogen into glucose more rapidly. Digestion all but stops, blood vessels constrict, heart rate increases, blood pressure increases, the air passages expand, pupils dilate, blood gets re-distributed away from the brain and less vital organs and towards the muscles. In response to the release of adrenalin, the pituitary gland stimulates the release of cortisol, which can have long-term effects on the body and often results in weight loss, reduced auto-immunity and subsequent illness.

Critically for a fighter, however, given that we aren't too concerned about future weight loss when we are about to get kicked in the face, is the simple fact that adrenalin can utterly exhaust you. The purpose of adrenalin is to give the body superhuman strength for a brief time, which it does very effectively – think about mothers lifting cars off of trapped babies. However, the price to pay for that brief physical ability is exhaustion, and you don't want to be exhausted before your fight has even begun!

If you perform best whilst psyched up and with adrenalin pumping, I recommend saving it until the moment of competition. I don't perform my best whilst under the influence of adrenaline – given that my style is more suited to calculated, efficient movements than wild brawling – and so the principle goal for me leading into a fight is to relax and to be as calm as possible. I play card games, read books, take naps, listen to calming music, and distract myself by talking to people about mundane, everyday things.

Even when the fight begins, I want to be calm and relaxed. The worst thing that could happen for me in a ring is to be robbed of my ability to think critically whilst on the move. Mental agility is my strongest advantage that I take into a fight – my sharpest weapon. Recognizing in myself that getting flustered, anxious and wild are not conducive to optimal performance, I have mastered the art of staying calm. The more chaotic and fierce the environment, the more powerfully my mental training takes hold, and the more I slow things down. As I've said before, that's the whole point of combat training. A fundamental re-wiring of the brain. My training has turned anxiety into calm clarity, and hesitation into aggression.

Breakfast was a light and generic affair. Bacon and eggs – something familiar. Today wasn't the day to start experimenting with unusual Asian foods. If I had been smart about it, I would've eaten a large serving of carbohydrates the night before so as to carbo-load and give my body plenty of reserve glycogen to turn into glucose during the fight. I hadn't done that, but I'd survive. I am a healthy guy and I didn't think fitness or energy levels would be a problem for me come fight time. They'd never been a problem before. It's another benefit to approaching the fight in a relaxed fashion.

I ate alone. Just me and my thoughts. I wondered briefly what my family was up to back home. I hadn't told them that I was fighting that night. That reminded me that I needed to remember to pass on my next of kin details to Stuart before the fight. It was one of those little details that would be easy to forget.

I would be disappointed if Stuart didn't come along to be in my corner. I expected him to be there. He'd said he would. We had spent a great deal of time training together, and sparring and clinching together. It was a bonding experience – one that we would forever share and one which was ours alone. He'd confided in me about a rash of troubles he was facing upon his return to England. Personal problems that involved a lovely woman, a violent ex-partner, and the matter being brought before the authorities. He was a good man. A solid man. Reliable.

I like the British.

They can be brutal, vicious, world-conquerors, but they believe, as I do, that a fight, regardless of how violent or savage or cruel it may be, must always be fair. It is the only type of fighting that I will ever condone. A fight must always be fair. Front on.

The day will come when I will lose a fight, and on that day, if the fight was fair and I lost to an honest fighter, then I will be happy to acquiesce to his superiority and acknowledge him as being better than me. That day will come, and I welcome it.

Christ, that day could be today…

I hadn't really considered the prospect of losing this fight, and I decided that I wasn't about to start now. Breakfast was done, and I still had more time to kill before going to meet with Ame and Lek at the stadium.

I ordered another glass of orange juice. A little Vitamin C couldn't hurt.

I haven't spoken very much about confidence thus far, or the role of confidence in combat sports and physical performance. I don't really consider confidence to be a key factor in deciding performance or outcome, provided you can identify the disconnect between thoughts and reality. Your thoughts can be different from your actions, and vice-versa, and so I don't consider insecurities or a lack of confidence or self-esteem to be sufficient roadblocks on the road to optimal performance. As it so happens, I am a very confident fighter, but I do not believe that my confidence in any way affects my ability to perform, whether it be as a fighter, or as a person. I do believe that standing straight and looking people in the eye and speaking slowly and clearly are all beneficial to a person's societal contribution, and I do believe that confident body language can be a powerful tool in a person's arsenal, however, I also believe that a shy, nervous introvert is capable of standing up straight and looking people in the eye. Lacking confidence is not a valid excuse for not trying. In order to be brave, one must first be afraid, and it's in overcoming one's fears that confidence is built. Confidence is not something that gets stumbled upon in unexpected places. Confidence is built. Layer upon layer.

After breakfast, I wandered over to the stadium, taking the time to look around and soak it all in. I'd be fighting there later in the evening. I nodded to the dwarf as he tended to his bar, sweeping the floors with a small-handled broom and straightening the whiskey bottles. There was just something about that tattooed, mean-looking dwarf – something that I couldn't put my finger on or enunciate in any meaningful way – that made me want to smack him with the business end of a wet, rolled up towel and then see what happens.

Ame and Stuart were already in the ring, training hard. The sound of pads being hit was ringing throughout the empty stadium. It sounded louder from this vantage point than it did in the ring. There was an echo that I hadn't noticed before, perhaps bouncing off the old sheets of tin on the roof. It was strange to watch training and not be a part of it. To not be in there, suffering and laughing alongside Stuart.

"Here he is!" Stuart panted as he finished a round of pad work and leant against the nearest rope. "How are you feeling, champ? Got the wind in your sails?"

I nodded and raised my hand in greeting. "I feel good thanks mate," I said. "How's it all going?"

"Usual," Stuart said, still trying to catch his breath.

I nodded my understanding and turned to look at Lek, who was sitting on the side of the ring, waiting for me.

"How's it going, Ame?" I called up to the young Thai warrior in the ring.

"Hey, Michael!" he called back, raising a Thai-padded hand in warm welcome. "Tonight fight, uh?"

"Looking forward to it," I said.

Lek stood and greeted me with a curt nod. "In the ring," he instructed. "Wai Kru."

I nodded and climbed into the ring with Stuart and Ame.

This wasn't a training session. Before a Muay Thai fight, it's customary for both competitors to perform the Wai Kru – a traditional warrior dance – blessing the ring and offering respect to the respective coaches and to the sport of Muay Thai itself. Most coaches have their own, distinctive tweak that they put on the dance so that their fighters can be marked apart from the rest. The various moves can all mean different things, depending on what the coach wants from his charge.

Lek spent fifteen minutes teaching me the dance. His personal touch was minor – a whip-cracking movement performed over my head and directed at the corner of my opponent. It was meant to signal a declaration of war between the two of us, and to signal that it was my intention to attack him. I figured that it was a respectful thing – 'just letting you know, mate, I'm gonna start punching you now, mmk.'

After performing the Wai Kru twice to Lek's satisfaction, I climbed out of the ring. The next time I stepped in there, I would be stepping in to fight for real.

"Short, have?" Lek asked, grabbing his own colourful, Thai kickboxing shorts.

I shook my head. "No, I don't have any."

Lek nodded. "Ok. I bring for you… Have Thai oil? Hand tape?"

I nodded. "Yep, I got it from the pharmacy, as you said."

Ame leaned over the top rope with a cheeky look on his face. "You buy for Stu? Condom for…?" he gestured to the shuttered doors of the nearby *Ladyboy Bar*.

"Oi!" Stuart roared, punching Ame playfully in the back.

We all laughed and then Lek turned serious again.

"Ok. You bring tonight, uh? Hand tape, Thai boxing oil, ok?"

I nodded. "Sure."

Lek looked at me sternly for a moment. It was a fatherly look. Proud, discerning and hard. "Come with me, uh?" he said, gesturing down the side-alley that I had first entered the stadium via, almost a whole month ago.

I shrugged. "Sure," I said, following him out of the alley. I wasn't sure where we were going, but I had nothing else to be doing for the rest of the day.

Lek led me to a waiting motorbike. He kick-started it into action and then gestured for me to climb onto the back. I obliged, and we set off along the rickety, pot-holed alleyways and backstreets, bound for destination: no idea.

I thought that maybe he was taking me to show me his house and to introduce me to his family. That's the sort of thing Thai people like to do. They're a hospitable, socially mature people, and being friends with foreigners is often seen as a status symbol.

We dove and raced between gaps in traffic as we wound our way through the narrow streets that were only wide enough for one car at a time, at best. At one point, we found ourselves road-blocked. There was a traffic jam of some kind up ahead. I was ready to settle in for the long haul, but Lek had different ideas. Changing down gears and gunning the throttle, we were soon racing along parallel to the stalled traffic, riding precariously along the raised guttering that hemmed the bitumen road.

I was peeking out over Lek's shoulder like a bewildered meerkat, readying myself to leap clear of some horrifying, inevitable wreckage that Lek appeared eager to instigate. We shuddered over a series of bumps in the guttering and I was almost thrown clear off the back of the bike, but I clung on to the underside of the wheel arch itself, gluing myself to the seat and feeling the hot air coming off the rubber of the rear tire, mere centimeters from my fingers.

Thailand is just crazy sometimes. There's the expected crazy, like the conspicuous displays of sexuality and the corruption and the market places, but it's the unexpected crazy that can really catch you unawares and shock you. Clinging on for dear life on the back of Lek's speeding motorbike on the day of my Muay Thai fight, I found myself briefly pondering how my family and friends back home might react to the news that I had perished in a fiery, high-speed motorcycle accident on some back alley in Chiang Mai.

"We really can't explain what your son was doing, ma'am. Witness reports suggest that he was seen flying through the air on the back of a motorbike which had just attempted to jump over a street vendor that was attempting to sell bananas... Please be quiet and let me finish, ma'am... Now, the rest is all a bit hazy, but we have a dwarf here testifying to the fact that he heard your son say that he needed to get bananas to feed his pet monkey, which he had just purchased at an illicit cockfighting event... I understand, ma'am, that this may not sound like the sort of thing your son would do, but we have witnesses... Yes, that's right, a monkey... Monkquisha, he called it... Suffice it to say, ma'am, that the purchase of monkeys is illegal here in Thailand, and you will be expected to foot the bill for the bananas."

Mercifully, my long-suffering mother was spared this long-distance, presumably crackly phone conversation when Lek eventually slowed and turned off into a quieter area, where he found a place to park his motorbike. The engine died and I climbed off, doing my best to appear indifferent and unshaken. "Where are we?" I asked.

"Buddha market," Lek replied, gesturing for me to follow. "Only Buddha market in Chiang Mai."

"Ok," I nodded. "Cool." A Buddhist market sounded peaceful and non life-threatening. I was happy to stay there right up until the moment of the fight if it meant not getting back on that motorbike with Lek at the helm. Give me 5 rounds with a Thai in a professional kickboxing fight any day.

I followed Lek as he walked into a large, quiet market place. It was dark in there, protected from the sun by an old, rusted tin roof. There were stalls everywhere selling Buddhist trinkets and statues and various other odds and ends that might aid the discerning customer in the practice of Buddhism.

I spent a little time perusing the market alleyways before Lek found me and called me over.

I was shocked to find that Lek had brought me a Buddhist amulet on a necklace. There was a small, silver coin with Buddhist engravings on it, which had been encased in protective glassware, and which was now dangling from a necklace.

"For luck, for fight," Lek said, showing me the amulet.

I didn't know what to say, though I stammered out something resembling a thank-you. Lek said he needed to have it blessed before I could wear it, and I followed him round like a stunned mullet in search of a monk.

Being a Buddhist market, Lek quickly located a monk and they had a soft conversation in Thai. There was lots of smiles and nodding from both sides, and then the monk took the amulet from Lek and gestured for me to approach.

Right there, in the middle of the market floor, the three of us sat cross-legged on the concrete whilst the monk sang and murmured over the amulet. Somebody brought forth a bowl of water, which the monk dipped his fingers into before flicking water over the amulet and over me. I bowed my head in submission to the blessing.

I had travelled in search of spiritual enlightenment before, but I believe that my pre-conceived notions of what to expect had clouded the experience. The unexpected nature of this encounter with Buddhism were hitting close to home, and I found myself on the verge of tears as the monk finally leant forward and placed the necklace around my neck. It was difficult to explain. I'm not quick to be moved. I didn't find Titanic to be a particularly sad or emotive film. But I won't ever forget that moment in the middle of Chiang Mai's Buddhist market, sitting on the dirty floor with Lek and a Thai monk and being presented with an amulet that had been blessed for luck and protection.

I've also never been big into personal decoration, but I would go on to wear that amulet necklace with pride.

Muay Thai: Peace, At Last

The return motorbike ride was uneventful, which was a relief, and Lek dropped me off out front of my hostel with a promise to meet me again at Loi Kroh stadium at 8pm later that evening to prepare for the fight.

I waved him off gratefully and returned to my room. I lay on my bed for a while, observing the amulet and pondering the implications that it held. After a while, I drifted off to sleep. It was as good a way as any to while away the time in the afternoon before a fight.

I woke up after a couple of hours and, realizing I still had a lot of time left, I decided to explore the hostel. The hostel itself was seven stories high, but only the bottom floor and the top two floors were in use. The rest were being renovated, albeit slowly. I hadn't seen a single construction worker in the weeks that I had resided there. Barring the unexpected, that would be my last night in the hostel before I set off towards Pai for a few days before returning home to Australia.

I wandered down the stairs and into the barren bathrooms and dorm rooms on the middle floors, just wandering mindlessly, thinking about life and love.

Life isn't something you should think your way through, I reiterated to myself. You should *feel* your way through it.

The British girls found me and asked me to go to dinner with them. We found a small, peaceful little place and we sat and talked quietly. I had my little plastic bag of fight gear by my side. We joked and laughed. I was deep into relaxation-mode now. I was proactively relaxing and calming myself. We exchanged funny travel stories and Rhiannon spoke lovingly about her Dalmatian puppy waiting for her back home. Pretty soon, it was nearly 8pm, and the time came for me to excuse myself. The girls promised me they would come to the stadium shortly. I wasn't expected to fight until later on in the evening, at closer to 10 or 11pm, and so there was no rush for them to leave their dinner. Just as I was getting up to leave, a Thai man walked past and pushed a flyer into my hand. I glanced at it briefly and then did a double-take. I was looking at my own face! It was an advertisement for the fights that night. Apparently I had been upgraded to the main-event of the evening. My picture was situated proudly above my name and the Australian flag. I laughed quietly and passed the flyer to the girls before making a beeline for the stadium. I had a date with destiny, and she wouldn't be pleased if I kept her waiting.

I strolled along the street, humming to myself and swinging my little plastic bag around. I saw the beggar in his same spot once again, with his legs amputated at the thighs. On a whim, I sat down next to him and watched the world go by for a few moments. I introduced myself with a handshake and we spoke a little bit about various things. I was running late for fight preparation now, but I was in no real hurry. I was relaxed and I was fascinated by the man as he told me the story of how he'd had his right leg blown off after stepping on a landmine in Burma. His left leg had been amputated shortly afterwards due to infection of the wounds that he had suffered. It was a horrifying story, made all the more so by the amiable, throw-away manner with which it was told.

I nodded gratefully to the man and shook his hand before getting on my way once again. A nice dose of perspective before the fight was probably exactly what the doctor would've ordered.

All the bars in the alley were open and they were doing a roaring trade, despite the early hour of the evening. An opening fight was already underway in the ring. It was two Thai boys fighting each other as hard as they could. A nice sized crowd was already seated, and I expected that it would build as the night wore on. The dwarf had a huge crowd in his bar, and I caught his eye and we nodded with a strange familiarity to each other as I walked past.

It was fight night, and I was ready.

Muay Thai: Peace, At Last

Do your worst, I'm somewhat bored; bored of you and me,
    You hang there like an idle truck suspended from a tree.
  You think I'm scared that possibly, your rope will someday tire?
The straightest straight is dull to me, your sparrows sing for hire.
    So go ahead, do your worst, I hear the creaking warn,
Let's walk in step into the dark and see who's there come morn.

CHAPTER 15
KILL ANYTHING THAT MOVES

"I've loved the stars too fondly to be fearful of the night."
– Galileo

I couldn't see Lek or Ame anywhere, but I soon spied Stuart reclining on a chair in one of the bars towards the rear of the stadium. He had empty beer bottles lined up in front of him and he was talking at the top of his voice, entertaining an audience in the bar.
Stuart roared his approval when he saw me approaching and quickly introduced me to all of his new mates and the half-naked bar girls. "This lad's gonna be fighting tonight!"
"You're happy tonight, mate," I observed, sitting down beside him and waving away shouted questions and offers of beer.
Stuart leaned over and hugged me, which was weird.
"Are you alright?" I asked him as he let me go.
"I'm having a baby," he said, and there was delight in his eyes.
I assumed a wide-eyed look of shock. "Jesus, should I get a doctor in here?" I asked, patting his belly before breaking into a huge grin. I was thrilled to see Stuart looking so happy. He had been having problems back home and this was terrific news that would hopefully bring some stability to his situation.
"I couldn't be happier," Stuart said.
"Wow," I said, shaking my head. "That's just excellent news, mate. I'm happy for you, I really am."
I was tempted to accept that beer just to share a drink with the man, but then Ame arrived and I remembered again why I was supposed to be there.
"Have you seen Lek?" I asked Ame after we all greeted each other.
Ame shook his head and accepted a beer from the bar girls. Moments later, the two Thais that had come along to training to spar with me arrived in the bar, wearing nice clothes. They greeted Ame, Stuart and I and then sat down. I was surprised to see them. They had come along just to watch me

in my fight. It was touching to see them. They had no real investment in my success or failure, they had simply come along to support our corner.

One of the fights finished and the crowd continued to build. I sat in the bar at the rear and tried to concentrate on the fights. The bar was packed full of eager, drunk tourists, and Stuart was shouting to everyone who could hear and pointing at me, telling everyone who I was and that I would be fighting soon. I had people coming up to me and asking to take photos with me and plying me with questions. I posed awkwardly for photos with strangers. I'm not a fan of photos. I don't hate them, I'd simply rather not be in them, given the choice.

I saw Darryl take a seat at ringside. He'd brought along a veritable harem of gorgeous girls. I counted four of them, and they all sat down alongside Darryl.

Lek finally arrived, and he had brought his entire extended family along with him! I was introduced to his parents and to his brother and to his grandparents and to his uncles and aunts and to his cousins and nieces and nephews. They all crowded around to see the farang whom their Lek had been training. I received gushing hugs from Lek's mum and dad and from his grandparents. They were so proud of their son, they said in broken English. They urged me to do him proud in the ring, and I promised them that I would do just that. I was shocked at how much of a big deal this was for Lek, to have brought his entire family along. I'd gotten a little bit carried away in thinking that this fight was all about me, but it appeared that Lek and even Ame had invested almost just as much into this fight as I had, emotionally, if nothing else. I was a little overwhelmed by the support from the huge Thai presence in my corner. Stuart and I probably looked out of place amongst them, though we certainly didn't feel out of place.

Out the corner of my eye, I saw Clark and the two British girls taking their seats next to Darryl, whom they clearly recognized from the hostel. I wasn't sure if they had all spoken to each other or not, but I could see Clark leaning across and eagerly chatting to one of the girls that Darryl had brought along.

The crowd was starting to really find its voice as the fights prior to mine turned into wars. I was the only foreigner on the fight card for the evening now. All of the other fights were entirely Thai affairs. There was a Frenchie who was supposed to fighting on the card also, but Ame told me that he had pulled out a few days prior.

"Pussy," Stuart said knowingly, giving me a proud little wink.

I nodded in agreement.

Lek gestured to my plastic bag and I handed it to him. Ame reached into another bag and pulled out a pair of bright red Thai boxing shorts that I would be wearing. I accepted them gratefully.

Lek and Ame both took a roll of tape and sat themselves on either side of me. Taking one hand each, they started taping up my hands and knuckles, making sure they were ready so that I could throw punches as hard as I pleased without fear of injuring my hands. The huge crowd of Thais all gathered around to watch Lek and Ame as they went about their work.

"Can't say they're not giving you their full attention," Stuart murmured in my ear, nodding towards the two Thai trainers who had been with us for the better part of the past three weeks.

I nodded in agreement, surprised by all the attention that I was receiving.

"Got your camera for me?" Stuart asked, perusing the little plastic bag and pulling out the go-pro. I talked him through how to use it whilst the hand-taping process continued. Stuart spotted my mouth-guard in the bag and tucked it firmly behind his ear, as you would a pencil.

I laughed at the site of him with a mouth-guard behind his ear, but Stuart appeared to be taking his role as mouth-guard-bearer quite seriously.

"See that guy over there?" Stuart nodded subtly towards a middle-aged, overweight Thai man who was seated at the end of the bar. One of the bar girls was sitting on his lap. "The girls were telling me that he is with the mafia," Stuart said warily.

I eyed the Thai at the end of the bar. It was rare to see an overweight Thai. I shrugged and turned my attention away. He didn't appear to be anything special, though I found it hard not to think about the article I had just read about the mafia related homicide that had occurred a few blocks away.

Then it was time to get dressed. There were no changing rooms, and so I stripped down to my underwear right there in the bar, next to the pool table. The bar girls *goohed* and *gahhed* for the sake of dramatic effect, and a few more people snapped photos as my trainers crowded in to tie the "box" over my manhood. The box was a hardened piece of plastic with ropes attached to it, and the ropes were tied underneath my legs and around my waist. It was uncomfortable, but I figured I would forget all about it when the fight began. Then the red shorts went on over the top, and then Lek, Ame and the two Thais who had come along for sparring crowded around me with tubs of Vaseline and Thai boxing oil, which they mixed together and then smeared all over my body, massaging it into every square inch of skin they could find. One of the bar girls decided to help, much to the amusement of the other bar girls, but then Lek's mum came in and shooed her away with a barrage of angry Thai. This was her son's moment, and she clearly wasn't going to let some uppity young thing in a bikini come along and steal his thunder. I tried not to laugh at the scene unfolding around me.

White-skinned tourists whose game of pool I had interrupted were shouting questions and suggestions at me. Are you gonna win? Are you gonna knock him out? You should knock him out with a head kick! No, knock him out with an elbow! Just throw the elbows like a fucking crazy man!

Meanwhile, as the scene around me grew ever more rowdy and the bar girls ferried more and more alcohol around to the crowded bar, I turned my attention inward and disappeared into my calm little bubble that I had pre-prepared.

This was my time now.

The Thais finished slathering me in oil, and then Lek pushed gloves onto my hands and strapped them on tightly. The fights prior to mine were proceeding apace, and they had all finished by way of brutal knockouts. I made a silent promise to the crowd that my fight would be no different. The crowd was deafening in the stadium – the noise of their stomping and roaring was echoing around the tin walls and was battering my eardrums. I had been to witness fight events held in this same stadium in the previous weeks, but they were all achingly silent affairs when compared to the size and the noise of the crowd that had come down on this Saturday night.

And I was the main event.

It was my face on the posters and the flyers that had been distributed and plastered all around the city of Chiang Mai. The crowd had piled into the stadium en masse and they were all gearing up to see the Aussie take on the Thai.

I poked my head up out of my bubble from time to time to allow myself a moment to soak in the atmosphere and the sheer *energy* of the crowd, and then I would retreat once again, finding my calm, grim place from which I would be plying my trade.

I caught my reflection in the mirror behind the bar. Covered in Thai boxing oil, my skin was shiny and reflecting the lights.

Lek approached holding a traditional Muay Thai headpiece that looks a little bit like a tennis racquet with the strings all missing. That headpiece is called a Mongkon, and each gym or trainer's is unique. The Mongkon represents the spirit and strength of the gym and of the master trainer. Lek pushed it onto my head and then bowed his head and touched his hands against my gloves to pray.

"If lose, no problem," Lek said to me quietly, so that nobody else could hear. "If hurt, ok… My family, Thai people, we no care for win." He touched my chest. "Heart," he said. "If lose, no problem, but heart – must have, uh?"

I nodded my understanding. "Thank you for everything," I replied quietly, trying to convey every ounce of my gratitude. "Thank you for training me and for caring about me… Now leave the rest to me, ok? Try not to worry. I'll take it from here."

Lek and I bowed to each other in a mutual display of respect, and then, with the Mongkon proudly on my head, I turned my gaze towards the ring.

The fight immediately prior to mine was a one-sided affair, and judging by the chaotic behavior of the crowd, it was almost over. There was blood spattered all over the ring. Both of the fighters were covered in it. Someone in there was cut badly, though it was impossible at this point to tell which of them it was.

I looked around the extremities of the crowd, wondering where my opponent was, and wondering what he looked like, and what he might be thinking in that same moment. We would be meeting in a matter of moments, he and I.

The inevitable finishing blow was dealt by means of a knee strike to the liver, and the losing Thai crumpled to the ground in agony, defeated.

There was a mat nearby on the ground with other, similarly beaten Thais lying on it, some of them motionless, others writhing in pain. I watched as one of them got to his hands and knees and vomited on the ground.

I waited patiently as the defeated Thai was carried past me, dripping blood onto the concrete floor. Ame had his hands around my shoulders, restraining me and holding me still. He needn't have. I could've stood more still than any statue for however long it took.

Stuart swung the go-pro into my face and I couldn't help laughing. I explained to him that he had it facing the wrong way, and then somebody called through in Thai, and a bunch of people were talking, and then Stuart was gesturing to me, pointing towards the ring. "Time to go, Mike!" he called, camera at the ready.

I grinned and nodded to him and then I started the walk towards the ring. There was no walk-out music or fanfare. I was simply another commodity to be displayed for the purpose of entertainment. Whether or not I ended up lying on the mat with the losers or with my hand raised to the crowd, the promoters didn't care. I'd already done my bit. The crowd was assembled. They had paid for their tickets. Now, all that remained was for me to get in there and fight.

I heard the bar girls screaming their encouragement to me as I moved towards the ring. I ignored them. The crowd turned to look as I was led through a small, metal barrier that separated me from the rest of the crowd and led towards the steps that would lead me up to the ring. I caught the eye of my little support crew in the crowd. Darryl, Clark, Rhiannon and her friend, and the other girls that Darryl had brought along. I smiled to them and inclined my head, glad to see them there. They all had their cameras out and I squinted into the camera flashes.

I really don't like photos.

I waited at the base of the steps. Ame and Lek pushed past me into their positions in the corner. I could hear Stuart running a constant stream of commentary about the crowd and the situation. I wasn't sure if it was supposed to be for my benefit or if he was talking for the camera.

It's traditional for Thai fighters to kneel at the base of the steps and offer up a prayer of protection, but I decided I didn't want to do it.
No, I'm doing this on my own. I don't need Your help.
Ame walked up the steps and pressed his weight down onto the top rope, and Lek gestured for me to go on up.
It was time.
I bounced up the steps and leapt over the top rope in one bound. I heard the crowd suddenly get louder as they all began their judgments and commentaries with their companions regarding the new fighter in the ring. *'So, this is the Aussie, huh?'* There was scattered applause and cheering, led by my eager cheer squad of Thais and backpackers.
My opponent wasn't in the ring yet. I strolled out into the centre of the ring and bowed to the four sides of the stadium, offering up my humble subservience to the crowd. I was public property from the moment I stepped into that ring. My duty was to entertain.
"Oi, Mike!" Darryl called from the crowd, waving me over to the rope nearest him. I obliged, happy to have something to pass the time as I waited for my Thai opponent. Darryl was gesturing to a couple of guys that were seated in the row in front of him. "These guys are from Australia!" he called.
I bobbed my head in greeting to the two men. "Yeah? Wherabouts?" I called to them.
"Tasmania," one of them called back. He was young and cocky. Your typical Aussie, really.
"Ah, that's not Australia," I said, waving them off dismissively – equally as brash and cocky. There were cheers and catcalls amongst the crowd as different folks took it in turns to level insults at the two Tasmanians.
"I'll bet you twenty bucks you get your head kicked in!" the guy from Tasmania shouted up at me, standing up angrily.
I turned back and shrugged casually. "Sure thing. Happy to take your money."
"Mike!" It was Stuart, gesturing me back to the corner. "Focus," he said seriously, glaring at the guys in the crowd. The guy who had stood up sat back down and there was a distinctive *crack* as the leg of his plastic chair broke and he tumbled to the ground amidst a torrent of cursing. Another cheer went up around the crowd when they saw who had gone down.
"Ignore them," Stuart insisted, grabbing my shoulders and steering me away from the tourists in the crowd.
The situation was very rowdy indeed, and I was loving it.
I nodded and turned back around just in time to see my opponent stepping over the ropes and into the ring. I eyed him impassively, trying to study his movements and learn as much as I could about him before the fight began.

He was shorter than me, and stockier, which bothered me a little. His chin would be better protected than mine, and he would be able to generate power and balance through his strikes. I could combat this height difference in one of two ways. I could choose to fight tall, and use my reach advantage to keep him at bay, deploying regular jabs and thip kicks. However, fighting tall means sacrificing power, and I wanted to knock this guy out, so option two was far more appealing to me. I would fight short, with bent knees and hips, spreading my balance further between two points and being able to call upon the power in my legs and hips whenever I wanted it. In my opinion, fighting short is easily the most devastating and effective means of fighting, but it is taxing on the body. It requires a lot of energy and lactic acid endurance, especially in the legs. That's where all the running, skipping and pad work that I had done in recent weeks would come in to play. My legs were strong, and if I couldn't finish the fight within the first three rounds and if I felt that I was getting tired and slow, I could revert back to the easier, less energy intensive style of fighting tall for the final two rounds and see if I could tease out a points victory.

I nodded to myself. The game plan was decided, barring something unforeseen. I would fight the power game in the opening rounds and look to win by knockout. Failing that, and assuming I got tired, I would reassess and change the game plan for the latter rounds.

The referee came to our respective corners with a roll of tape and scissors in his hands. He taped up the wrists of our gloves firmly and tightly so that they wouldn't come undone.

Suddenly, the Thai music started up – a flute-like klaxon instrument wailing and warbling over the top of rhythmic drumming – signaling the start of the Wai Kru. It was time to dance.

I sighed to myself and began the dance. I had actually forgotten about the dance. I was too eager to get on with the fight itself.

To begin, I walked around the perimeter of the ring, with my right glove touching the rope, symbolically sealing the ring from bad spirits. Out the corner of my eye, I saw my opponent doing the same thing. I noticed that he was further around the ring than I was, and I grinned to myself. He was nervous. Anxious, possibly. I took my time, stopping at each corner. Lek had told me to offer up a prayer at each corner – I was supposed to be praying for luck for myself and for my opponent. Instead, when I stopped at each corner, my message was to myself, and it was crystal clear. *Kick the fuck out of his legs. Kick the fucker in half. Kill everything that moves. Crush his face with your elbows. If he doesn't die, it doesn't count.*

I was in a murderous place, and it felt familiar. It's a place that most people know and understand – fighter or not – it's a very human place, though it may not feel very human at the time. They say that people who cannot kill will forever and always be subject to those that can, but I believe that every able-bodied person is capable of killing if they really had to.

I could hear the crowd cheering as we went through the movements of the Wai Kru. There was a Thai commentator speaking over the top of the music, announcing our names. My name was preceded by my country of origin, and it drew a deafening cheer from around the stadium. I bowed slightly to acknowledge the cheer from the crowd. To my slight surprise, they were heavily in my corner, possibly because I was something different to what they had been seeing all night long. The tourists in the crowd, in particular, were pulling for me, raising their beers and standing up to pump their fists in my direction whenever I stopped in their section of the ring and looked out towards them. I could see all of their faces clearly from my vantage point up in the ring. It felt very high up there, with everyone seated or standing at my feet. I looked down at the crowd, looking into individual faces and trying to acknowledge as many of them as I could with direct and lingering eye contact. This fight was for them, after all. I wanted them to feel intimately involved. I wanted them to flinch with every kick and every blow that I would take.

Halfway through the dance, I noticed that my Thai opponent had stopped and chosen to kneel facing his corner. It was a clever move, and one that I knew to be commonly employed by the more experienced Thai boxers against the presumably nervous foreigners. His corner was trying to make me feel lonely in the ring, so that I would feel every eye on my movements. They wanted me to feel nervous and shy about dancing on my own under the bright lights in front of so many people, but it was the wrong tactic for the wrong guy. I am a very confident guy, and in response to the absence of my opponent, I decided to take up a little more time by extending the dance, repeating my whip-cracking movement in the direction of my opponent and stomping my feet in challenge, channeling the New Zealand All Blacks and their notoriously intimidating Haka. The crowd whooped it up with every challenge, until I decided enough was enough and I returned to my corner. The music stopped the moment I was back in my corner, and suddenly the only noise was that of the crowd as it came to life for the big moment.

The referee called my opponent and I into the centre of the ring, and we stood there facing each other and received our final instructions. I had absolutely no idea what the ref was saying, given that he was speaking entirely in Thai, but I nodded along politely. It didn't matter. I knew the rules – this was all just a formality at this stage.

"You look lovely tonight," I said to my opponent.

He smiled respectfully and bowed to me, which I returned. Evidently, my opponent didn't understand any English. We touched gloves and went back to our corners.

Stuart met me in the corner and we touched our hands and heads together. It was supposed to be Buddhist prayer time, but Stuart didn't know what to say. "Well, good luck then," he said, and then he removed the Mongkon from my head. Traditionally, Lek would've been the one standing on the skirt and removing the Mongkon, but Stuart had asked if he could do it and Lek had obliged.

"Thanks mate," I said, punching Stuart lightly in the shoulder and offering him a grin. "I'll see you later."

He took the mouth-guard from behind his ear and I chomped down on it. I turned around and faced the middle, banging my gloves together eagerly and nodding to the crowd.

The mind games had begun with the Wai Kru, and I knew in that moment how I wished to proceed.

The referee chopped his hand down in the center of the ring and the music started up again.

"Round one," the commentator called over the speakers.

The crowd roared its approval.

I leant back casually against the top rope and stretched out my chest, and I saw my opponent doing the same thing in the opposite corner, and then we strolled forwards, right at each other. I offered my left glove and he touched it with his own in a sign of respect, and then we stepped back and it was time to fight.

Muay Thai: Peace, At Last

You've ravaged all or so you think, there's nothing left to steal.
Nothing you can see at least, and nothing you can feel.
You've taken girls, you've taken friends, you've taken life and limb,
You've taken theirs, you've taken mine, you've taken on a whim.
And yet, how strange, that there remains, one thing you cannot see;
And hear it state forevermore, "You've never taken me."

CHAPTER 16
A CLASH OF SHINS

"Freedom lies in being bold."
– Robert Frost

Neither of us wasted any time.

The Thai threw a heavy roundhouse kick at my head immediately after stepping back. I blocked it on my arms and returned the kick right back at him, throwing it as hard as I could.

Twin *smacks* echoed around the stadium and the crowd shouted and stomped. They were on their feet!

I pressed forward with as much disdain as I could express, dropping my hands down by my side and sneering at the Thai's initial kick. *Is that all you got?* The Thai backed off towards the rope, maintaining the jab distance between us.

In truth, it had been an immensely powerful kick, but I expected nothing less from the short, stocky Thai, and I knew for certain that I could kick just as hard as this guy when I wanted to. There were no shin guards now. No protective gear. The only thing now that could stop an elbow or a shin bone or a knee from crushing my face would be my training. This was the real thing.

I tried to close the distance immediately, looking to establish the clinch, but the Thai darted out to the side to avoid getting stuck against the ropes. He didn't want to clinch with me. Not yet, anyway.

I sighed at him and shrugged as if to say, *come on then, why not?*

He replied by throwing another heavy right shin at my head, which I again blocked on my arms. Those kicks would leave deep bruises on my forearms the next day – imagine getting hit on the bones of your forearms by somebody swinging a baseball bat – but in that moment I didn't feel a thing and I shrugged again at my opponent.

I was walking and bouncing him backwards around the ring. I focused on trying to cut him off and trap him into a corner, but the Thai was a wily chap and he countered my movements by throwing more kicks aimed directly at my head. I blocked them all and tried to force myself through the barrage, but he very cleverly followed up his final kick with a stunningly powerful right hand, which surprised me and landed flush on my jaw and stopped me in my tracks.

I was a little rattled. The floor and the ceiling all got a little confusing for half a second, but then I was back and it was as if nothing had happened. I grinned and gestured for my opponent to try again. He did so, clearly thinking that he had hurt me, and I covered up easily and stood my ground whilst he battered my arms and gloves with powerful, searching punches. I lowered my gloves and slipped left and right to avoid the next two punches, which dissuaded him from throwing any more. He backed off hurriedly before I could counter-strike. I was slightly annoyed at not getting in some counter-strikes, but I wasn't too bothered either. I was having a great time putting on a show. By laughing in his face and chasing after him even though *he* had been the one throwing the punches, I was trying to show my opponent that I loved getting hit, and that he was in the ring with a madman, which was entirely possible – I haven't quite decided yet.

I was getting tired of my opponent's ability to strike and then run away without me getting in a counter-strike, and so that meant that I would have to get in first the next time. This guy was good, there was no doubt about it. He was an experienced campaigner. He was a master at managing distance, which can be half the battle in the fight game, and he was a powerful striker, but I also felt that I had the upper hand, despite his having landed far more strikes than I. I felt as if he was uncomfortable in the ring, and I felt as if he had been too quick to pull the trigger with the barrage of heavy punches that he had thrown. He had been trying to finish the fight early, but he risked exhausting himself by punching uselessly against my forearms. He was anxious in there, and I felt supremely confident that I was in far better physical condition than he was. I was more calm and relaxed, and I was pressing the action.

All I needed was one clean shot.

It's all I've ever needed.

Just the one.

Aware of the screaming crowd, I decided to put on a little show, and so I put my hands down and gestured at my opponent, offering for him to come forwards and try to hit me. *Ok, instead of running away all the time, why not come in and take a free shot, hmm? Just come a little closer…*

He began to edge closer, and just as he did, I switched into southpaw and pretended to throw a left body kick. Just as my shin came up towards his body and my opponent was moving to intercept, I used the momentum and the coil in my standing leg to leap forwards into a left superman punch, which hammered home on the Thai's face, snapping his head back and sending him staggering back against the ropes. He darted away again, skipping out to the side and even breaking into a slight jog as I chased after him. I broke into a jog as well and finally managed to trap him in my own corner, where Stuart, Lek and Ame were shouting encouragement at me. I banged a few punches into the Thai's gloves to set up what was supposed to be the knock-out right hand. I launched everything into the right hand but the Thai saw it coming and ducked underneath it. I over-committed and ended up in the corner *with* the Thai, and we clinched up awkwardly. The referee stepped in quickly and pushed us further into the corner to stop us from fighting before pulling us out of the corner and separating us.

The crowd was deafening. It was plain for all to see that the two guys in the ring were trying to end the fight in a brutal fashion, and the ever-present possibility of danger and a violent knockout had everyone up and out of their seats, not wanting to blink for fear of missing something.

This was Thailand, after all. There was no instant replay.

The referee chopped his hand down in between us and I looked into the eyes of my opponent and a fleeting moment of silent communication passed between us for the first time since the fight had begun. He looked weary now, with defeat written across his face, as if the end was going to be painful and inevitable. I acknowledged the defeated expression on his face with a grim shrug of my own, as if to say I was sorry, but that I had a job to do. "Come on then," I said, gesturing him closer with my gloves.

I instigated the next engagement, threatening with my left jab and then slamming a savagely satisfying kick into the Thai's left thigh. The kick thudded in with what must've been an excruciating connection, and I saw pain flash across the Thai's face and he skipped away out of range once again.

The crowd cheered as I stalked him down. I threw another leg kick, exactly the same, and it landed just the same. Savage and painful.

He responded instantly this time, throwing a kick that had nothing held back. It was a desperate kick, thrown with reckless force, risking injury not only to me, but to himself as well. Unfortunately for me, I never even saw it coming, and it slammed into the left side of ribs. I felt pain flare up immediately and shoot right through my torso. I didn't know it at the time, but that kick had broken a rib.

With easy disdain plastered permanently on my face, I took a half-step back. I was planning on chatting to the Thai and taking my time, because I wasn't ready to engage again just yet, but then the bell clanged and the music stopped.

Round one had ended.

I nodded to the Thai and we touched our left gloves together as we walked past towards our respective corners. The pain in my left side had completely disappeared and I forgot all about it, grinning to Lek and Ame as they climbed into the ring to meet me. Someone slid a metal tray into the ring with a lip on it, so that water wouldn't spill onto the canvas, and there was a plastic stool in the middle of the tray. I stepped into the tray and sat down on the chair, and Ame went to work immediately, pouring ice over my chest and massaging my limbs vigorously.

Lek took my mouth-guard out and then held a bottle of water to my lips, which I sipped from and then nodded to indicate that I'd had enough. I felt fine. Better than fine, actually. I couldn't wait for the 2nd round to begin so that I could get back into it. I'd already forgotten about the pain in my ribs. So far as I could tell in that moment, I was 100% healthy and ready to go again.

"Ok," Lek crouched down in front of me and nodded. He was calm and relaxed, which I was grateful for. I didn't need anybody shouting in my face. I am a calm fighter and I require the same from my corner.

I smiled to Lek again. "He's not bad," I said.

Lek nodded. "Him strong," he said. "Good power. I think him have many fights."

I nodded in agreement. This was no ordinary Thai I was in the ring with. He was an experienced campaigner. I even suspected that there had been an attempted set-up. It's not unusual for promoters to put master Thai boxers in the ring to kick the crap out of the foreigners. With the Mafia guy in the crowd, it was entirely possible that I was in the middle of an attempted gambling rort, but now wasn't time to be concerning myself with such matters. That was Lek's job, if he felt it necessary, but he didn't appear too concerned. In fact, he asked me to turn around and pose for a photo with him in the corner. His brother took the photo and then Stuart leaned his head through the ropes. "I have it even, Mike," he said. "He got in more strikes but you were the one pushing forwards. I have it even, that round."

I nodded. "Yeah, thanks."

Ame continued to massage my body, which I ignored.

Lek offered me more water and I shook my head.

I could hear my friends in the crowd shouting encouragement to me, trying to get my attention.

I wanted them all to be quiet so that I could think about my strategy going in to round two. I hadn't expected the Thai to move around so much. It's unusual for Muay Thai fights to be so mobile around the ring - they're usually stand in the middle of the ring and bang propositions. I needed to think of a way to force this guy to engage with me. I needed to close the distance. I hadn't been able to secure the clinch with him in the first round, and that was somewhat problematic. I thought about the leg kicks that I had landed. His being so backwardly mobile meant that he was pushing a lot of weight through his front leg, which made it vulnerable to those sorts of kicks. I decided that I would change into southpaw to begin this round and look to step forwards into orthodox each time the Thai backed off and then step again immediately into a right leg kick to his lead thigh. I needed to trap him into corners and then work patiently once I got him in there.

The referee came over and said something, and Lek and Ame cleared out of the ring, taking the seat and the metal tray with them. I turned into the corner so that Lek could proffer the mouth-guard again, and I chomped down onto it.

The bell rang and the warbling Muay Thai music started up once again. "Round two!" the commentator called over the speakers.

I stretched out on the ropes again and the Thai did the same thing in his corner. We met in the middle of the ring and touched our left gloves and nodded to each other. "Fight for real this time," I said to him as we stepped back and readied ourselves.

I slid into southpaw and I saw the Thai's eyes flick down to my feet. He was watching carefully.

I lifted my right knee, feinting a right thip kick and then hopping forwards when the Thai predictably moved backwards. I kept my hands extended just in case he tried to catch me coming forwards, and I stepped my left foot forwards into orthodox and then swung my right shin into another leg kick. It landed with a loud smack that echoed all around the stadium, and the crowd cheered. The Thai flinched and backed off further, and I chased him back into his own corner, trapping him there. He leant back all his weight on his rear leg and raised his lead knee to defend himself with thip kicks. He pushed me back a couple of times before I managed to time a right high kick, which connected across the Thai's arms. I tried to follow up with another but the Thai pushed me away with another thip kick and used the space to slip out along the ropes and circle away.

I followed him and caught him on the ropes. I threw another high kick, this time aimed at his head. It was one of the fastest kicks I had ever thrown, but the Thai saw it coming and leaned back at the waist, just out of range. The kick whipped around, mere centimeters shy of the Thai's jaw, and I spun around full circle. The crowd *oooohed* at the near miss. That would've been game over had that landed. I laughed at the Thai and reclined a little, looking around at the crowd. I heard laughter from the crowd in response. "That was close, mate," I said to the Thai.

He smiled and inclined his head to acknowledge the near miss and then threw a right leg kick. This time, finally, I managed to block it with my raised shin, rather than with my arms, and I grinned as the Thai winced and his leg buckled slightly when he put his weight back on it. Our shins had clashed with a loud thud, and I heard the crowd exclaim and recoil at the violence of it. In hindsight, I believe it was that moment - that shin check - which signaled the beginning of the end.

I hadn't felt a thing.

I closed the gap again, using punches to disguise my forward press, and then, finally, I managed to clinch with the Thai and force him backwards a few steps until he was pressed up against the ropes. I had planned to use the clinch to throw knee strikes, but the Thai raised one shin and pressed it horizontally across the front of my thighs, preventing me from throwing my knees. I growled at him, angry now that I couldn't utilize my clinch dominance to hurt him, and so I pulled him back off the ropes and threw him to the canvas in disgust. His sacrifice of his lead leg to push against my thighs was effective in preventing my knee strikes, but it made throwing him very easy.

The crowd roared its approval as the Thai went sprawling to the floor. The referee leapt forward and pushed his arm across my chest to allow the Thai the space to get to his feet. I glanced into my corner and saw Lek standing there and leaning over the top rope, gesturing with wide-eyed eagerness, telling me to chase after the Thai and finish him off following that display of clinch dominance.

I banged my gloves together and marched forwards the moment the referee moved out of the way. The Thai responded differently this time, leaping forwards into a jumping elbow. It was a desperation move. He was trying to knock me out in one fell swoop. He had dug into his arsenal and pulled out his finishing move. I defended easily with a raised knee, and I felt the elbow crash into my forearms. I shoved him back and across the ring and marched after him again. Once more, the Thai leapt at me, leading with the elbow. Once again, it crashed uselessly into my forearms.

The crowd sounded almost hoarse from screaming. They could sense that the fight was in its final moments. One of us was about to get knocked out, and there was no telling who it was going to be.

The Thai leapt forward for a third time, and again he came up short. On his fourth try, I pre-empted the leap and charged forwards, stopping him in his tracks by pushing my gloved hand hard into his face. I followed this up by marching him backwards across the ring and slamming two leg kicks into his already battered left thigh, one after another. There was anger behind those strikes now. He fell back against the ropes and I initiated the clinch again, wrenching on his neck. He didn't raise his shin across my thighs this time, and I could *feel* that his will to fight had broken. There was no power in his neck anymore. He didn't even try to return the clinch, instead just desperately pushing his forearms across his abdomen to try to protect himself from the inevitable knee strikes that were coming his way.

I ignored the torso and went instead for the unprotected face, slamming my left knee up into his mouth and nose. The crowd roared, and I could hear Lek shouting something. He was shouting in Thai, which wasn't much good to me, but I didn't need him to tell me what to do. I threatened with a follow up knee and then threw my left elbow instead – twisting from the hips, driving through the legs – with my full bodyweight behind it. It connected clean as a whistle to the Thai's head and he became an instant dead weight - only being held up by my arm and shoulder crushing his neck. I let him go and the Thai crumpled to the ground and rolled partially out of the ring beneath the bottom rope.

The crowd was going bananas.

The referee rushed forwards and I stepped back, away from my fallen opponent. The referee gestured me towards the furthest neutral corner and began counting out the Thai.

I strolled calmly across to the corner and reclined against the padded turnbuckle. I crossed my right leg over my left and waited.

The referee waved him arms over his head and turned hurriedly to the Thai corner, urging them into the ring to attend to their fallen fighter.

It was over.

I had won.

Lek was waving his arms to me and pointing me over to the fallen Thai. We had talked about this in training, after he had taught me the Wai Kru. "If you win, knock-out. You go, and this, uh?" he had said, getting to his knees on the canvas and bowing to the imaginary fallen foe. It was a sign of respect.

There was nothing imaginary about it now.

I nodded to Lek and walked over to the valiant, fallen Thai. His corner-men were already at his side. I knelt down beside them and pressed my head against the canvas beside my opponent's prone form. I sat up straight and his corner-men patted me appreciatively on the shoulder. One of the corner-men offered me a drink from their bottle of water, and I sipped from it gratefully.

The Thai was coming around and I helped him to his feet and into the arms of his corner-men. The crowd cheered as the Thai was carried out of the ring...

That was the last I would ever see of him. I never learnt his name, or anything about him. For a brief moment in time, our paths had crossed, and in a most violent way. We had met for the first time in the middle of a Muay Thai ring, and now we would never meet again.

The referee seized my wrist and raised it into the air as the commentator announced my name and described my victory by way of knock-out in the 2nd round. I walked a full circle with the referee holding my wrist firmly, parading the victor in front of the assembled audience. I didn't want to be in the ring any longer. I bowed my head as we walked around. It was over. I wanted to get out now.

I thanked the referee and bowed quickly to him once he had let go of my wrist. He patted me on the shoulder. I bowed to each corner of the audience as per the custom and then went to my corner and stepped out through the ropes and into the waiting arms of Ame, Lek and Stuart.

They were shouting hoarsely and thumping me on the back.

I returned the group hug, wanting nothing more than to find someplace quiet to retreat to. Someplace isolated.

Lek took my mouth-guard out of my mouth and passed it to Stuart, who tucked it firmly back behind his ear, clearly not bothered by the fact that it had just been in my mouth.

I skipped down the steps and back onto the concrete floor, through the crowd.

I pointed at the Tasmanian when I spotted him. "Twenty bucks," I called out. He threw his head back and laughed in acknowledgement and then pumped his fist to me. "Good fight, mate," he called back.

"Can you get these off?" I asked Stuart, holding my gloves out to him. He was pointing the go-pro camera at my face.

Lek appeared with scissors, and together, he and Stuart ripped the tape off my gloves, along with the wrapping tape on my knuckles, and my hands were free once again. Mine was the last fight of the evening, and so it seemed as if the entire audience had gotten out of their seats now and most of them were milling around me, calling things to me and taking photos. Chief among them were two young boys, who I later learned were French. They shoved their way up to me and shouted my name. I happily gave them a high five and their father asked me to take a photo with his two sons. I obliged and the three of us clenched our fists and posed for the photo.

"Thank you," the father said, shaking my hand eagerly. "They loved you in there. It's good for them seeing another white person fighting. Inspirational for them, truly."

I nodded and glanced back at the two boys. I guessed their ages at around eight and ten.

"They were screaming the whole fight," Stuart said in my ear, watching the French boys. "They were on the other side of the ring but I could hear them from where I was."

"That's pretty cool," I said thoughtfully, wondering how I might've felt as a young boy attending a Muay Thai fight in a strange and unfamiliar country. It was probably the kind of thing that can have a significant impact on a young man.

"You look like them, I guess," Stuart said with a shrug.

I shook hands with a cacophony of people as I made a slow and steady way back to the bar where it had all began. I'd left my jeans, shoes and shirt there and now I wanted them back. People crowded in from all sides to congratulate me on my win.

"One of the best fights I've seen," a guy with a beret and a rather pompous bearing said, pumping my hand. "Vicious. Just vicious. Bravo, young man."

Lek asked me to take a photo with his entire extended family, and of course I obliged them all, smiling for the camera and posing with the huge Thai crowd. I loved the fact that I'd had Thais in the crowd cheering for me. That meant more to me than anything else, although it was also nice to consider that I may have had an impact, however slight, on the lives of those two young French boys.

Stuart shepherded me through the rest of the crowd just as my friendly backpacker contingent arrived, cheering loudly. I suspected that they were all drunk. "I'll be back in a sec!" I called to Darryl. "Gotta get changed."

"Oh, Jesus," Stuart suddenly exclaimed, and I felt hands on my shoulders. "Check out the welts on you, man. *Fuck,* that must hurt!"

I examined my torso and discovered that I had a series of large, red, painful-looking welts on my left side, from where I had been kicked. My ribs, my left arm, and even my back on the left side was lumpy with the welts. They were as a result of those blitzkrieg body kicks from the Thai.

I remembered the brief jolt of pain I'd experienced at the end of the first round and tenderly poked and prodded at the inflamed areas, but I couldn't feel anything unusual. I shrugged to Stuart. "I feel fine," I said. "No pain or anything… Just give me a second, would you? I'm going to see if I can get changed."

The bar girls had kept my clothes for me behind the bar, and I accepted them gratefully. One of the girls steered me around to a dank looking hallway which led me out to the back, which was outside in the hot, humid night air. There was a tap on the wall connected to a suspended water tank with a release valve. I thanked the girl and then turned the water on and stepped underneath the cool water, shorts and all. I figured I'd have to return those shorts to Ame, so it would be rude to not try and clean them a little. They were drenched in sweat as they were.

I undressed under the water and showered for a few minutes longer than was necessary, enjoying the peace and quiet and taking the opportunity to reflect on the chaos that had been the previous hour of my life.

The back door suddenly banged open and there was Clark, the Irishman, as drunk as only an Irishman can be. "Oh, shit, sorry," he said, seeing me standing under the water. "Everybody's waiting for you inside, man. They all want to go out and party… I just needed a place to piss."

I shrugged, not caring about very much at all in that moment. "Whatever, man," I said.

Clark relieved himself in the shadows of the alley whilst I stood under the water. We steadfastly ignored each other. I sighed once Clark had left and turned the water off. I got dressed once again, wincing occasionally as I noticed a slight pain shooting through the left side of my rib cage. I hadn't thought to bring a towel or anything to dry myself off, but it was a hot night and I didn't really care.

I didn't want to go back inside. I just wanted to be alone with my thoughts for a while, someplace quiet.

I'd won my fight. I'd achieved what I set out to do. I'd had more than enough violence for one night. Now, all I really wanted was some peace and quiet.

I wondered how the Thai I had fought was feeling now. Would he have been taken to hospital? Was he alright?

I didn't really know how to feel. Some feelings don't have words. I wasn't relieved, because I'd expected to win. I wasn't elated in triumph. I wasn't feeling giddy with a sense of my own self-worth, or anything like that. If anything, I felt small and thoroughly humbled. I'm not a violent person. I'm a fiercely competitive person, but I'm not inherently violent… Or am I?… It's a grey area, I suppose. People aren't built in blacks and whites. Or greys, for that matter, now that I think about it… People are built in layers. I was nervous as a child. Introverted and caring, with a sarcastic sense of humor and a silly laugh. I was a little boy who loved reading and playing with his toys on his own in his bedroom. I cared about others and I cried when others cried. I didn't like it when other people were hurt, and I still didn't like it in that moment, after my fight. People don't simply shed one skin and assume another, as we so often assume when people appear to have changed with the passage of time. Change doesn't work like that. People simply add layers. The old layers are still there. They always will be. I'm still that nervous, introverted, caring little boy I once was – the same boy who cried when other people cried and the same boy who loved playing with toys – but I've added new layers since then. It's true that amongst those layers, there are now some with labels like; cruelty, aggression, hatred and violence, but I believe those are a necessary part of growing up as a man in a harsh world. They don't define who I am. There are no words to accurately label or describe a human being. Attempting to do so is foolish, in fact. Even calling someone a fighter is ridiculous. I'm not a fighter. I'm a person who has fought before, but that doesn't make me a fighter. I love to write, but it doesn't make me a writer. You can describe what people do, but never who they are.

You're either alive or you're dead. That's something that you can put a label on. And on that warm night in Chiang Mai city, I was alive.

Michael Goodison

The maps are filled, the edges drawn,
    There's nought for you and me.
        No hidden place, no Distant shores,
            No place you're first to see.
Adventure then, has changed in time,
And now we see it clear;
Turn inside and Close your eyes,
There's danger lurking near.

CHAPTER 17
PEACE, AT LAST

"It's only after you've lost everything that you're free to do anything."
— Chuck Palahniuk, *Fight Club*

Lek wanted to take me out to a restaurant with his family to celebrate in Thai style. That sounded terrific to me, but it had just passed midnight, which meant the military curfew would be enforced and nothing would be open. Lek and Ame spoke animatedly in Thai and we agreed to meet again at the ring the following morning. They said they would take me and Stuart to a nearby lake that they knew, and we would relax together and unwind.

Lek's parents and grandparents bowed to me before giving me a quick hug each. I thanked them for coming and told them Lek was an excellent trainer.

Ame thrust an envelope into my hand. I opened it up to reveal 4,000 Thai Baht. It was my prize money. Roughly $120 AUD. Even though they were being paid by the gym, I thrust another thousand baht each into the hands of Lek and Ame, and then pocketed the rest. We said our goodbyes and went our separate ways.

"Want to come back to our hostel?" I asked Stuart, gesturing at the waiting backpackers. "It's just down the road."

Stuart nodded. I think he liked the look of the girls. "Sure," he said.

We went into a 7/11 on the walk back home and managed to sweet talk the girl behind the counter into letting us buy alcohol, even though it was after midnight and the curfew was in effect. I had to lift up my shirt to show her my welts and bruises before she would finally relent.

Back in the hostel common room, Darryl decided he was going to try and find a party with the Dutch girls that he had brought along. Clark decided to join them, and they all left, leaving me and Stuart with Rhiannon and her friend. We sat at a table and shared and swapped beers and whiled away a couple of hours telling stories and talking to each other. I told the girls Stuart's news about his girlfriend being pregnant back home in England.

Stuart told the girls about the training that he and I had been doing together over the past couple of weeks, and they reflected again upon the fight itself.

"You rocked in there," Rhiannon said proudly. "It's like nothing can hurt you."

"You *did* take some hard shots," Stuart agreed, looking at me with concern on his face. "Any pain?"

I shrugged. Truthfully, I was starting to feel a burning pain creeping into the left side of my ribs. "I feel fine," I said. "Like nothing even happened… Do you still think you're going to have a go at fighting?" I asked him.

Stuart grimaced and shook his head. "I'm a father now," he said. "And after watching that, I don't think I can do it. Just those hours before the fight, lad. Those are the worst. Watching all the fights before yours. I was so nervous for you in there. I reckon I was more nervous than you were."

The girls agreed with the sentiment.

After a few quiet drinks, Stuart caught a tuk-tuk back to his hotel and we said goodbye. Despite his promises to see me the next day at the ring, that would be the last time that we would see each other.

Climbing the ladder into my top bunk that night was torturous. My left side was grating and crying out with every movement. I wrote briefly into my travel diary about the fight and how I felt about it, and then I drifted off to sleep.

I arrived at the ring the very next day to find the two French boys were there with their father once again. All three of them were in the ring and training with Ame. I grinned at the scene and sat down quietly in the back row to watch for a while. Ame, I was surprised to discover, could speak fluent French.

Lek arrived shortly afterwards and sat down with me to watch. The session finished within a few minutes and Ame called out to us in greeting. The French boys asked to take more photos with all of us, and so we all climbed back into the ring – I tried to disguise my ginger movements – and posed for more photos with the French family.

"They want to be Muay Thai fighters now," the father told me with a wry little smile. "They're up all night telling me how they want to fight and be famous fighters. I think it is good for them, no?"

"There are plenty of worse things they could be interested in," I said with an affirmative shrug. "You look like you're having fun as well?"

"Oh, it's too difficult for me," the Frenchman said bashfully. "I have not the flexibility, I think."

We said goodbye to the French family and then waited a little longer to see if Stuart would arrive. We gave him half an hour and then piled into a waiting car. One of the other Thai men that I had sparred with was in the driver's seat. Lek, Ame and I joined him and we set off, bound for the countryside.

It was a nice drive, and it was nice sharing the car with the three Thai men. It felt like a unique cultural experience, simply to sit there quietly and listen to the Thai radio station played through the car speakers, and listening to the three Thai friends chatting and joking with each other in their native language. I was more than happy just to listen quietly. I was in the mood for nothing else, really. I didn't want to talk to anyone, or do anything more strenuous than slow walking. I had booked a bus ticket across to Pai for 3 o'clock in the afternoon, and Lek had agreed to have me back at the hostel by that time. I was due to fly back home to Australia at 11pm on the 18th, which meant that I only had two more nights remaining in Thailand.

The lake was called Huay Tung Tao, and it was beautiful and serene. We arrived just before noon to find the place deserted. Lek told me that it's rare to find tourists at this lake, and so the local establishments that have sprung up along its banks cater primarily to local Thais.

We drove around and found a lovely little corner of the lake, where there was an array of bamboo huts erected along the shore line. I followed along in their wake as the three Thais picked a place with a beautiful view over the water, and we all got comfortable in our very own little bamboo hut that was raised up off the ground. There was a breeze blowing through, taking the edge off the heat, and it made me feel lethargic and at ease.

There was a mood of celebration in the air. Ame produced a smart phone and a small speaker, and soon the reggae sounds of Jack Johnson and Bob Marley mingled with the conversation. We ordered Thai beer from the waitress, and then Lek went a little crazy as he tried to order the most outrageous and unique Thai foods so that I could give them all a try. I was a little wary about all of this. I usually eat pretty bland foods, and I'm not a massive fan of spices. We watched as a group of Thai men waded determinedly out into the lake in front of our hut, and Lek leaned over to explain. "Them catch food for us," he said, smiling.

"Ohhh," I turned back to watch with renewed interest as the men slapped the water in a rough semi-circle and then lifted up a net to reveal several large fish. The fish they selected was on our table within twenty minutes, complete on a rice bed and with a variety of fruits and vegetables arranged around the side. We all shared the meal, leaning around each other to pick the tender, exquisitely fresh meat from the delicate bones of the fish. More meals arrived, and I was shocked to find that our next course was still alive. Lek passed around a container of insects which looked a lot like grasshoppers, and were difficult to grasp. The Thais ate them whole, and I followed suit, trying not to flinch when I felt the insect wriggling around in my cheeks, trying to escape. There were soups, mangoes, seeds of some kind, and yet more beer. By the time we were finished, I could hardly move for how much I had eaten, and almost all of it had been entirely new to me.

I paid for the meal, which was incredibly cheap given how much there had been and how brilliantly and freshly prepared. It was cheaper for the four of us to eat several courses (and consume a lot of beer) here by the lake than it was to buy a meal for myself from a fast food joint back home in Australia. The three Thais were shocked that I had paid for all of them, and they tried to force their money into my hands, but I refused. It was cheap, and I didn't really need the prize money that I had kept from the fight the night before. I should've given all of it to Lek and Ame, in hindsight, so it was the least I could do to buy them lunch.

After lunch, the four of us strolled out into the lake and floated about for a brief time. I was ever wary of my sore torso. I was wondering what I had done to it. I figured that it would go away in a few days, though it would end up being more than a month before the pain would eventually recede.

I was back in Chiang Mai in time to catch the 3pm bus across to Pai. The last time I had made this journey, I had been with Romy, from the Netherlands, but this time I reclined on the bus on my own, staring out the windows at the spectacular mountain scenery with music playing softly through headphones in my ears. I was listening to my favoured grunge music. It was 90's music, mostly. Pearl Jam, Red Hot Chili Peppers, Nirvana, Alice In Chains, and their like. I enjoy almost all music that isn't pop music – I even like country music – but grunge rock will always be my first love.

It's difficult to imagine what the world would look like were it not for grunge music… There would probably be an all-consuming, overwhelming wave of sickening commercialization of people with no real talent, presenting to the masses a myriad of narcissistic songs that relentlessly and repetitively paint pictures of mirrors, and all the while the teeming masses would probably end up dancing and trying to connect with music that is created by soulless computers… But it's hard to believe that an intelligent society would ever allow that to happen… How can music ever be made by a computer and still be called music? It's foolish to call something music when it isn't music and then expect it to be music. It doesn't work that way. Someday, when the world is cold and dark and regimented and completely devoid of any emotion or feeling, and human beings are soulless automatons that are branded with barcodes and inserted with computer chips and exist for the sole purpose of consuming – then someone may pose the question: where did this coldness begin? What was the *source* of this awful heartlessness?

Well, I'll tell you now.

Computers masquerading as musicians was the catalyst for the heartlessness. And people listening to sounds made by computers and *believing* that it's music was the tipping point.

Don't say I didn't warn you…

Muay Thai: Peace, At Last

If you're ever afraid that you've lost track of your life and come to realize that you have no idea what real music sounds like, go and listen to *Mr. Tambourine Man* by Bob Dylan. That's a good place to start. And if you're lucky enough to have the opportunity to listen to it whilst travelling the twisting road between Chiang Mai and Pai, through the forested, mist covered mountains and valleys, then you're another step closer again to understanding why art means so much to the human race.

I was born into the twilight years of the 20th century, and I've been clinging onto it ever since. I feel sorry for the generations that will never get to experience the 90's. Now it's all whining boy bands and narcissistic feminism screeching painfully across the airwaves. I remember a time when real men played rock n' roll, and I'm clinging on, waiting for the wheel to turn.

I arrived in Pai and I was soon back in the same room that I had stayed in on my previous trip with Romy. It was a nice place, with the swimming pool and the quiet atmosphere. As good a place as any to recover from a Muay Thai fight. I could read and relax, do some writing, eat and drink, and try not to move too much.

That's precisely what I did.

The following day, I rented a scooter and rode it out of town and into the surrounding valleys. I visited every café along the way, and I took my time. I was enjoying the leisurely feel of not having to train or think about fighting in any way, shape or form. I met an English girl along the road who was also on a scooter on her own, and we stopped in at a place called Pai canyon, which is a series of precarious, twisting gravel paths and cliffs. We explored the area and took some photos and then continued on with our scooters. We passed elephants that were grazing along the side of the road with their Thai handlers napping on their enormous backs. In the late afternoon, we found a resort with a treehouse as the main feature. I was delighted. I love treehouses. We climbed up the treehouse and explored the various levels and intricate woodworking. There were rooms to rent up high in the canopy, and we chatted for a time with a South African couple who were honeymooning in the treehouse resort.

We lazed about in a giant hammock swing for a while until finally, after it had long since gotten dark, we got back on our scooters and rode back into Pai. We met up with James and the two British girls once again, and we all exchanged stories and had a few drinks together. I left them all to it after a little while. I wasn't in the mood for a late night. I returned to my room and floated in the pool for a while before turning in for the night.

The next morning was my last in Thailand. I needed to be back in Chiang Mai by 11pm to catch my flight back to Bangkok and then onwards to Melbourne. I was sad to be leaving. I'd been there for a month, though it didn't feel like it. Time flies when you're having fun.

I spent the morning at a bar in Pai, where I bumped into the same English girl I had met the day before on the scooters. We played a few games of pool together and then it was time for me to catch the bus back to the big smoke.

I would miss that sleepy, hippy little town of Pai. There's really nothing to do there, and it would probably get boring after more than a few days, but for someone who enjoys just lounging about and reading and writing, it was like Heaven on Earth for a short while. Who really wants to go to Heaven though? There would be nobody even remotely interesting or fun there to hang about with. It would be the most boring, pretentious place I can possibly imagine. Little cherubs playing harp music isn't bad I guess, but after too long of that I'd need something with a bit of distortion and a decent drum line.

Thailand had been a lot of fun. I felt as if I could write fiction all my life and still not come up with stories that are as exciting as that which transpires in the real world. Thailand is the perfect kind of a place for craziness to unfold. It's like a breeding ground for craziness. The world's greatest playground, where anybody can play and there are no rules and no safety guidelines and no parental supervision.

Nothing so exciting ever seems to happen in Australia. Australia is safe and secure and regulated and dull. To my mind, and in contrast to the Government's apparent thinking, there is no linear correlation between the words "safer" and "better." I have friends in Australia whom I only catch up with rarely, due to circumstance and lack of effort, and six months may pass in between meetings and then we will catch up for a cup of tea again and the inevitable question will get asked: So, what have you been up to since I last saw you? and I'll sit there and think about everything I've been up to in the prior six months and then I'll think about it some more and I'll compile a list of the top three things that I've done to try to make sure it's all condense and concise so that I don't end up talking all about myself for too long and then I'll go over those things again and put it all together at the front of my mind so that I can access all of the necessary information in order to give the most honest and accurate response. "Absolutely nothing," I answer. How is that even possible? Six months of nothing? Who does nothing for six months? Well, me, apparently. And then I come to Thailand for 30 days and I can write an entire book's worth of stories? Perhaps I should make a new life rule along those lines. *Live your life as if you have to write a book about it at the end of each month.* Maybe something like that. I'll think about that one some more before I go ahead and commit to my mental rule book. Maybe I'll do a trial phase and see if I'm broke after the first month. If that ends up being the case then it was probably a bad idea. A bad idea every now and again doesn't hurt though. Bad ideas can be a whole lot of fun. My memory bank is bursting with a kaleidoscope of images that were the result of bad ideas. You regret them at the time, but you laugh about them when you're older and you're even proud and grateful to have made those mistakes.

Mistakes are a part of who we are…

At the end of the day, the most important thing in your world is your mind. Your mind is *you*. Your mind is where you live. You can focus all of your energy on your body and on your surrounds as much as you want to, but the mind is everything, and if your mind doesn't get the attention that it needs, then someday it's gonna let you know all about it, and it's gonna let you know by completely fucking you up. Whether it's a stupid decision, or a personality disorder, or depression, or anxiety, or a stress related illness, if you don't give your mind the attention that it needs, it's going to force you to give it attention. The mind requires training and maintenance, the same way that the body does if you want it to keep working at maximum capacity. I'm a believer in the existence of a soul, and I'm including the soul in that assessment. Your soul needs attention, too. There's a lot more to health than just the physical.

Spend all your time and energy focusing on your bank account and you'll soon come to see what I mean. Energy deserves the right to be invested as carefully as you would invest your money.

Upon returning to the developed world, there seems to be an overwhelming feeling – or belief, rather – in the concept of progress. Progress has become something akin to a disease gone global. Some new form of intellectual parasitism, like religion of old and political-correctness of new. The modern day driver of misery and dejection is the notion and the desire and the relentless pursuit of *progress*. But what does progress entail, exactly? Why do we want it so badly? Why are all of our systems – monetary, reward, fiscal, political, social – geared towards progress and with progress being the sole yard stick for success?

The hell with progress, I'm happy right here.

In fact, I was happy 10 years ago.

I don't need the latest of everything in order to feel like I'm a worthwhile human being.

What kind of thinking is that? Is it conservative, or is it so progressive as to have gone full circle and re-emerged on the right side of the spectrum once again?

Is it love or fear?

I have a fear of robots. Robots give me the heeby-jeebies.

Lions, snakes, spiders, clowns; no big deal. But robots? No, thanks very much. I'll pass.

I don't really like air conditioning, either…

The interesting thing about the modern day notion of progress is how little it has to do with evolution in the biological sense. Rather than improve ourselves, we'd rather try to improve our surroundings. It's like building a house and starting with the roof tiles. In fact, it appears to be a sliding scale. The parts of the world that have experienced the most *progress* are also the parts of the world where obesity and mental health crises are slowly and quietly killing everyone. By contrast, the less-developed world appears healthier and happier.

Why are people so afraid to turn their energies inwards? How shallow have we become when other people's opinions of our extremities mean more to us than how we *feel* about ourselves?

The thing that bothers me most about progress, innovation and advancement is the tradeoff, which often tends to go undiscussed and falls by the way side. It's easy to talk about what progress and advancements have given us, but what have they taken away? I mean, sure, mobile phones have given us instant communication, but we have largely lost a great many opportunities for genuine human interactions for favour of interacting with screens.

Shouldn't we discuss these sorts of things *before* we press on with further advancements?

Apparently not.

The world we live in and the people that surround us and the media that we consume tends to encourage big dreams and upward thinking, and I feel obliged now to challenge that notion, for it often does more harm than good. Directing your tireless and relentless attention towards that which you don't have is precisely what capitalism requires of you, but it is also a recipe for hurt, disappointment, loneliness, gaping holes in your existence, and a failure to appreciate that which you *do* have. I'd happily make a bet with you that 99% of people whom cheat on their partners are big dreamers and upwards thinkers. By contrast, it is those that are content to enjoy what they already have whom find happiness and contentment in life. Capitalism, advertising and motivational videos have us all brainwashed into being ultra-competitive beasts, with grand designs and misguided hearts. Happiness is no longer the simple act of getting in a car and going for a drive, it's in driving an Aston Martin.

My time spent fighting and my time spent in poor countries has proven to be a spiritual journey, as much as a physical one. My overriding compulsions in life now are no longer competition, desire and ambition, but gratitude and contentment. It's no longer an all-consuming drive to find happiness in the acquisition of more, but in finding happiness by living contentedly with less.

It may very well be that the overwhelming consensus disagrees with me on this. We went to war and our soldiers fought and died defending capitalism, so how could the consensus really afford to suggest otherwise?

However, there's a danger that lies at the heart of a consensus – that being the idea that a general consensus wouldn't be a consensus were it not correct, and therefore the majority opinion of the time simply *must* be correct, even if it's not. I hate decisions made by means of a vote, for that very reason. After all, how many religions have there been throughout the history of mankind? Thousands of them, right? Maybe even millions of different religions, and they all shared a localized, common belief that their religion was true and correct, and, because the majority of people agreed with it, that became the adopted thinking of the time and place. The problem emerges and makes itself quite clear when you step back and realize that there have been thousands and maybe millions of different religions throughout the ages, and they can't all be right, which therefore suggests that on thousands and maybe millions of occasions, the majority opinion was actually wrong. What's the message to take from this? Well, it's the idea that, regardless of how overwhelming a consensus may be, there are thousands and maybe millions of reasons for a lone voice to stand up and challenge the established thinking, because the odds are pretty good that the consensus is wrong.

I believe that human-beings are animals – if highly evolved animals – and I also believe that all animals have an optimal way of living – one which is most conducive to biological evolution, the betterment of the planetary eco-system, the welfare of the individual, and the connectivity between all things and energies. I also believe that modern human-beings are way off the mark. The vast majority of us are not even close to living our most optimal lives to fit the aforementioned criteria.

I am of the sincere belief that physical fighting is one step back in the right direction for me as an individual. A step back towards an optimal way of life, and of thinking. Nothing – not the internet, not books, not my schooling, not television – has taught me as much about what it means to be alive and to be human as fighting has.

Remove, alienate and vilify fighting and combat sports in society if you feel you must, but do so knowing that it's another step down the slippery slope of bullshit.

EPILOGUE
LIVE, LOVE AND DIE

> *"And if you gaze long enough into an abyss,
> the abyss will gaze back into you."*
> – Friedrich Nietzsche

I mentioned right at the beginning that my story wasn't your typical fighter's story.

I had a wonderful childhood. Everything was all very comfortable. I was loved and supported and life was easy. I didn't come from a broken family, I had never suffered a real loss of someone close to me, I had never experienced poverty or genuine hardship. I had the greatest childhood a kid could ever hope to have. I built little huts in the trees, played games with my siblings and watched Space Jam religiously. I have no doubt that I was the cause of many a mystified cleaning session, where my poor mum would try to clean fingerprints off ceilings and walls. I wasn't a spoilt child, but I was always given the opportunities to use my imagination and be creative and have fun. I spent a lot of time outdoors on my own little adventures. My parents were wonderful, selfless and caring. My childhood is not even close to what you might expect from a professional fighter. You would expect to see hardship, but you could look all day and you wouldn't see hardship in my upbringing. My life was cozy, comfortable and easy. It was all laid out for me, lined up nice and neatly, just one ticked box at a time towards becoming a middle-income man living in a nice house in the suburbs with a pretty wife and two kids attending the local private school. Life was easy for me.

And *that's* why I wanted to become a fighter.

I chose to become a fighter because I believe that suffering is the greatest instrument of human happiness.

In order to appreciate warmth, you must first know cold. I take a great many things from that lesson and I apply it wherever I can. It's easy to take things for granted, and that's a cursed existence that I refuse to allow for myself.

Our biological reward system, developed over hundreds of thousands of years of evolution, is a perfectly tuned machine. Perfectly tuned, that is, to a world that no longer exists. That same reward system is where our sense of fulfillment and purpose comes from. For people that grew up like me – very cozy and comfortable – our biological reward system is rendered almost entirely obsolete, and that's problematic. It creates confusion. Confusion that can lead to unexplained and seemingly unreasonable stress and angst.

We each possess within ourselves certain evolutionary drives. Oxygen, water, food, sleep, sex, safety, comfort, and a sense of belonging. Those are the things that drive the human machine on a daily basis – that give our lives meaning and a sense of purpose and subsequent reward. However, when all of those things are so easily attainable that we can take them for granted, then the mechanical drive and the evolutionary sense of purpose dries up, and with it, so disappears the sense of reward.

In a world so developed as the one that I was born into – a world sheltered and comfortable, with everything that I needed readily available and easily attained – it is easy for a person to become numb. We find ourselves asking questions about the meaning of life. We ask ourselves what the heck we are supposed to be *doing* on a daily basis, so as to feel industrial and needed, but there's nothing of any real worth left for us to achieve – nothing that can enrich the lives of those around us – nothing that hasn't already been done. Indeed, same in society as in travel, the blank edges of the map have all been filled in, and now there is nowhere else left to explore.

Those who still feel that nagging compulsion at the base of their spine – that ancient desire – are often left feeling numb.

For a very long time, I felt numb.

I was too comfortable. My life was too easy.

I once heard an expression that states: there is no such thing as pleasure, only the relief from suffering. I have no idea who said that, but it is a philosophy that I subscribe to. The greater our suffering, the greater the relief. The greater the pleasure. Yin and Yang. Taijitu. Duality. The deeper we dive, the more sweet the surface.

Fighting is extremely challenging.

It is scary and it is painful.

It's exceedingly hard.

And that is why I fight.

Through fighting, I have rediscovered what it means to feel alive. Now, success is measured by the sacrifice that was invested.

Fighting has given me gratitude and appreciation – the healthiest of all human emotions. It's more than just fists and elbows and push-ups and blood.

Fighting is a spiritual experience.

It is in fighting that I found peace within my soul. Those troubled waters – so deeply stirred by an unscratchable itch – are now glassy calm...

Without a doubt, and despite my reservations about life in the developed world, the best part about travelling is returning home. It's all about that appreciation. That's the gift that travelling gives so generously and tirelessly. Appreciation for home and for family and friends. It's not until you've gone without them that you can truly appreciate what you have.

There are lessons in life that only fighting can teach us, and the first lesson is that not all fights are physical, and not all fights take place in a ring, and not all fights are fair. But we learn that it's ok to break. It's ok to falter. Sometimes, things don't go according to plan. Relationships don't work out, you get sick, you lose your job, the world falls apart.

There is a Japanese profession called Kintsukoroi, which is the repair of broken pottery with the use of gold or silver lacquer seams. The Japanese understand that the pottery can be made more beautiful for having been broken. They do not attempt to hide the cracks. Instead, they highlight them and turn them into something remarkable and unique.

Do not be afraid to die.

It is death that allows us to live.

If something is worth fighting for, then it's worth fighting for.

"The test of literature is, I suppose, whether we ourselves live more intensely for the reading of it."
– Elizabeth Drew

AUTHOR'S NOTE

Thank you for reading this book, I hope you enjoyed the adventure of Thai Boxing in Thailand!

I write stories to inspire, and I hope that this book has inspired you.

I have my emails all set up on my phone now, like a 21st century person probably should, and since writing this book, I have greatly enjoyed hearing from so many of my readers. I've been inspired by reading about your stories in life – we all have our battles, and the hardest fights don't typically occur in a ring with a referee. I'm honoured to receive your stories, and I read and reply to every one of them.

As a storyteller, I believe that stories are the fabric of our society. I believe that sharing stories brings people together, and I also believe that all great stories begin from a place of hardship.

When you write to me, you have the luxury of skipping the small talk. Please, when you write to me, tell me the story of the greatest hardship you've faced in your life. Tell me all about it, big or small, it's different for everybody, and tell me how it changed your life, for better or worse. Tell me about your fight. Open your emails, type in my email address, and open a vein and bleed.

My email address is: astoryworthtelling@hotmail.com

www.michaelgoodison.com
www.facebook.com/michaelgoodisonauthor
@michaelgoodisonauthor

Please read on…

ALSO BY THE AUTHOR

When Fighters Dance

From the critically acclaimed author of "Muay Thai: Peace, At Last," comes another in the Combat Sports book series.

Sam Benton is known around the world as the future star of boxing, when a single moment of violence alters his path dramatically. A hero to some. A villain to most.

Finally granted a second chance at his freedom, Benton dedicates himself to the task of enjoying the little things, as far away from the spotlight as possible. When events intercede and destiny sets him on a path towards boxing glory, Sam comes face to face with the ghosts of his past, and he must will himself to the top.

In a world where sports and politics collide in a violent fashion, When Fighters Dance is a story of willpower, family, and the overwhelming need to fight.

Read on…

When Fighters Dance
An Introduction

CHAPTER ONE
STAR-CROSSED LOVERS

Sam Benton was fifteen years old when he first killed a man. It would be another fifteen years before he would kill again. Two deaths – different from one another in so many respects, but similar in one meaningful way. Both kills were attributed to Sam Benton's bare hands.
More specifically, his closed fists.
At the age of fifteen, Sam Benton was being talked about in wide circulation. If the commentary swirling around him was to be believed, then you would have it on good standing that young Sam Benton was on track to someday becoming the greatest boxer in the long and star-studded history of that sport. Unquestionably, the world's most popular combat sport.
Boxing was about to get a new star.
On the night of December twenty first – the year was 1981 – all of that changed. The anticipation surrounding the Aussie boy with the big future went up in smoke. Gone with the wind.
Sam, like most red-blooded boys from the north shores of Brisbane, had been chasing a girl. In his case, the girl in question was one, Sandy Heatherton – daughter to nobody important, but a girl who would turn laps up and down the walking track that ran right alongside main street, just on the off chance there was someone who hadn't noticed her latest form-fitting outfit. At the age of seventeen – two years senior to Sammy Benton – Sandy Heatherton was harbouring a conspicuous resonance with the American west-coast brand of anti-Vietnam, Woodstock-toting, breast-flashing hippies. She had just about completed her transformation, right down to the roller-skates and the burgeoning American colloquialisms – she

would never know the gravity of the day that was to come when the calendar turned its page to December twenty one.

Sandy was smitten with Sam Benton. She knew about the big future that he had in store for himself.

Every night, after finishing work at her after school job, Sandy Heatherton would catch the 8:48 north shore loop. It was the last bus of the regular schedule, and the next bus wouldn't come along for another ninety minutes. And every night, *he* was there. The creepy guy. Staring at her from across the way. His head lolling about madly with every bump and turn that the bus made, but his eyes always remaining locked – *fixed!* – on her.

Sandy would breathe a little sigh of relief every night when the bus reached her stop and she could finally get off. Away from the creepy guy and his constant stare.

And like that wasn't bad enough, Sandy remembered the thunderbolt of fear and the sudden thudding of her heart the time that he had followed her from the bus. At the last moment, as if by some afterthought, the man had flung himself out the door and out onto the street behind her.

Doing her best to ignore him, Sandy had walked as fast as she could towards home. She tucked her large, curly blonde hair as tightly as she could behind her neck, the better that she could see out the corner of her eye when she glanced back over her shoulder. And each time she looked, the man was still there, keeping pace with her. Large, purposeful strides. The fear was real then. Painfully real.

The worst part was the key in the front door.

The sweaty, shaking hands. The impossibly delicate task of inserting the key and opening the door to her home as quickly as possible. Slamming it shut and locking it behind her. The surreptitious peek through the blinds from the living room.

It continued like that for three days. He would follow her all the way home, and then he would stand out the front for a while, and then he would walk around the track that led to the park down the side of Sandy's house, and he would loiter there even longer. She would watch him through the curtains, making sure the room was dark before she peaked through the blinds. She could see him there, even in the dark, standing there, occasionally pacing, but always returning to stare at the house and the windows. Eventually, he would leave.

To Sandy Heatherton, three days felt like a lifetime of terror. The nights were the worst. She couldn't sleep, so tightly wound was she to the slightest rustle or creak. All through the night, she would find herself creeping back to her window and parting the curtains to make sure... To make absolutely sure...

On the fourth day, after deciding not to tell her parents for fear of having her liberties severely restricted, Sandy confided in the hardest, toughest son of a gun that she knew. Sam Benton. Fifteen years old and powerful enough to stun a charging bull with his fists. Sam made her feel safe. Sam would protect her.

It was the morning of December twenty first, 1981.

Upon hearing the tale of the creepy guy from the bus, Sam's eyes had narrowed eagerly. Sandy still remembered the way that he had looked. Like a lion cub that finally had a chance to make good. Together, they had hatched a plan. A simple plan.

Sandy would catch the bus after work later that same night. The same way that she always did. She would walk home. She would run if needed. She was a good runner. And when she got home, Sam would already be there, waiting in the shadows in the park beside Sandy's house. They'd never actually discussed what he would do at that point. Even Sam had never stopped to consider what might happen next. The plan ended at that juncture. The creepy guy would walk down the side of Sandy's house, to the park, and Sam Benton would be there waiting for him.

As it so happened, it all went according to plan...

The local newspaper carried the story in the weekend edition, and within twenty-four hours, the story had made its way around the globe and all of the way back again. Back to the north shores of Brisbane, where Sandy Heatherton was sleepwalking her way through a nightmare.

She described to the police officers how she had watched through her bedroom window. It had been dark outside in the park, but she had seen enough. Seen her would-be boyfriend leap on her stalker, catching him by surprise. The pair had stumbled and fallen, landing in the dirt. Sam had been the first to his knees, and Sandy watched him lash out with a punch. The punch had missed, and the man had tackled Sam and ended up on top of him. The stalker landed three clumsy but fast punches to Sam's face, breaking his nose with one of them. In his amateur boxing career, hardly anyone had managed to land a punch on Sam Benton, but in the dark, with no referee there to keep an eye on things, the drug addict was landing savage blows.

Sam bucked and struggled. In that position, the young boxing star became suddenly and frightfully aware of the physical differences between fifteen year old boys and grown men – even drug-addled, untrained men.

Panicking, Sam sunk his teeth into the man's neck, holding on by his teeth like a Pitbull as the man reared away, and suddenly Sam was on top, and now the star boxer cut loose. One punch, two punches, three, four… Ten, eleven, twelve… Nineteen… Twenty…

The stalker's name was Nicholas Crior.

Somewhere in the midst of those battering punches, Nicholas Crior died. Thirty-eight years old. A career felon. Beaten to death in a park by boxing's golden boy.

Sandy told the story of how Crior had followed her home. How he had followed her the previous three nights as well. How he had stood outside and watched the house. Her parents were stunned. The police took statements.

The nightmare was only just beginning.

It was red meat to the media people. Half of them were claiming that it was self-defense, that it was justified. Sam Benton was the noble hero, the defender of his friend – a young woman who had turned to him in her time of need.

Others were calling for life imprisonment and an end to combat sports of all forms. This "latest" incident was clear evidence that sports like boxing promoted the use of violence in a manner that extended beyond the gym.

Being a juvenile, Sam Benton's identity was supposed to remain private, but that injunction lasted about fifteen minutes before it was open season. He was an international star, even at fifteen years old, and there were jurisdictional issues concerning his privacy, and pretty soon the media people had thrown caution to the wind and Sam Benton's photo was making front and back page appearances.

In Australia, the sport of boxing enjoyed a sudden and immense revival, as men and women around the country signed up to local gyms en masse. The hugely publicized case of Sam Benton and Sandy Heatherton only reinforced what everybody had been saying in recent times. That it was dangerous out there. That we needed to be ready for anything. And, clearly, the sport of boxing carried with it one hell of an effective self-defense resume.

Sandy Heatherton was next in the firing line, and her story twisted and turned in perhaps the most bizarre fashion of all. At first, she was the innocent victim – every woman's, every parent's worst nightmare come to life. Yet somehow, over the course of a few short days, Sandy had become widely accepted as a villain of the story. Why had she enlisted her friend to help in the first place? Why hadn't she done the sensible thing and gone to her parents, or to the police? What did she think was going to happen? How dare she manipulate a young man who clearly had feelings for her into such actions? A young man couldn't be expected to back away from something like that, could he? His pride couldn't possibly allow it. She should have known better.

And then the photos started appearing. Photos of seventeen year old Sandy in her tight skirts, her barely there crop-tops, her roller blades, her crimped hair and her bubblegum. Her friends started answering questions about her. Telling stories. Describing her. *She* was the cause of all of this, and now a man was dead and a fifteen year old boy's promising future was in ruins.

The fact that she was two years older than her accomplice was the final straw. *She* had been the mastermind in all of this. *She* had manipulated Sam Benton. Sandy Heatherton was to blame for the entire affair. Sam Benton was behind bars and facing a murder charge, Nicholas Crior was dead, and she was at home with her parents.

In the boxing world, they mourned the loss of a future star. Sam Benton had been training hard for the '82 Olympics, and it was expected that he would have taken the opportunity to stamp his authority as the emerging superstar everyone believed he was. Following the alleged murder of Crior, raw footage emerged of Sam Benton in action. Those who were in the dark about Benton were quickly informed. In his early amateur bouts, his boxing IQ was on full display, but it was his footwork which left the boxing pundits stunned. Never had a fighter looked so delicate in a boxing ring. So… *pretty*. Benton's dazzling footwork combined with his ring smarts and viper-quick lead hand left his early opponents looking like bumbling fools. How could a young man so violent seem so beautiful in the way that he moved? It looked like violence without fighting.

Benton's training videos showed an adolescent boy with a lot of physical development still to come, but his skills were without question. He hit the speedball with his eyes closed, he skipped rope, but most of all, he danced in the ring with his sparring partners. In there – the squared circle of dreams – he was without peer.

The wheels of justice turned slowly. Inexorably.

Eighteen months after waiting in the park and pouncing on the strange man, beating him to death with his fists, Sam Benton's final legal appeals were exhausted. He was sentenced in an out-of-session hearing to a term of sixteen years in prison. Given time already served, he could be eligible for parole in twelve years. He'd celebrated two birthdays already behind bars, recently turning seventeen. If he was released on good behavior after twelve years, he would be twenty nine years old. He still had one more year remaining in juvenile detention before he would be transferred to an adult correctional facility.

On the one hand, he would have a chance at a relatively full life. On the other, twenty-nine was almost old age for a boxer. It was dementia and arthritis and trivia. It was downhill from there. Especially after nearly fourteen years spent incarcerated. There was commentary and discussion, but most everybody agreed that this was the end of Sam Benton the boxer. Maybe he could come back and make a real contribution to the world in another way. If he got out before he was thirty, he would still have plenty of time at his disposal.

The professional boxing world moved on.

Elsewhere, behind other closed doors, the nightmare was the same. Sam's parents tried desperately to keep their wits about them.

Can you believe it was that Benton boy? Little Sammy Benton, from North Shores public high school? Can you believe he really killed that man?

In their darkest moments, both of Sam's parents gave voice to their own, private anxieties. Was all of this somehow their fault? How was it possible that they, the two of them – two honest, hard-working people of good community standing – how was it possible that *they* could have raised a killer?

"A hero," Sam's dad would growl, when confronted. "My son is a hero. A damned hero. He was protecting that girl. I bet if it was your little girl being followed, then you'd have something different to say to me."

But Sandy's parents never said a word to Sam's parents.

Not during the police phase. Nor the media phase. Nor the courtroom and the lawyers phase. Sandy's parents never breathed a word to the family of Sam Benton.

And it would be almost fifteen years before Sandy Heatherton would set eyes on or speak a word to Sammy Benton again.

In fifteen years, the entire world can change.

New technologies are created, new industries rise up from nothing, wars are fought. Leaders are installed and toppled. Two teenagers from a small section of beachfront in Queensland would be swept up in the currents of the world. One of them a murderer. The other, mostly to blame.

The gap that exists between man and boy can be decade, or a day – it just depends on the day. Sam Benton was eyeing his future behind bars, surrounded by insurmountable barricades on all four sides. His long-distance vision would not be used for a decade and a half. After having already spent eighteen months behind bars whilst his legal defense toiled away, Sam was resigned to his new lifestyle. His new reality.

In his concrete hell, Sam found a natural outlet for his anxieties. He shadowboxed. For countless hours, he set traps for his invisible opponents, drawing them into his favourite pull-counter, maintaining the distance with his snake-like jab, parrying and turning on a dime. Within a few weeks, he could box in his cell with his eyes closed and know precisely where he was in relation to the walls. He worked up a heavy sweat, his breath coming in sharp pulls and hissing exhalations as he returned straight punches at his worthy foe. Sometimes he would fight multiple attackers at once.

Barefoot, Sam built hard callouses into the soles of his feet, pivoting and twisting, dancing and skipping away, the master manipulator of time and space in a boxing match.

Every day, Sam fought. Sometimes as many as one hundred fights in a single day, against all manner of different opponents. Some fights were first round knockouts, others were merciful corner stoppages, and others went the full distance.

The guards lingered to watch sometimes. This kid was supposed to have been the next big thing in boxing, and now they were the only ones who ever saw him going through the moves.

For his part, Sam rarely even noticed them. He lived in his own little world. He was allowed a notebook, and in it, he drew up tournament schedules, and he fought his way through them, winning some and occasionally losing on the scorecards to worthy opponents whom he would later defeat in the hotly-anticipated rematch.

His sister visited on occasion, and she reported back to her parents that Sam had gone crazy. He was muttering about his arch rivals; running through their vital statistics, their height, weight, reach, their fighting style. None of these people existed. But Sam was in the heat of battle against them every single day.

It was difficult to explain, but Sam was happy.

He had his mission.

Sam Benton celebrated his eighteenth birthday in prison. His parents visited, along with his sister. And they ate birthday cake. Sam's mum put on a brave face and Sam's dad made a show of how fast the time was passing, and making sure Sam was being proactive with his time. Learning new skills, keeping up with developments in the real world.

The next day, Sam was transferred to an adult prison, where he would spend the remainder of his term. If his good behavior continued, he would be eligible for parole in just eleven more years.

This was a big deal for Mr. Benton, now a voting age citizen, because he was being transferred out of Queensland and down to a medium security prison in Victoria. It felt as far away as the moon. Sam's parents had been informed of this move several months earlier, which had given them time to settle up their affairs in North Shores, Brisbane. Sam stayed quiet when his dad informed him that the family would be moving down to rural Victoria in order to stay close to him. He couldn't bring himself to protest or insist that his family keep their lives where they belonged. He was traumatized by his own weakness in those moments, when he realized how desperately he needed his family close by whilst he served out his time.

Sam met his cell mate. A greying, bony man who had already staked out his space. Neither man was big on talking, so they were well suited to each other.

After a few days of awkwardness, Sam started up his shadowboxing routine again.

His cellmate went by the name Bonehead. Maybe because his bald skull had weird knobbly bits on it. Sam didn't care. He just did his best to ignore Bonehead whilst he moved around, learning the new space. Bonehead was an intrusion on his imagination, and it bothered

Sam immensely, but there was nothing that he could do about it. Acceptance was all that he had left.

Or I could just kill him, Sam considered, on occasion. His mind was betraying him, and he recognized it. But acceptance was all that he had left.

It was several weeks of this before Bonehead did more than his typical grunting routine. "What are yer then, uh?" he said, swinging his legs around to address his young cellmate. "Suppoze ter be a boxer, is dat right is it?"

Sam was in the midst of one his shadowboxing battles, but it was one of his journeyman opponents who he had been toying with easily, so he took a moment to dispatch of the contender before glancing across the small space at Bonehead. "Supposed to be," he answered at length, catching his breath and checking to make sure the ref had called the fight to a merciful end.

Bonehead just nodded, as if a burning question had been answered, and he returned to his favourite position on his bunk, his feet crossed, his hands folded across his chest, his eyes on the ceiling.

Welham Correctional Facility had an exercise field, and a library, and a computer room. It was a grown-ups version of what Sam had gotten accustomed to during his time spent behind bars. There were counsellors here, and programs that were offered. There was a non-denominational Chapel service held four times a week. There was an alcoholics anonymous group.

Sam was growing up in prison, and he was finding his feet. He started engaging with the prison guards, most of whom he discovered were decent and likeable folks just trying to find their way to the end of their shift so that they could return home. Nobody wanted trouble. Some of the guards started talking with Sam about boxing, and pretty soon Sam was running impromptu skills sessions, demonstrating his famous footwork in lengthy displays to excited guffaws from the guards.

But there was a female guard.

Sam hated her on sight.

It took several more of his regular sessions with his psychologist before he became aware of how powerfully he felt towards the girl. The psychologist must have made a recommendation, and the girl was moved to a different part of the large facility. Sam Benton, it turned out, was harbouring a deep-seated and simmering resentment towards women. And it was worse, far worse, for women to whom he was attracted. They burned him up. It was almost inexplicable, and were it not for his psychologist, Sam might never have understood it.

Sam blamed Sandy for everything that was happening to him. Before and ongoing. Everything bad that ever happened to him would forever be Sandy's fault, unless Sam could find a way to conquer those feelings. And in lieu of expressing those feelings to Sandy – having never achieved closure – Sam was attaching those same feelings of rage to other young women.

He was dangerously angry, the psych warned him.

Dangerous enough to hurt someone, if the wrong thing was said, the wrong wound reopened. He would need to fight this particular demon, and it was a fight that Sam Benton might never win.

"You're making progress," the psychologist said. Sam wasn't sure if the man was just supposed to say that.

Given the growing popularity of the facility's new boxing star, the sport of boxing itself was on the rise within the population. The inmates were asking for a heavy bag to be hung in the yard, and even the guards were often there, exchanging chit-chat about perfect technique. Skipping ropes were strictly forbidden. They were an easily converted murder weapon.

But Sam Benton didn't require much in the way of equipment to continue his boxing training. All he needed was a few square feet of room, and he could shadowbox for hours on end. Getting a heavy bag to hit though, was a dramatic breakthrough. After countless hours spent imagining the sensation of impact, it was such an overwhelming sensation of release to finally hit something. To punch with real heat, real impact. An electrifying experience, and Sam's training sessions took themselves out to the exercise yard, and to the newly installed heavy bag there.

Within moments, he would draw a crowd of intrigued onlookers.

It wasn't unusual for men in the yard to hit the heavy bag. It was one of their favourite pieces of exercise equipment.

But the way that Sam Benton hit that bag… It was *different*.

A man hitting a heavy bag was a spectacle of labour and of grit. Of heavy feet and heavy shoulders and of big movements. Beasts of burden. Hitting a heavy bag was an ugly thing to behold. Lots of grunting. Lots of underlying human angst.

But Sam Benton didn't look ugly when he hit the heavy bag. He performed with it, like it was a dance partner on a ballroom floor, a performance fit for tuxedos and ballgowns.

"Not every strike needs to be thrown as hard as possible," Sam said one day, when asked to explain himself. He fired his jab in with a sharp snap. He head-faked and walked, it seemed, *twirled* to the far side of the bag. "We call it the game of boxing. Not the game of punching… I want to tell my opponent a story, but it is a lie. I want him to like me. I want him to feel comfortable. I don't want to pressure him, I want to offer a suggestion, and he trusts me, so he will follow my lead. Watch… I'll draw him around…"

The guards stood shoulder to shoulder with the inmates, watching Sam, just listening to him speak.

The kid was only eighteen years of age, and he was a master of something.

How rare it was to achieve mastery in this life…

ALSO BY THE AUTHOR

Jack Burgoyne & the Treehouse by the River

Jack Burgoyne & the Treehouse by the River is fun for the whole family!

Jack Burgoyne is thirteen years old, and he has been looking forward to working with his friends on his treehouse project over the summer holidays. He has no idea the trouble that awaits him.

An adventure filled summer at the Burgoyne Bed & Breakfast, affectionately known as The Lodge, turns deadly. When Jack's older brother invades a weekend camping trip at the treehouse, the consequences are beyond imagining...

Is the Burgoyne Bed & Breakfast – their family's lifelong home and business – doomed?

This adventure story, set in the Australian countryside, sees larger than life characters set loose in a world full of intrigue and possibility.

Read on...

Michael Goodison

Jack Burgoyne & the Treehouse by the River
An Introduction

PROLOGUE
JURRAH BEND

Time moved slower back then. Or so it seemed. It's only now, now that I am older, that I can truly hear the infernal ticking of the clock. There is evil in that sound, I am sure of it.
Ah, but we were children once!
We were young, innocent and carefree.
What a time it was…
It's been many years since I last visited the town of Jurrah Bend – the town of my youth. I was born and raised there, semi-wild amongst the trees, many worlds removed from those city lights.
My parents, Pete and Loretta, owned the Burgoyne Bed & Breakfast, although it was more affectionately known then as "The Lodge." They had built it by hand when they were young and starry-eyed.
Nestled in amongst the trees, and hugging the river that ran along the northern edge of the town, The Lodge was a large, sprawling series of timber cabins and outbuildings, all surrounding the main building – the beating heart of the place – which was the administration lobby, the staff quarters, the function hall, and the riverside restaurant. Access to The Lodge was only possible over a small, rickety old timber bridge, which ensured the guests their privacy from the rest of the population of Jurrah Bend. It was a place for the city slickers to travel on the weekends to escape the hustle and bustle. To "get away from it all," as they liked to pontificate in the lobby.
Us kids, we were intrigued by the out-of-towners.
Living in a travel lodge was an adventure all on its own. My brother and our little sister would join my charge as we barreled around the

buildings and the grounds, searching for new, undiscovered hidey holes. Often times we would sneak out at night and see owls sitting atop the old street signs which offered directions to the guests of the lodge. This way to the river, that way to the restaurant. The owls would suddenly tense, their prey spotted, and a moment later their wings would unfurl and they would launch forward on silent wings, swooping low to the ground before rising again into the trees to swallow their catch in one large, gruesome gulp.

We would invite all of our friends from the town.

My brother and I were kings of the town back then – or so we liked to believe – and when the call went out that the Burgoyne brothers were on the march, the others would come, even if it meant sneaking out of bedroom windows in the middle of the night and quietly traversing the town, sticking to the shadows... All to be a part of the goings-on that we had organized out at The Lodge.

We would build treehouses and rope swings over the river, and when the summer heat was relentless, we would strip off our clothes bravely in front of each other and then swim for hours, the young boys and girls in the nude and looking for reasons to sneak up on each other from under the water, shrieking in delight, because we knew that nobody could hear us out there, and nobody ever came looking. We were free to play.

Hell, we were free...

We had phones and things back then, but not the way the city kids had them. Ours were mostly attached to walls, and we would be required to answer several questions from an adult on the other end of the line before we were finally put on to speak with our friends. And we built bonfires the way the city kids built resumes, easily and carelessly, and just for something to do. We fished in the river and we ghosted bottles out of the liquor cabinet, and one of the boys from the town was learning to play the guitar, so sometimes we sang the same song over and over again by the crackling fire. We were as tight as thieves, us kids of Jurrah Bend. It was the best of times, and we were the best of friends.

The adults used to tell us how stressful their lives were, with bills to pay, businesses to run, responsibilities on all fronts. None of that was any of our concern, and we had our own issues to deal with – our own anxieties to keep us awake at night.

I was thirteen years old and my friends called me Jack.

I remember that summer like it was yesterday.

We were home for the Christmas holidays, summer in the southern hemisphere, and all was going according to plan up to that point. The seconds, minutes and hours moved at their proper pace.

Maybe it was inevitable that we would grow up. Maybe it would've happened one way or another. Maybe everyone experiences it in much the same way.

That summer, we crossed a line somewhere. We stopped being kids, but we weren't quite adults yet, either. We saw things, we *did* things… and nobody ever warned us about those things. We never saw them coming.

Now, people call me Mr. Burgoyne.

But it wasn't always the case…

Please read on more by the author, Michael Goodison.

ACKNOWLEDGMENTS

To my brother, who designed the front and back cover for the hard copy of this book. To Lek and Ame of Chiang Mai, for their precious time and energy that they gave to me. To the Red Hot Chili Peppers and Pearl Jam, just because.

To Sarah, my fiancé, whom I first met whilst writing this book. Thanks for tolerating me, especially when I am in writing mode. Ours will be the great adventure of life.

And to my readers… A book is 50% writing and 50% reading. Were it not for you, this would be just paper and ink, so thank you for completing this with me, and thank you for being readers.

Until next time,
Michael Goodison.

Printed by Amazon Italia Logistica S.r.l.
Torrazza Piemonte (TO), Italy

56008509R00118